FIRST COURSE IN COST AND MANAGEMENT ACCOUNTING

T. LUCEY

M.Soc.Sc., F.C.M.A., F.C.C.A., J.Dip.M.A.

Terry Lucey has been an accountant and consultant in industry and has had over twenty years examining and teaching experience at all levels of professional studies and for diploma and degree courses in business studies. He was previously Head of Department of Business Studies at the Polytechnic, Wolverhampton and is now a consultant and visiting Senior Teaching Fellow at Aston Business School, Aston University.

Amongst his other published works are:
'Investment Appraisal: Evaluating Risk and Uncertainty', 'Accounting and Computer Systems' (co-author), 'Quantitative Techniques', 'Management Information Systems, Management Accounting'; Costing and several ACCA Study and Revision Manuals including, Cost and Management Accounting 1, Cost and Management Accounting 2 and Quantitative Analysis.

DP PUBLICATIONS LTD.
Aldine Place
142-144 Uxbridge Road
Shepherds Bush Green
London W12 8AA
1990

ACKNOWLEDGEMENTS

EXAMINATION QUESTIONS

The author would like to express thanks to the following for giving permission to reproduce past examination questions.

Association of Accounting Technicians (AAT)
London Chamber of Commerce and Industry (LCCI)
Royal Society of Arts (RSA)

Each question used is cross referenced to the appropriate examination board and the title of the paper.

ISBN 1 870941 54 3

© T. LUCEY.

First Edition 1990

Printed in Great Britain by
    The Guernsey Press Co. Ltd.,
    Guernsey, Channel Islands.

Pageset by
    Kai, 21 Sycamore Rise,
    Cinderhill, Nottingham.

PREFACE

AIMS

This book provides a broad introduction to cost and management accounting for those who have not previously studied the subject. It is written in a clear, straightforward fashion without technical jargon or unnecessary detail.

It will be found useful for any course requiring an introductory non-specialist treatment of cost and management accounting including: B/TEC courses in Business Studies and Finance, Royal Society of Arts, London Chamber of Commerce and Industry, Association of Accounting Technicians, Management and Supervisory courses, Business Studies and Marketing courses, Access courses, Purchasing and Supply courses and many others.

APPROACH

No previous knowledge is assumed and each technical term and principle is fully explained and, where necessary, illustrated by a worked practical example or diagram. The book is sub-divided into three sections corresponding to the main areas of the subject. It should be studied in the sequence of the chapters which have been arranged so there is a progressive accumulation of knowledge.

To gain genuine understanding of any technical subject constant re-inforcement of knowledge and practice in answering problems is vital. Special attention has been given to this and the book contains:

- Review exercises at the end of each chapter (with answers)
- An Assessment section at the end of the 3 main sub- divisions of the book containing:
  Multiple Choice Tests (with answers)
  Examinations Questions (with and without answers)
  Assignments for single or group activity.

DEVELOPMENT OF SUBJECT MATTER

Readers who wish to explore any topic in greater depth or to study the subject at a higher level, are recommended to consult the author's other books, *Costing and Management Accounting* also published by DP Publications Ltd. These books are on the recommended reading lists of the major professional accounting bodies and are sold internationally.

NOTE FOR LECTURERS

This book is suitable both for topic based teaching or student centred learning using the questions without answers and the assignments provided in the Assessment sections.

A Lecturers' Supplement is available free to lecturers adopting this book as a course text. The supplement contains:

- Answers to the questions in the book
- Guidance notes on the solutions to the Assignments
- OHP masters of key diagrams from the book.

T. LUCEY
1990

CONTENTS

Section 1
Cost Analysis and Cost Ascertainment

The first part of this book describes the ground rules of cost and management accounting. These include expenditure analysis, the calculation of product and service costs, and costing principles. These are routine, but important matters which must be thoroughly understood because a sound, well organised costing system is the foundation stone upon which more advanced information systems are built.

1 INTRODUCING COST AND MANAGEMENT ACCOUNTING

OBJECTIVES

After you have studied this chapter you will

- Understand the purpose and scope of cost and management accounting
- Know the three major subdivisions of the subject
- Understand, in outline, how cost and management accounting can assist management
- Have been introduced to some basic definitions
- Have had an introduction to the rest of the book.

WHAT IS COST AND MANAGEMENT ACCOUNTING (CMA)?

CMA is one specialised aspect of the whole subject of accounting. CMA is a key part of the internal information system of an organisation and is equally applicable to manufacturing firms, service industries such as banks and building societies, local and central government, hospitals and so on.

In summary, CMA provides vital financial information to management in three inter-related areas:

- Cost analysis and cost ascertainment
- Planning and control
- Decision making and performance appraisal

These three areas are described more fully in the following paragraphs and developed in detail in the rest of the book.

Note that cost and management accounting may be sub-divided into costing (or cost accounting) and management accounting. This sub-division is frequently found in professional examinations but any form of sub-division is quite arbitrary and is not particularly useful for someone approaching the subject for the first time.

COST ANALYSIS AND COST ASCERTAINMENT

Fortunately, for most of us, our private lives are relatively straightforward and we have little need for a formal system to tell us in detail what we have spent money on or what things have cost. If, for example, we want to know what our car has cost to run we can find this out accurately enough by looking at old bills, checking on our bank statement and perhaps relying on our memory.

However, this happy go lucky approach has obvious deficiencies and managers trying to run any organisation or business in an efficient and profitable manner need to know, in detail, exactly what has been spent, on what materials or services and what the materials or services have been used for. Furthermore, management need to know what products or services cost to produce or provide and what it costs to run each department. This type of detailed information cannot be provided without some form of CMA system.

Such a system could provide answers to countless questions, for example:
- What were the salaries in the Rates Department last period?
- What is the cost of producing 1 tonne of cement?
- What does an open heart surgical operation cost?
- What did we spend on stainless steel last month and what was it used for?

and many, many others.

To provide answers to questions such as these a systematic method of analysing all expenditures must be followed together with agreed methods of calculating costs. These must be tailored to the exact requirements of the individual organisation. It follows from this that the CMA system in an organisation will, in some respects, be unlike any other although it will follow generally accepted principles and methods.

The foundation of any CMA system is knowledge about both the *nature* of the expenditure e.g. materials, salaries etc., and the *location* or *use* of that expenditure. This two-fold analysis is carried out by using a coding system containing two distinct elements: Nature of expenditure/location or use.

For example: expenditure for salaries in the advertising department might be coded as follows –

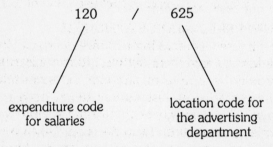

whereas salaries in the design department might be coded as follows:

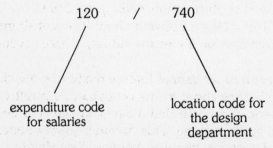

The codes thus determine in which accounts the expenditures are recorded and form the basis of all subsequent analyses. It should be noted that similar principles are used whether the CMA system is dealt with manually or is fully computerised.

PLANNING AND CONTROL

Planning is a primary management task and means deciding in advance *what* is to be done and *how* it is to be done. When the plans are implemented, control takes place by ensuring that operations proceed according to the plan. Control is usually carried out by comparing actual results with the plan (alternatively called a target, budget or standard) and making what adjustments are necessary.

Planning and control require information from numerous sources and of various types e.g. information about sales, quality, rejects, costs, and so on not all of which comes from the CMA system. However, as most plans have financial implications and control of expenditure is always necessary, the CMA system is one important source of internal information to management for planning and control purposes. Indeed one particular CMA planning and control technique, that of budgets and budgetary control, is familiar, at least by name, to virtually every person.

Budgets are plans expressed in money terms and budgetary control is a formal system in which actual results are compared, item by item, with the budget and the differences (called budget variances) reported to management.

Budgeting is a valuable and widely used technique but to be effective, requires a sound system of cost analysis and recording, properly organised management structures together with an awareness of how people will react to the discipline of the system.

DECISION MAKING AND PERFORMANCE APPRAISAL

Decision making means, in essence, making a choice between alternatives and is considered by many to be the key management activity. In organisations, decisions need to be taken continually. They may be long term, strategic decisions taken by top management, for example, should the company invest money to set up a branch in Europe in anticipation of 1992? Alternatively, they may be day-to-day operational decisions taken by the lowest level of management, or medium term decisions taken by tactical or middle management; for example shall we sub-contract work over the next month because of increased demand?

It is important to realise that all decision making relates to the future; if something has already happened we cannot take a decision about it. Accordingly any information of use for decision making must also be about the future; future revenues, future costs, future volumes and so on.

Although it is self-evident that we cannot foresee the future, a well organised CMA system can provide valuable guidance about future outcomes by careful analysis of past patterns and behaviour. For example, assume that a decision needs to be made about whether or not to introduce second shift working. This decision largely depends on estimates of how all the various items of cost are likely to behave. Examination of the cost records and analysis of past cost behaviour will provide valuable guidance in predicting what the costs are likely to be if a second shift is introduced. We will be in a better position to judge which costs are likely to increase (and by how much) and which are not likely to change much.

Costs which alter when activity levels change, are known as *variable costs*; examples include, materials, labour, power usage and so on. Those that tend to remain the same even though the activity level changes are known as *fixed costs* and examples include, rent, rates, most salaries and so on. Note that 'activity' is a general term used to describe the various ways of measuring the level of operations e.g. level of sales or production, number of shifts worked, orders processed and so on.

Organisations are frequently sub-divided into departments and operating divisions, each with managers responsible for their successful performance. Senior management need to be supplied with suitable information about the way the departments and divisions are working and how well the operating management are performing. This type of information is called performance appraisal information and the CMA system is a key provider.

Figure 1.1 opposite summarises the major parts of CMA and shows the chapters dealing with the various topics.

PRACTICAL NATURE OF CMA

CMA is not a complex, highly technical subject. It is a collection of common sense rules and procedures designed to be of practical help to managers. Indeed the only justification for any facet of CMA is that it must provide practical assistance – if it cannot be used or understood by management – it is of no value.

No advanced mathematics are required to gain a sound understanding of CMA. The ability to add, subtract, multiply and divide is all that is required to understand and use virtually every aspect of CMA, including many of the more advanced topics not included in this introductory book.

KEY POINT SUMMARY

- CMA provides financial information to management
- CMA includes; cost analysis and information for planning, control, decision making and performance appraisal
- A primary requirement is knowledge about the type of expenditure and its location or use
- Planning means deciding what is to be done; control is the process of monitoring actual results in order to keep to the plan
- Decision making means choosing between alternatives
- When activity levels change a fixed costs tends to stay the same but a variable cost alters in sympathy.

REVIEW EXERCISES

1. Give five examples of information supplied by a CMA system and their uses.
2. What is the two-fold analysis of expenditure?
3. What is the relationship between planning and control?
4. What are the key features of decision making?

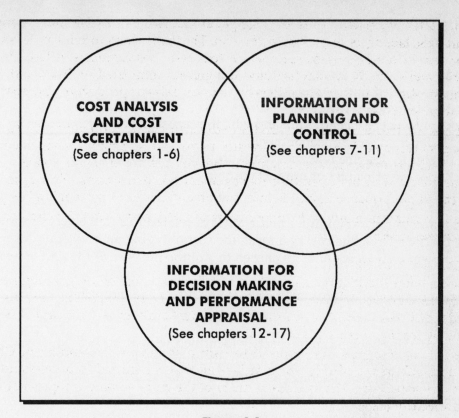

Figure 1.1

AN OVERVIEW OF COST & MANAGEMENT ACCOUNTING

2 COST ANALYSIS

OBJECTIVES

After you have studied this chapter you will

- Be able to define direct and indirect costs
- Know what cost centres are and why they are used
- Understand cost apportionment
- Be able to describe how overheads are accumulated
- Know the principles of product costing.

COSTS AND COST UNITS

A cost is an amount of expenditure and is always related to some object or unit. For example the cost of a book, the cost of a meal, the cost of typing an invoice and so on. These units are known as *cost units* and are chosen to suit the purpose of the cost ascertainment exercise and the organisation.

An important primary classification of costs is into direct and indirect:

DIRECT COSTS

Direct costs are those which can be directly identified with a product or service. They can be sub-divided into direct labour (or wages), direct materials and direct expenses. As an example, in a firm that manufactures a telephone set the direct costs might be as follows:

Direct Labour:

All the wages of the people directly engaged in making the individual components, testing and assembling the instrument.

Direct Materials:

All the materials incorporated in the finished telephone i.e. wire, components, metal, plastic etc.

Direct Expenses:

These are less commonly encountered but are fees, tool hire, royalties and so on directly associated with the final product so that if the firm had to pay a designer or inventor a royalty per instrument this would be a direct expense.

The total of direct costs is known as *Prime Cost* thus:

Direct Labour + Direct Materials + Direct Expenses = Prime Cost.

INDIRECT COSTS OR OVERHEADS

All costs which cannot be identified as direct are indirect costs or *overheads*. There are many more items of overheads than there are direct costs and the tendency in manufacturing firms is for overheads to become an increasing proportion of total expenditure. Examples of overheads include: salaries, running costs of machines, telephone costs, heating costs, rates, insurance, advertising and so on.

Expenditure on overheads is not wasted expenditure. It provides the essential support and organisation for production and it follows that the total cost of a product should include both the identifiable direct costs plus a suitable proportion of overheads thus:

Direct costs of product + share of overheads = Total cost of product.

By their nature, the direct costs of a product can be easily identified but several steps are necessary to determine what amount of overheads should be included in the product cost.

THE BUILD-UP OF OVERHEADS

A major difficulty associated with overheads can be illustrated by considering one particular item, that of Rates. Rates are levied as one sum on the premises as a whole yet clearly all departments and sections benefit from having premises to work in and should thus bear a proportion of the total Rate bill. In effect, a system is required to accumulate for each department or section all the overheads specifically identifiable with that department *plus* a reasonable share of general overhead items such as Rates.

The first step is to sub-divide the whole organisation into *cost centres* which, for control purposes, are normally the responsibility of a single person. Each cost centre is given a location code as mentioned in Chapter 1. Examples of cost centres are: the Personnel Department, the Typing Pool, the 50 ton Power Presses, Sales Representatives and so on. Thus a cost centre, which need not be a physical location, is a 'pigeon-hole' to accumulate overheads. These may be those specifically identified with the cost centre e.g. the salaries of the staff in the Planning Department or those overheads, such as Rates, which are shared between all cost centres. The process by which common costs are shared out between cost centre is known as *cost apportionment*.

COST APPORTIONMENT

Where two or more cost centres share the benefits of a common expenditure it is reasonable that the cost should also be shared between them; ideally in the proportions in which they receive the benefits. The basis on which the apportionment is carried out varies from cost to cost but some typical bases are shown below:

BASIS	Examples of costs which may be apportioned on this basis
FLOOR AREA	Rates, Rent, Heating, Lighting
VOLUME OR SPACE OCCUPIED	Heating, Lighting, Building Depreciation and Maintenance
NUMBER OF EMPLOYEES IN EACH COST CENTRE	Canteen, Welfare, Personnel, Administrative costs.

7

EXAMPLE OF COST APPORTIONMENT

An organisation has total heating costs of £25,000 and wishes these to be shared out fairly over its 10 cost centres. It has been decided that space occupied is the fairest basis of apportionment.

Cost centre	Space occupied (cubic metres)	Percentage of total	Share of heating costs
No 1 *	750	6.5%	1,625
2	750	6.5%	1,625
3	3,500	30%	7,500
4	250	2%	500
5	750	6.5%	1,625
6	250	2%	500
7	2,250	20%	5,000
8	1,000	9%	2,250
9	750	6.5%	1,625
10	1,250	11%	2,750
Total	11,500	100%	£25,000

* each apportionment is dealt with in the same way e.g

$$\frac{750}{11,500} = 6.5\% \text{ and } 6.5\% \text{ of } £25,000 = £1,625.$$

FINDING THE OVERHEADS FOR A COST CENTRE

The total overheads for a cost centre are thus a mixture of those directly spent by the cost centre, for example, the salaries of the people employed in it and an appropriate share of general costs such as rates, heating and so on.

In a manufacturing company some cost centres are directly concerned with making the product and are known as Production Cost Centres, for example, Machining, Assembly and Spraying and so on. The rest, which are non-production cost centres, are usually grouped under titles such as Administration, Marketing, Financial, Design and others, to suit the particular organisation. Each classification of cost centre naturally has different types of overhead but the general principles of gathering overheads by cost centre are universal.

Figure 2.1 overleaf summarises the build-up of overheads by cost centres.

FINDING THE PRODUCT COST

Earlier it was stated that the total cost of a product should include its direct costs plus a suitable share of overheads. To ensure that each product does carry an appropriate amount of overheads a two-stage process is necessary. Firstly, overheads are collected by the cost centre system described above. Then the overheads of the cost centre are spread over all the products passing through that cost centre by a process known as *overhead absorption* or overhead recovery.

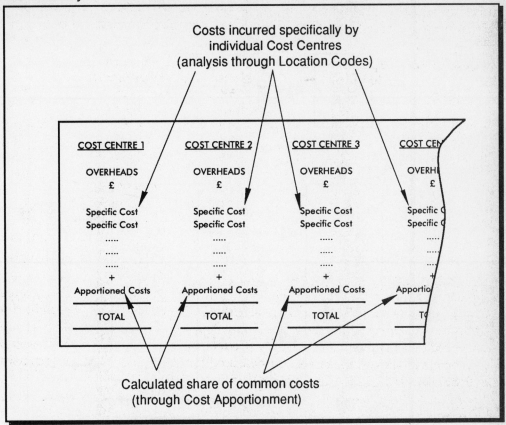

Figure 2.1

THE BUILD-UP OF OVERHEADS BY COST CENTRE

Ideally, each unit of product would receive a share of overheads which exactly reflects the load that producing that unit places on the cost centre. Naturally, this ideal is difficult to achieve but if the time is recorded that a product takes to pass through a cost centre and overheads are absorbed in proportion to the time taken, (measured as labour hours or machine hours) then reasonably accurate results can usually be achieved. Overhead absorption is developed in more detail later in the book.

Fig. 2.2 overleaf shows the outline of product costing which can be thought of as the units of production flowing through the organisation gathering overheads as they move along.

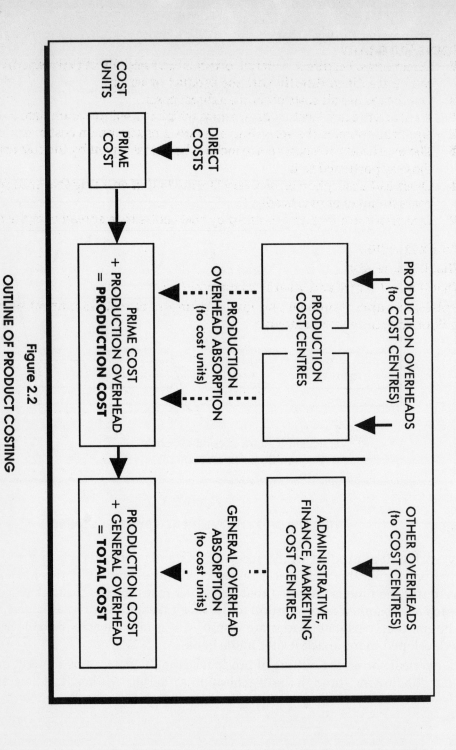

Figure 2.2
OUTLINE OF PRODUCT COSTING

KEY POINT SUMMARY

- Direct costs, i.e. direct material, direct labour and direct expenses, are those that can be identified directly with the product or service
- Overheads are all costs other than direct costs
- A cost centre is a location or function which is used to accumulate overheads
- Apportionment is the spreading or sharing of a common cost over cost centres
- The overheads of a cost centre include both costs spent by the cost centre and those apportioned to it
- Overhead absorption or recovery is a method of ensuring that each cost unit bears its share of overheads
- Overheads are first accumulated by cost centre then spread over the cost units.

REVIEW EXERCISES

1. What is prime cost?
2. What is a cost centre and what is its purpose?
3. Explain cost apportionment and give 3 examples of costs that might be apportioned on floor area; number of employees.

3 | MATERIALS AND LABOUR

OBJECTIVES

After you have studied this chapter you will
- Know the functions connected with materials
- Understand the reasons for issue pricing systems
- Be able to describe and use the main issue pricing systems; First in – First out, Average Price and Standard Price
- Understand the difference between time based and output based wage systems
- Know the difference between straight and differential piecework
- Be able to describe a typical bonus system.

PROBLEMS WITH DIRECT COSTS

Direct costs comprise direct materials, direct labour and direct expenses. Direct expenses are rare and are easily identified but there are several problems with the control and ascertainment of direct material and labour costs which are dealt with below.

DIRECT MATERIALS

These are bought in materials, parts, components and so on which are to be incorporated into the finished product. Direct materials often represent a substantial proportion of expenditure and it is essential that there is close control over all stages dealing with materials. These include; Purchasing, receipt and inspection, storage, issue to production and control of scrap and wastage during production. Key features of these stages follow.

PURCHASING

The Purchasing Department have an important function to fulfil. They have to ensure that the correct quality/specification of material is ordered, at the best price, with a delivery date which suits Production. After selection of the supplier, an official Purchase Order is sent. The issuing and signing of Purchase Orders must be closely controlled and no goods or invoices accepted unless covered by an Official Purchase Order.

RECEIPT AND INSPECTION

Goods received must be carefully inspected for quality and quantity and a Goods Received Note (GRN) raised. The GRN is used to check the supplier's invoice for the goods.

STORAGE AND ISSUE

Frequently, but not always, materials are taken into storage and then issued to Production as and when required. An Issue Note is raised for each issue which shows the quantity and description of the material issued – the description usually being a code. This is a vital stage as far as CMA is concerned because this is when the cost unit is charged with the direct material cost or, if an indirect material is concerned, the overheads of the appropriate cost centre are charged. The issue price used by the CMA system is not as easily determined as would be expected and various issue pricing methods have been developed which are explained later in this chapter.

SCRAP AND WASTAGE

Materials and components are expensive and excessive scrap and wastage must be avoided although some may be unavoidable because of the nature of the production process e.g. swarf, offcuts, trimmings and so on. All scrap must be weighed or counted and sold where possible and material that can be used again returned to stores. An important practical means of control is to issue just enough material to make the quantity required, allowing for normal scrap. If more is requested it immediately pinpoints that there has been excessive wastage which can be investigated there and then.

Note that the direct material cost of a product normally includes an allowance for unavoidable scrap.

PRICING ISSUES

In practice, the stock of materials and parts is made up of numerous deliveries often bought at different prices. As a consequence, it is difficult or perhaps impossible to identify an item with its delivery consignment and hence find the actual price paid.

Accordingly, it is normal to price issues from stores using a materials pricing system rather than try to trace the actual price paid. The system used should charge issues on a consistent and realistic basis and should be easy to use. Numerous systems are possible and three important ones; First in – First out, Average Price and Standard Price, are described below, followed by a worked example.

FIRST IN – FIRST OUT (FIFO)

Using the FIFO system, issues are priced at the cost of the oldest batch in stock until all that batch has been issued when the cost of the next batch is used and so on.

This system reflects good storekeeping practice whereby oldest items are used first but it does mean keeping track of the number or quantity in each batch which causes extra clerical work.

(There is a complementary pricing system where the price of the *newest* batch in stock is used; this is known as Last in – Last out or LIFO system.)

AVERAGE PRICE

This is a straightforward system whereby the issue price is the average price of all items in stock. The average price is recalculated after each receipt.

The average price method makes cost comparisons between jobs easier and requires less clerical work than the FIFO system.

3. Materials and Labour

STANDARD PRICE

A *standard price* is a planned price for a period which is used for all issues and returns.

This is the simplest system to deal with clerically and is best suited to stable conditions otherwise there is difficulty in deciding upon an appropriate standard price.

Note: The choice of issue price also determines the value of the closing stock

EXAMPLE OF ISSUE PRICING

The following data relate to Part No. X200 for the month of May

May 1st	Opening stock	1,000 items	@ £4 each
3rd	Issue	600 items	
6th	Receipt	400 items	@ £4.20 each
12th	Issue	500 items	
25th	Receipt	700 items	@ £4.30 each
26th	Issue	200 items	

The firm is considering using a Standard Issue Price of £4.15 per item but wishes to compare this price with the issue prices if FIFO or Average Price were used. Also the firm wishes to know what the closing stock values would be using the three systems.

SOLUTION SUMMARY

Issue Prices & Stock Valuations

Stock Movements		Standard Price (see Note 1)	FIFO (see Note 2)	Average Price (see Note 3)
		£	£	£
May 1 Stock	1,000			
3 – Issue	600	600 @ £4.15 = 2,490	600 @ £4 = 2,400	600 @ £4 = 2,400
New Stock	400			
6 + Receipt	400			
New Stock	800			
12 – Issue	500	500 @ £4.15 = 2,075	(400 @ £4)	
			(100 @ £4.20)=2,020	500 @ £4.10 =2,050
New Stock	300			
25 + Receipt	700			
New Stock	1,000			
26 – Issue	200	200 @ £4.15 = 830	200 @ £4.20 = 840	200 @ £4.24 = 848
Closing Stock	800	Stock Value= 3,320	Stock Value =3,430	Stock Value=3,392

Note 1

All issues take place at the Standard Price of £4.15 per item and total: £2,490 + 2,075 + 830 = £5,395.

The closing stock is also valued at Standard Price i.e. 800 @ £4.15 =   £3,320.

14

Note 2

The FIFO system uses the price of the oldest batch first, until it is all used up thus:

	Batch 1		**Batch 2**
Opening stock	1,000 @ £4		
600 Issue on 3 May	600 @ £4		
Balance	400 @ £4	Receipt	400 @ £4.20
500 Issue on 12 May is			
from 2 batches	400 @ £4 and	Issue	100 @ £4.20
		Balance	300 @ £4.20
			20 Issue on
		26th	200 @ £4.20
		Balance	100 @ £4.20

Note that the FIFO system may require issues to be drawn from more than one batch which means that several prices may be included in one issue.

The total issue value using FIFO is £2,400 + 2,020 + 840 = £5,260 and the closing stock value is found as follows:

OPENING STOCK + RECEIPTS - ISSUES = CLOSING STOCK

$£(1,000 \times 4) + (400 \times 4.20 + 700 \times 4.30) - 5,260 = 4,000 + 4,690 - 5,260 = £3,430$

The closing stock valuation can be proved as follows:

Closing stock, 800 items made up of

100 from Receipt on 6th May	= 100 @ £4.20	=	£420
700 from Receipt on 25th May	= 700 @ £4.30	=	£3,010
		=	£3,430

Note 3

The Average Price system uses the average price of stock and is recalculated after every new receipt thus:

3rd May	Issue of 600 @ £4 (i.e. as opening stock) leaving a balance of 400 @ £4
6th May	Receipt of 400 @ £4.20
	∴ New average price = $(400 \times £4 + 400 \times £4.20) \div 800 = £4.10$
12th May	Issue 500 @ £4.10 leaving balance of 300 @ £4.10
25th May	Receipt of 700 @ £4.30
	∴ New average price = $(300 \times £4.10 + 700 \times £4.30) \div 1,000 = £4.24$
26th May	Issue of 200 @ £4.24 leaving a balance of 800 @ £4.24 = £3,392

Closing Stock Valuation proof

Opening stock + Receipts – Issues = Closing Stock

$= £4,000 + 4,690 - 5,298 = £3,392.$

DIRECT LABOUR OR WAGES

Direct wages are those paid to people directly concerned with manufacturing the product. Examples include; machinists, assemblers, sprayers etc. The wages paid to people who support and organise production such as foremen, inspectors, maintenance and so on, are not direct wages but are classified as production overheads.

There are numerous methods of calculating direct wages but the various systems can be classified into those that are based on *time* and those that are based on *output*. These are explained below:

TIME BASED WAGES

At the simplest, wages are paid at a basic rate per hour up to, say, 38 hours per week. Time worked above 38 hours would be classed as overtime and is usually paid at a higher rate, for example, 'time and a half' i.e. 1½ × basic rate per hour, depending on the number of hours worked and when the overtime was worked.

Time based wages are not dependent on the level of output but naturally output quantity and quality are still vital factors and it is normal for performance to be closely monitored. Time based systems are most appropriate where quality is all important or where output related schemes would be difficult or impossible to install.

Time based systems frequently also include bonuses and other payments. For example, timekeeping and shift bonuses, good housekeeping bonuses, safety bonuses and so on.

OUTPUT BASED WAGES

Schemes in which wages are dependent on output are usually known as incentive schemes. There are numerous types of these schemes, some apply to individuals, others to groups, some have minimum earnings guarantees and so on. Properly organised incentive schemes can benefit both the employee and the firm. The employee from the extra wages arising from increased production and the employer from the reduced overheads per unit of the increased production.

Incentive schemes can increase production and wages and thereby improve morale, but some schemes are difficult to administer and there can be problems in deciding upon performance levels and rates.

The commonest wages systems based on output are Piecework Schemes and Bonus Schemes which are explained below.

PIECEWORK SCHEMES

At their simplest, the worker would be paid an agreed rate per unit or operation, for the number of units produced or operations carried out.

> ### Example
> A machinist is paid on piecework at the rate of £1.80 per 100 components produced. During a week he produced 9,140 components of which 60 were rejected by inspection. What were his wages for the week?

Solution

Output for week	9,140	components
less rejects	60	
Net good output	9,080	

∴ Wages for week = 9,080 @ £1.80 per 100 = £163.44

Note that only good production is paid for.

Where, as in the example above, the same rate per unit is paid for all production, the system is known as *straight piecework*. On occasions, the rate is increased progressively at various output levels and this is then known as *differential piecework*.

Example

A worker is paid by differential piecework and the following rates have been agreed:

up to 500 units	25p per unit
501-600 units	27p per unit
601-700 units	30p per unit
701 and above	35p per unit.

During a week the worker produced 642 good units. What were his wages for the week?

Solution

Wages				£
500	@	25p	=	125
100	@	27p	=	27
42	@	30p	=	12.60
		TOTAL		164.60

BONUS SYSTEMS

There is a great variety of these systems which usually combine a flat rate per hour with a bonus for achieving a given output level. Often the bonus is based on the savings made between the actual time taken and the target time for a job.

Example

A worker with a basic rate of £5 per hour receives a bonus of half the hours saved on each job. In a 38 hour week he completes 2 jobs as follows:

Job	Target time	Actual time
A	32 hours	23 hours
B	16 hours	15 hours
		38 hours

What are his wages for the week?

Solution

Bonus hours:

Job A	= ½(32 – 23)	=	4 hours
Job B	= ½(16 – 15)	=	½ hours
Total Bonus Hours			5 hours
Total pay hours	= 38 + 5	=	43 hours
and wages	= 43 × £5	=	£215

WHEN DIRECT WAGES MAY BE CLASSIFIED AS INDIRECT

There are certain occasions when the wages paid to direct workers are classified as indirect i.e. they become part of overheads rather than part of direct costs. Typical examples are:

(a) when overtime is worked it is common to charge overtime wages above basic rates to overheads rather than direct wages. For example, if the basis rate is £5 per hour and overtime is paid at 'time and a half' then £5 would be charged to direct wages and £2.50 to overheads. The reason is that it is usually accidental which job is done in overtime and that job should not be penalised.

(b) when workers are paid by an incentive scheme and an unavoidable production stoppage occurs, the period during which no production takes place is known as 'idle time' and the workers usually revert to being paid at normal time rates. Idle time wages are invariably classified as overheads.

KEY POINT SUMMARY

- Close control must be kept over all stages dealing with materials: Purchasing, Receipt, Storage and Issue
- The material cost of a product includes an allowance for unavoidable scrap
- Materials are charged out from stores using a pricing system rather than actual cost
- The First in – First out (FIFO) system prices issues at the cost of the oldest batch in stock. The LIFO system prices issues at the cost of the newest batch in stock
- The Average Price system using the average price of all items in stock
- A Standard Price is a planned price for a period
- Time based wages include basic rates and overtime rates such as 'time and a quarter' and so on
- The simplest incentive scheme is Straight Piecework
- Differential piecework means that the rate per item is increased as output increases
- Numerous types of bonus schemes exist and are frequently based on the savings between actual and target time.

REVIEW EXERCISES

1. The following information is available about a component

Opening stock	1st May	5,000 at 20p each
Receipts	6th May	1,600 at 22p each
	18th May	1,800 at 23p each
Issues	2nd May	3,000
	16th May	2,100

Produce statements showing the issue prices and closing stock values assuming that issues are priced at

(a) LIFO

(b) Average price

2. Distinguish between wages paid by time and wages based on production.

3. A worker is paid by differential piecework as follows:

up to 300 units	40p per unit
301 – 500 units	45p per unit
501 – 800 units	48p per unit
801 and above	50p per unit

In a week 596 units were produced of which 22 were rejected.

What were the worker's wages for the week?

4 OVERHEADS

OBJECTIVES

After you have studied this chapter you will
- Know how to calculate an overhead absorption rate (OAR)
- Understand the way OAR's are used in calculating product cost
- Be able to explain why time based overhead absorption is generally preferred
- Understand and be able to calculate under or over absorption of overheads
- Be able to calculate depreciation charges using the straight line, reducing balance and production unit methods.

OVERHEAD ABSORPTION

It will be recalled from Chapter 2 that overheads are first accumulated by cost centre then shared out over the products passing through the cost centre by a process known as overhead absorption or overhead recovery. The objective is to spread the overheads of a cost centre over the products in a way which fairly reflects the loading that a product or job places on the cost centre.

The usual method by which this is done is to calculate, for each production cost centre, an overhead absorption rate (OAR) which is then used to find the overheads applicable to the product or job.

OVERHEAD ABSORPTION RATE (OAR)

OAR's are calculated using the overheads of a cost centre and the number of units of the absorption base considered most appropriate, say, labour or machine hours. Because the *actual* amounts of the overheads and the absorption base cannot be known until the end of a period and the OAR is required throughout the period it is normal to use *estimated* values for both factors and to make what adjustments are necessary later. Thus the OAR for a cost centre is:

$$\text{Predetermined OAR for cost centre} = \frac{\text{estimated overheads for cost centre}}{\text{estimated units of absorption base}}$$

Example 1

The Assembly cost centre has estimated overheads for Period 1 of £75,000. Labour hours are considered the most appropriate basis and it is expected that 12,000 hours will be worked in total during the period.

What is the OAR?

Solution

$$\text{OAR for Assembly} = \frac{£75,000}{12,000} = £6.25 \text{ per labour hour}$$

HOW IS THE OAR USED?

The factory or production cost of a cost unit comprises its direct costs (direct material, direct labour and any direct expenses) plus a share of the overheads of each production cost centre involved with the manufacture of the cost unit. The share of overheads is found by using the calculated OAR of the particular cost centre multiplied by the hours spent in the cost centre (assuming that time is considered the most appropriate absorption base)

Example 2

Job No. 525 is one of many jobs that pass through the Assembly cost centre during a period. The only work done on Job 525 is assembly work and its direct costs are

	£
Direct materials	65
Direct labour (5 hours @ £4)	20
Total direct costs	85

What is the total production cost of Job 525 assuming that the Assembly OAR is £6.25 per hour as previously calculated

Solution

Job 525

	Total production cost
	£
Direct materials	65
Direct labour (5 × £4)	20
Prime cost	85
+ Assembly overheads	
(5 × £6.25)	31.25
Total production cost	116.25

Note that the 5 labour hours are multiplied by the previously calculated OAR to find the total overheads of the job.

However unlike Example 2 most jobs pass through more than one cost centre and gather overheads from each of the cost centres involved in the manufacture of the job. For example:

Example 3

Job 854 is made in two cost centres, Assembly and Finishing, whose overhead absorption rates are £6.25 and £11 per labour hour respectively. The job details are:

	Assembly		Finishing
	£		£
Direct materials	120		25
Direct labour 8 hrs @ £4	32	14 hrs @ £5	70

What is the production cost of Job 854?

21

Solution

	Total Production Cost	
	£	£
Direct materials (£120 + 25)		145
Direct labour (£32 + 70)		102
= Prime cost		247
Overheads		
Assembly 8 × £6.25	50	
Finishing 14 × £11	154	204
Total production cost		£451

CHOICE OF ABSORPTION BASE

There are no hard and fast rules for deciding which is the most appropriate absorption basis; judgement is always necessary. What is required is an absorption base which realistically reflects the characteristics of the given cost centre and which avoids undue anomalies.

It is generally accepted that the time based methods (labour and machine hours) are more likely to reflect the load on a cost centre and one of these should normally be chosen. However, other absorption bases exist; for example, recovery on direct wages or materials or by cost unit, but these alternatives have numerous disadvantages and would rarely be chosen.

The characteristics of the time based methods are given below:

DIRECT LABOUR HOUR BASIS

This is best suited to a labour intensive cost centre where simple (and inexpensive) machinery only is employed. The system is easy to use as the hours taken are normally recorded anyway for wage payment purposes. However as production becomes increasingly mechanised, this method of overhead absorption is likely to be less appropriate in the future.

MACHINE HOUR BASIS

This basis is most appropriate for mechanised cost centres. In such cost centres overheads are related to machinery and machinery usage (power, maintenance, depreciation and so on) so absorption using a machine hour rate reflects the occurrence of overheads in a reasonably accurate way.

The machine hour OAR of a cost centre is calculated using estimates of the total machine hours and overheads expected in the cost centre, in a similar fashion to the labour hour method described previously.

UNDER OR OVER ABSORPTION OF OVERHEADS

Each job or cost unit passing through a cost centre absorbs, through the OAR system, some of the overheads of the cost centre. This happens progressively so that at the end of the period the total amount of overheads absorbed by production is known. Because the predetermined OAR's are based on estimates of production and overheads, invariably the total of absorbed overheads does not agree with the actual overheads incurred.

If overheads absorbed by production are *greater* than actual overheads, this is known as *over absorption*.

If overheads absorbed by production are *less* than actual overheads, this is known as *under absorption*.

An example follows:

Example 4

Cost centre 210 data for Period 8

	Estimated	Actual
Overheads	£85,000	£82,605
Machine hours	7,500	7,210
Prime cost		£126,500

The machine hour basis of overhead absorption is considered the most suitable for cost centre 210.

What is the amount of under or over absorbed overheads?

Solution

OAR based on Machine hours $= \dfrac{85,000}{7,500} = \underline{£11.33 \text{ per hour}}$

∴ overheads absorbed by actual production = 7,210 hours × £11.33 = £81,689

It will be seen that the total of absorbed overheads, £81,689 is *less* than the actual overheads of £82,605 so there is *under-absorption* in this instance.

i.e.   £82,605 − 81,689 =   £916 *under-absorption*

WHAT HAPPENS TO UNDER OR OVER ABSORBED OVERHEADS?

It is important to realise that it is *actual* costs and overheads which determine the final profit. This means that the total of actual costs must be used to find profit and not merely the calculated product cost; which includes actual prime costs plus absorbed overheads based on a predetermined OAR.

Thus the amount of under absorbed overheads should be added to total costs before profit is calculated and conversely the amount of over absorbed overheads should be subtracted from total cost.

This is illustrated, using the data from Example 4

Actual Prime cost		Absorbed Overhead		Calculated Production cost		Under Absorption		Actual Production cost
£126,500	+	81,689	=	208,189	+	916	=	209,105

to Profit calculation.

Note: The under absorption has had to be added to the calculated production cost to bring the total up to the actual costs incurred. This may seem to be a long winded way of getting to actual costs but it is necessary because individual job costs are required right through the period and it would be highly inconvenient to have to wait until the end of the period before they could be calculated. Accordingly predetermined OAR's are used, based on estimates, and errors in the estimates are compensated for at the end of the period, using the under or over absorption process described above.

ABSORBING NON-PRODUCTION OVERHEADS

Many of the overheads of a typical company are incurred outside the production cost centres. They include overheads relating to: Administration, Selling and Distribution, Research and Development, Marketing, Advertising, Finance and numerous other non-production cost centres.

Naturally these general overheads must be included in the total cost of a product together with the prime cost and production overheads dealt with previously. Because of the difficulty of relating general overheads to individual products the absorption of general overheads is usually done by taking, either a percentage of product cost or percentage of sales value. For the same reasons given earlier, predetermined OAR's are used.

Example 5

The general overheads of a firm comprise those relating to Administration, Marketing and Research. For Period 6 the following estimates were made:

	£
Estimated total general overheads	45,000
Estimated total production costs	75,000

(a) What is the General Overhead Absorption rate assuming that absorption based on production cost is considered the most appropriate?

(b) What amount of general overheads would be absorbed by the following two jobs?

Job No.	Total production cost
168	£6,050
243	£2,900

Solution

(a) General OAR $= \dfrac{\text{estimated total general overheads}}{\text{estimated total production costs}}\%$

$= \dfrac{45{,}000}{75{,}000}\% = 60\%$

(b)

	Job 168	Job 243
	£	£
Production cost	6,050	2,900
General overhead	(60% of 6,050)	(60% of 2,900)
	3,630	1,740
Total cost	9,680	4,640

DEPRECIATION

Most assets decline in value due to wear and the passage of time. This decline in value is known as *depreciation* and the amount of depreciation in a period is included as part of the overheads of the period.

Although depreciation is an important item of overheads it differs from other overhead costs in two ways. Firstly, the amount of depreciation to be charged in a period is decided by the organisation itself. With most other forms of overheads, for example, electricity, telephones, rates and so on, the organisation has little or no control over the amount charged. Secondly, a typical overhead cost entails money being paid out from the organisation. Examples include: salaries, electricity, insurance and so on. In contrast, a depreciation charge does not cause a movement of cash; the charge being a book-keeping entry only. This does not mean that depreciation is unimportant. It would be unrealistic not to include the cost of expensive machinery and buildings in the cost of a product and depreciation is the most practical way this can be done.

DEPRECIATION METHODS

Numerous methods exist but they can be grouped in two categories:

(a) Where depreciation is based on *time*

(b) Where depreciation is based on *volume of production*

Two time based methods; Straight line and Reducing balance, and the Production Unit method based on volume are described below.

STRAIGHT LINE DEPRECIATION

This method, also known as the equal instalment method, reduces the value of an asset by an equal amount each year thus:

$$\text{Depreciation charge per year} = \dfrac{\text{Asset cost}}{\text{Estimated life in years}}$$

Example 6

A welding machine cost £25,000 and is expected to last 10 years. What is the depreciation charge per year?

Solution

$$\text{Depreciation per year} = \frac{25,000}{10} = \underline{\text{£2,500 per year}}$$

This means that £2,500 per year would be included among the overheads of the cost centre in which the welding machine was situated.

Each year the asset is assumed to decline in value by the amount of the calculated depreciation. Thus, the welding machine in Example 6 would have a net value (known as the written down value or WDV) at the end of year 1 of £25,000 – 2,500 = £22,500.

At the end of year 2 the written down value would be £22,500 – 2,500 = £20,000 and so on. Thus at the end of 10 years, in each of which £2,500 had been charged, the welding machine would have a written down value of zero.

REDUCING BALANCE METHOD

Using this method a percentage of the written down value is charged as depreciation each year. The percentage chosen would be sufficient so that, over the life of the asset, its original cost will be reduced approximately to zero.

The effect of the reducing balance method is that *decreasing amounts* of depreciation are charged each year, as compared with the straight line method where *equal amounts* are charged each year.

Example 7

A boiler costs £30,000 and is expected to last 20 years. The firm uses the reducing balance method of depreciation and a rate of 40% is normal for this type of asset.

What is the depreciation charge for each of the first 5 years?

Solution		£	
Year 1	Cost	30,000	
	40% of 30,000	12,000	Year 1 depreciation charge
		18,000	Written down value
Year 2			
	40% of 18,000	7,200	Year 2 depreciation charge
		10,800	Written down value
Year 3			
	40% of 10,800	4,320	Year 3 depreciation charge
		6,480	Written down value

Year 4

40% of 6,480	2,592	Year 4 depreciation charge
	1,888	Written down value

Year 5

40% of 1,888	755	Year 5 depreciation charge
	1,133	Written down value

and so on.

Note how the yearly depreciation declines each year; from £12,000 in year 1 to £755 in year 5. Naturally the process continues over the life of the asset and the reducing balance method thus produces heavy charges in the early years and much lighter charges later on.

One possible criticism of the two depreciation methods described above is that they do not take account of the amount of production in a year; the same depreciation being charged whether production is low or high or indeed non-existent. This is considered incorrect for certain types of assets, especially those directly concerned with production where volumes can easily be recorded. In such circumstances the production unit method of depreciation can be used.

PRODUCTION UNIT METHOD OF DEPRECIATION

This method bases depreciation on the production volume in a period using a previously calculated depreciation charge per unit thus:

$$\text{Depreciation charge per unit} = \frac{\text{Asset cost}}{\text{estimated units of production over life of asset}}$$

Example 8

A blanking machine costs £25,000 and it is estimated that it can produce 1,000,000 parts over its lifetime. During the first two years, 110,000 and 155,000 parts respectively were produced.

What is the depreciation rate per unit?

What are the depreciation charges for years 1 and 2?

Solution

$$\text{Depreciation rate per unit} = \frac{£25,000}{1,000,000} = 2.5p$$

Depreciation charges

Year 1	110,000 × 2.5p	=	£2,750
Year 2	155,000 × 2.5p	=	£3,875

27

KEY POINT SUMMARY

■ Overhead absorption *shares the overheads over production*

■ Overhead absorption rates for a cost centre are calculated thus

$$OAR = \frac{\text{estimated overhead}}{\text{estimated units of absorption base}}$$

■ Overhead absorption based on labour or machine hours is generally preferred

■ If absorbed overheads are more than actual overheads there is over-absorption; if less, then there is under-absorption

■ The under or over absorption calculation is needed to bring absorbed overheads in line with actual overheads

■ Non-production overheads are usually absorbed either as a percentage of production cost or sales value

■ Depreciation is the decline in value of an asset and is an important part of overheads

■ Important depreciation methods include: straight line, reducing balance, and production unit.

REVIEW EXERCISES

1. Distinguish between overhead apportionment and overhead absorption.

2. What is the overhead absorption rate for the following machining cost centre? Overheads for the next period are estimated to be £85,000 and it is expected that 7,700 machine hours will be worked.

3. In the event, the actual overheads for the machining cost centre mentioned above were £82,681 and 7,328 machine hours were worked. What is the amount of under or over absorbed overheads?

4. What is depreciation and how does it differ from other overheads? How is the depreciation charge per year calculated using straight line depreciation?

5 | COSTING METHODS: JOB, BATCH AND CONTRACT COSTING

OBJECTIVES

After you have studied this chapter you will

- ■ Understand the two main categories of costing methods: order costing and continuous costing
- ■ Be able to define Job Costing and know where it can be used
- ■ Know how to calculate a Job Cost
- ■ Understand the relationship between Batch and Job Costing
- ■ Understand the characteristics of Contract Costing
- ■ Be able to calculate the profit or loss on uncompleted contracts and the closing asset and liability valuations.

COST ANALYSIS PRINCIPLES

So far the basic costing principles have been described. These include; expenditure analysis, apportionment, absorption and so on. These principles underpin all costing systems but it is also important that the method of costing is designed to suit the way goods are manufactured or services provided. The method of costing that suits a car manufacturer would not be appropriate for an oil refinery or a local authority, and vica versa. However, organisations in the same line of business are likely to have costing methods with recognisably common features.

CATEGORIES OF COSTING METHODS

As previously stated, the costing method must suit the organisation and the type of production or way services are provided.

There are two broad categories of costing methods; Order costing and Continuous costing.

Order costing is used where the work consists of separate jobs or contracts which generally are different from one another. This type of costing would typically be used by contractors, builders, jobbing engineers, accountancy firms, garages and so on. The cost unit is the job or contract and the costing system shows the profit or loss on individual jobs or contracts.

Continuous costing seeks to find the average cost per unit during a period for a number of identical cost units. The key feature is the presence of a continuous series of processes or operations producing identical or near identical products or services. Continuous costing can be used in any form of process industry, for example, oil refining, food and drink manufacture, mining and so on. It can also be applied to suitable service industries, for example, the provision of meals, hamburgers and so on in fast food outlets.

These categories and their main sub-divisions are shown in Figure 5.1 overleaf.

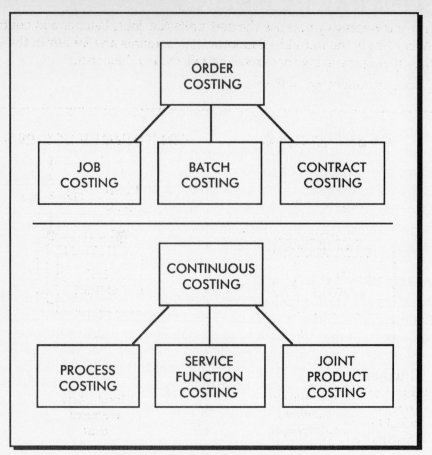

Figure 5.1

CATEGORIES OF COSTING METHODS

Order costing is dealt with in detail in this chapter and continuous costing in Chapter 6 following but first a key difference in the way that the cost elements (material, labour and overheads) are dealt with, must be understood.

COST ELEMENTS IN ORDER AND CONTINUOUS COSTING

Using Continuous Costing *all* costs i.e. labour, materials and overheads, are charged to a cost centre then the total is divided equally amongst the cost units produced. This simple, one stage procedure is possible because identical cost units are being produced.

This differs from Order Costing where only direct materials and labour can be charged directly to the cost unit. Overheads must be charged first to cost centres then spread over the cost units by the absorption process.

This procedure is necessary because the cost units (i.e. jobs, batches and contracts) are all different. Accordingly the individual amounts of materials and labour in the jobs and the varying times spent producing them must be reflected in their cost.

This difference is summarised in Figure 5.2

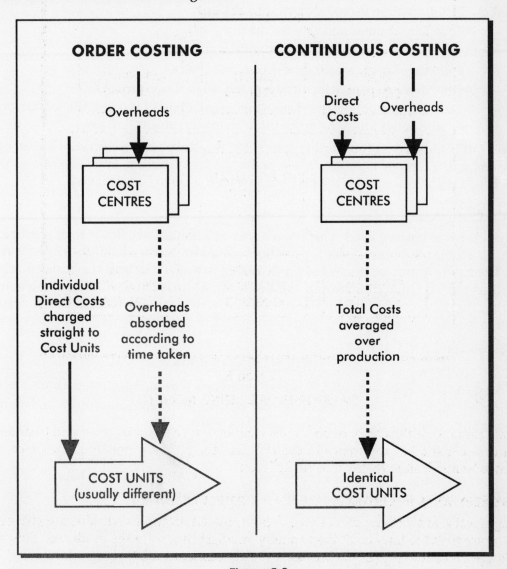

Figure 5.2

ORDER AND CONTINUOUS COSTING COMPARED

JOB COSTING

The main objective is to charge all costs incurred to the particular job. This is done by creating a Job Card (or equivalent entry on a computer file) for every job; each of which is given its own number.

The following information is recorded on the Job Card:
- Actual labour times and grades/rates of pay
- Actual issues of material, with quantities and prices
- Actual time spent in each production cost centre
- Actual direct expenses incurred e.g. special tool equipment hire
- Absorbed production overhead (this is calculated by using the labour or machine hours times the appropriate overhead absorption rate)

When a job is finished its Job Card is completed by adding to Production Cost an appropriate amount of General Overheads (e.g. Selling, Administration, Finance and so on). This gives Total Cost which enables the profit or loss on the job to be calculated.

BATCH COSTING

This is a form of costing used where a quantity of identical articles is manufactured in a batch. In general the procedures for costing batches are very similar to those for costing jobs. The batch would be treated as a job during manufacture and the costs collected as described above. On completion of the batch the cost per unit would be calculated by dividing the total batch cost by the number of good units produced. Batch costing is common in the footwear, clothing, engineering and similar industries.

Example 1

JOB/BATCH COSTING

An order for 150 brackets at £45 was received and was manufactured as Job No. 875.

Job No. 875 passed through three cost centres; Blanking, Assembly and Finishing whose overheads absorption bases and rates were:

Blanking	– Machine Hour Basis	– OAR	£20 per hour
Assembly	– Labour Hour Basis	– OAR	£9 per hour
Finishing	– Labour Hour Basis	– OAR	£12 per hour

The following production costs and data were recorded:

Direct Materials			£630
Labour	80 hours	Blanking at	£5.50 per hour
	140 hours	Assembly at	£4 per hour
	60 hours	Finishing at	£4.50 per hour

40 machine hours were recorded in Blanking and General Administration overheads are absorbed at 10% of total product cost

Calculate the total cost of the batch, the unit total cost and the profit per unit.

Solution

TOTAL COST JOB No. 875

		£	£
DIRECT MATERIAL			630
DIRECT LABOUR			
Blanking	80 × £5.50	440	
Assembly	140 × £4.00	560	
Finishing	60 × £4.50	270	1,270
PRIME COST			1,900
PRODUCTION OVERHEAD ABSORPTION			
Blanking	40 × £20	800	
	140 × £9	1,260	
	60 × £12	720	2,780
PRODUCTION COST		4,680	
+ GENERAL OVERHEADS (10% × 4,680)		468	
TOTAL COST		5,148	

$$\text{Cost per unit} = \frac{£5,148}{150} = \underline{£34.32}$$

$$\text{Profit per unit} = £45 - 34.32 = \underline{£10.68}$$

CONTRACT COSTING

Contract costing has many similarities to job costing and is generally used for work which is:

(a) Of relatively long duration (usually longer than a year)

(b) Site based

(c) Frequently of a constructional nature e.g. bridges, road building and so on.

Because of the self contained nature of most site operations, many costs normally classed as indirect can be considered as direct and charged straight to the contract. Examples include; power usage, site telephones, transportation, supervisory salaries and so on.

Cost control is a problem on many contracts because of their scale and the size of sites. Difficulties include; wastage, pilferage, vandalism, problems of labour control and so on. Good on-site management can help to reduce these problems but there are no perfect solutions.

As with job/batch costing the objective of contract costing is to find the final profit or loss on the completed contract. However, because many contracts last for several years it becomes necessary to consider interim profits and losses as the contract progresses, rather than wait until completion for the final result. This is explained below.

INTERIM RESULTS ON UNCOMPLETED CONTRACTS

Because of the scale and duration of many contracts it would be misleading if the firm ignored interim assessments of the profits or losses and stock valuations for contracts which are uncompleted at the year end.

The recommendations governing interim assessments are complex and detailed but the main principles are given below:

PROFITS / LOSSES ON UNCOMPLETED CONTRACTS

(a) If it is estimated that an overall contract profit will be made, taking into account costs already incurred and expected future costs to completion, then it is correct to take credit in the current period for a reasonable proportion of the expected total profit.

(b) If a loss is expected for the contract as a whole then this should be provided *in full* in the current period's accounts.

The effect of the above points is that a conservative view is always taken. This is entirely reasonable given the unexpected difficulties which can occur in contract work. Examples include; adverse weather, ground problems, material shortages, labour difficulties and so on. There are several methods of deciding what is a 'reasonable proportion' of Total profits and a common way is to obtain an Architect's valuation of the work done to date. However, whatever method is used it is important that interim profits are not overstated.

An example follows which illustrates the above principles.

Example 2

Profit/Loss on Uncompleted Contracts

Apex Developments had two contracts in progress at their financial year end as follows:

	Contract No.83 £'000s	Contract No.77 £'000s
Contract value	250	186
Costs incurred to date	65	140
Estimated additional costs to final completion	130	55
Architect's value of completed stages	78	150
Cost of completed stages	63	140

What profits or losses, if any, would be included in the current year's accounts in respect of the two contracts?

Solution

Contract No. 83

	£'000s	£'000s
Contract value		250
less costs to date	65	
Estimated costs to completion	130	195
Estimated total contract profit		55

As it is estimated that the contract will give an overall profit it is correct to take a reasonable proportion into account in the current period thus:

	£'000s
Architect's value of stages completed	78
less costs of completed stages	63
Profit for current period	15

Thus £15,000 profit from Contract No. 83 would be included in the firm's results for the year.

Contract No. 77

	£'000s	£'000s
Contract value		186
less costs to date	140	
Estimated costs to completion	55	195
Estimated total contract loss		9

As an overall loss of £9,000 is expected *all* of this would be taken into account in the current period.

Note that it is the estimated total contract result (in this case, a loss) which determined what is taken into account in the current period not the notional surplus of £10,000 between the Architect's valuation and costs incurred (i.e. £150,000 – £140,000).

BALANCE SHEET ENTRIES FOR UNCOMPLETED CONTRACTS

A balance sheet can be simply described as a statement of an organisation's assets and liabilities, i.e. what it *owns* and what it *owes*. All the various activities of the organisation result in assets and/or liabilities, including the transactions relating to uncompleted contracts. These translations include expenditure on the numerous costs (labour, materials and so on) and also the periodic receipt of money from the client when agreed stages are completed; for example, foundations complete, first floor level reached and so on. These interim payments are known as *progress payments* and are a normal feature of contract work.

The main principles concerning assets and/or liabilities arising from uncompleted contracts are:

(a) The stock valuation for an uncompleted contract (usually known as work-in-progress or WIP) is the total costs incurred less any costs used in interim profit calculations less foreseeable losses (if any) and payments on account.

(b) Debtors (i.e. someone who owes you money; an asset) arise if progress payments received are less than the agreed sales value of the completed stages.

(c) Creditors (i.e. someone you owe money to: a liability) arise if progress payments are greater than the agreed sales values of completed stages after allowing for any WIP value.

The following example illustrates the above principles.

Example 3

Balance Sheet Entries for Uncompleted Contracts

The data used in Example 2 are reproduced below together with details of the progress payments received for the work done to date on the two contracts.

	Contract No.83 £'000s	Contract No.77 £'000s
Contract value	250	186
Costs incurred to date	65	140
Estimated costs to final completion	130	55
Architect's value of completed stages	78	150
Cost of completed stages	63	140
Progress payments received	82	138

Calculate the asset and/or liability values of the two contracts for balance sheet purposes.

Solution

Contract No. 83

WIP calculation	£'000s
Costs incurred to date	65
less Costs of sales (i.e. completed stages)	63
= Work-in-Progress	2

Debtor/Creditor calculation

	£'000s
Sales Value (i.e. Architect's valuation)	78
Progress payments received	82
Difference = surplus of payments received	4

As there is a *surplus* of payments received of £4,000 this is equivalent to a creditor, i.e. a liability.

Thus this contract has produced an asset value of £2,000 for WIP and a liability value of £4,000 for creditors. These would be netted to produce a single figure of £2,000 for creditors thus

$$\begin{array}{lcl} \text{WIP + CREDITORS} & = & \text{NET CREDITORS} \\ \text{£2,000 + £4,000} & = & \text{£2,000} \end{array}$$

(If the WIP valuation had been greater than creditors, naturally the net balance would be a WIP value).

Contract No. 77

WIP calculation

	£'000s	£'000s
Costs incurred to date		140
less costs of sales (i.e.completed stages)	140	
Overall estimated loss	9	149
		−9

Thus what would normally be an asset has been turned into a liability of £9,000 which is, of course, the amount of the estimated loss. This would be entered on the liability side of the balance sheet as a £9,000 provision for contract loss.

Debtor/Creditor Calculation

	£'000s
Sales value (i.e. Architect's valuation)	150
Progress payments received	138
Difference = Shortfall of payments received	12

As there is a deficiency of payments received of £12,000 this is equivalent to a debtor, i.e. an asset.

Thus Contract 77 has produced two balance sheet entries, a liability (provision for Loss £9,000) and an asset (Debtors £12,000).

KEY POINT SUMMARY

- The costing method used must suit the method of manufacture or service provision
- There are two broad categories of costing methods: order costing and continuous costing
- Order costing generally deals with dissimilar cost units; continuous costing is used where similar cost units are produced
- Using continuous costing all costs are averaged over units whereas with order costing a more individual method is necessary
- Using Job Costing, individual costs are recorded on the Job Card to find the profit or loss on the job
- Batch costing uses similar principles to Job Costing. The final cost is averaged over the number of good units in the batch

- Contract costing is typically used for site based work of relatively long duration
- Where a profit is expected on the contract as a whole a conservative proportion can be taken at interim year ends
- Where an overall loss is expected this would be provided for in full at the interim stage
- Balance Sheet entries (assets and/or liabilities) arise from uncompleted contracts for WIP valuations and debtors or creditors.

REVIEW EXERCISES

1. What is the key difference in the treatment of the cost elements (material, labour and overheads) between order and continuous costing?

2. What would be the likely effects of absorbing all overheads on labour hours when some jobs contain mostly labour, and little machining whilst others contain many machine hours but little labour? Selling prices are based on cost.

3. What are the broad principles upon which interim profits are calculated for long term contracts?

6 COSTING METHODS: SERVICES, PROCESS AND JOINT-PRODUCT COSTING

OBJECTIVES

After you have studied this chapter you will

- Know when to use service costing and understand the problems in choosing suitable cost units
- Understand the principles of process costing
- Be able to distinguish between normal losses and abnormal losses and gains
- Be able to calculate the number of equivalent units in any partly completed production
- Be able to define a joint-product and understand how joint products are costed
- Understand the physical unit and sales value methods
- Know what a by-product is.

CONTINUOUS COSTING

It will be recalled from the previous chapter that continuous costing is used where identical or near identical cost units are produced. All costs can thus be averaged over production, greatly simplifying the costing and recording systems required. There are three subdivisions of continuous costing; service costing, process costing and joint product costing, all of which are dealt with in this chapter.

SERVICE COSTING

Service costing is concerned with the costs of *services* provided, not items of production. The services may be for external sale, e.g. public road, rail and air transport, hotel accommodation, restaurants, power generation and so on. Alternatively, the services may be those provided within an organisation. Examples include; canteen facilities, libraries, stores and so on. The costing of internal services is necessary where the organisation uses an internal pricing system and also as a way of providing information to management about comparative costs and efficiency.

COST UNITS FOR SERVICE COSTING

A particular difficulty is to define a cost unit that represents a suitable measure of the service provided. Frequently, a composite cost unit is considered to be the most useful. For example, a hotel may use 'occupied bed-night' as an appropriate unit for cost ascertainment and cost control.

Typical cost units used in service costing are shown below:

SERVICE	Possible cost units
HOSPITALS	Patient-days, number of operations
TRANSPORT	Tonne-miles, Passenger-miles, miles travelled
ELECTRICITY	Kilowatt-hours
COLLEGES	Full time equivalent student and so on.

Whatever unit is used the cost per unit is found thus:

$$\text{Cost per service unit} = \frac{\text{Total costs per period}}{\text{No. of service units supplied in the period}}$$

Example 1

Service cost unit calculation

A transport company with three lorries has expenses per week as follows:

	£
Drivers wages	640
Loading costs	370
Diesel	845
Repairs	490
Depreciation	550
General expenses	280

The journeys in a week were:

Journey	Tonnes carried (one way)	One-way distance (kilometres)
1	20	1,125
2	12	480
3	8	80
4	31	965
5	24	740
6	9	1,320
7	27	685
8	23	750
9	14	900
10	12	1,205

Calculate the average cost per tonne-kilometre.

Solution
Tonne-kilometres

Journey	Tonnes	Kilometres (one way)	Tonne/Kilometres
1	20	1,125	22,500
2	12	480	5,760
3	8	80	640
4	31	965	29,915
5	24	740	17,760
6	9	1,320	11,880
7	27	685	18,495
8	23	750	17,250
9	14	900	12,600
10	12	1,205	14,460
			151,260

Total costs = £640 + 370 + 845 + 490 + 550 + 280 = £3,175

$$\text{Cost per tonne-kilometre} = \frac{£3,175}{151,260} = £0.021$$

(Note that only the distances when carrying loads are used in the tonne-kilometre calculation).

PROCESS COSTING
This method of costing is used where a series of sequential processes produce identical units.

Process costing normally has the following characteristics:

(a) Accumulation of all costs (material, labour and overheads) by process cost centre.

(b) Accurate recording of units and part units produced, and costs incurred by each process.

(c) Averaging the total costs of a process over the total production of that process.

(d) Charging the cost of output of one process as the raw materials input cost of the following process.

Process costing is widely used in industries such as: food manufacture, chemical and drug manufacture, oil refining and so on.

The basis of all process costing systems is shown in Figure 6.1.

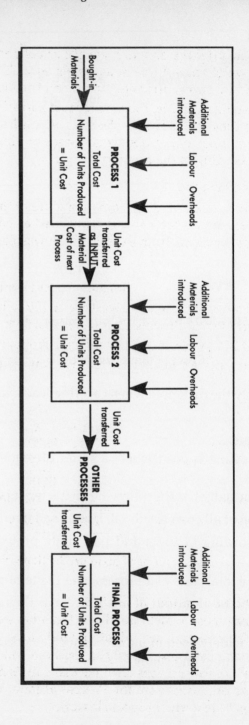

Figure 6.1

PROCESS COSTING OUTLINE

PROCESS LOSSES

In many process industries the quantity, weight or volume of the process *output* will be less than the quantity, weight or volume of materials *input*. This loss is due to various reasons including, evaporation, swarf, breakage, testing and so on.

If the losses are at standard levels they are termed *normal process losses*. If they are above or below expectations they are known as *abnormal process losses or gains*. It is necessary to find out whether there are normal or abnormal losses or abnormal gains because the costing treatment varies according to the category.

NORMAL PROCESS LOSSES

These are unavoidable losses arising from the nature of the production process so it is logical that the cost of these inevitable losses is included as part of the cost of good production. If any money can be recouped from the sale of the wastage this helps to reduce total costs.

Example 2

Normal process losses

A chemical process has a normal wastage of 10% which can be sold as scrap at £8 per tonne. In a period the following data were recorded:

Input material 260 tonnes at £45 per tonne, Labour and overheads £5,450

What is the cost per tonne of good production assuming that losses were at normal levels?

Solution

	Tonnes	£	
Input material	260	11,700	
Labour & overheads		5,450	
	260	17,150	
less Normal loss	26	208	(income from scrap sales)
= Net good production	234	16,942	

$$\therefore \text{ cost per tonne of good production} = \frac{£16,942}{234} = £72.40$$

ABNORMAL PROCESS LOSSES OR GAINS

Abnormal losses are those which are above the level expected. They cannot be foreseen and are due to factors such as; plant breakdowns, inefficient working and so on. Conversely there may be unexpectedly favourable conditions and actual losses may be lower than 'normal' losses and thus an abnormal gain is made. The cost effects of abnormal losses and gains are excluded from the Process account which will thus contain only normal costs (which include normal process losses).

Abnormal losses or gains are costed on the same basis as good production and so, like good production, carry a share of normal losses.

Example 3

Abnormal Process Loss

Assume the same data as Example 2 except that actual good production is 229 tonnes. Calculate the abnormal loss and show the cost calculations for the process

Solution

Abnormal loss	=	Actual Loss – Normal Loss
	=	(260-229) – (10% of 260)
	=	31 – 26
	=	5 tonnes

Cost calculations for Process

	Tonnes	£	
Input material	260	11,700	
Labour & overheads		5,450	
	260	17,150	
less Normal loss	26	208	
less Abnormal loss	5	362	Note 1
= Net good production	229	16,580	Note 2

Note 1

The 5 tonnes abnormal loss is costed at the net cost of good production, £72.40 per tonne i.e. 5 × £72.40 = £362.

The 5 tonnes of abnormal loss can also be sold as scrap for £8 per tonne so that the net cost of the abnormal loss is £322 (£362-40). This will be charged to the firm's Profit and Loss account.

Note 2

The net output of the process is 229 tonnes at £72.40 ie. £16,580. This becomes the material input to the next process. The effect of the above is that only normal costs remain in the process account even though losses are greater than normal.

Example 4

Abnormal Process Gain

Assume the same data as Example 2, except that actual good production is 236 tonnes. Calculate the abnormal gain and show the cost calculations for the process.

Solution

Abnormal gain	=	Normal Loss – Actual Loss
	=	(10% of 260) – (260 – 236)
	=	26 – 24
	=	2 tonnes

Cost calculations for Process

	Tonnes	£	
Input material	260	11,700	
Labour & overheads		5,450	
Abnormal gain	2	145	Note 1
	262	17,295	
less Normal loss	26	208	
= Net good production	236	17,087	Note 2

Note 1

The 2 tonnes of abnormal gain are costed at the net cost of good production £72.40 i.e. $2 \times £72.40 = £145$ (rounded).

Because of the 2 tonnes abnormal gain there were only 24 tonnes of scrap (instead of the 'normal' 26 tonnes) available for sale. Thus the benefit of £145 from the abnormal gain must be reduced by £16 ($2 \times £8$), the amount of scrap sales lost before the firm's Profit and Loss account is credited.

Note 2

The net output of the process is 236 tonnes at £72.40 i.e. £17,087 (rounded). This becomes the material input to the next process. As previously, only normal costs remain in the process account even though losses are less than normal.

EQUIVALENT UNITS IN PROCESS COSTING

At the end of a period it is quite normal for there to be some units which are only partly complete. It is clear that some of the process costs are attributable to these units as well as to those that have been fully completed. In order to spread total process costs fairly over both part finished and fully complete units it is necessary to calculate the number of equivalent units contained in the partly finished units. The number of equivalent units is the number of equivalent fully complete units which the partly complete units (i.e. the WIP) represent.

For example, assume that production was 3,400 complete units and 800 partly complete units. The partly complete units were deemed to be 75% complete.

Total equivalent production $\quad$ = Completed units + equivalent units in WIP
$\qquad\qquad\qquad\qquad\qquad\quad$ = 3,400 + ¾ (800)
$\qquad\qquad\qquad\qquad\qquad\quad$ = 3,400 + 600
$\qquad\qquad\qquad\qquad\qquad\quad$ = 4,000 units

The total costs for the period would then be spread over the total equivalent production

$$\text{i.e. cost per unit} = \frac{\text{Total costs}}{\text{total equivalent production in units}}$$

EQUIVALENT UNITS AND COST ELEMENTS

On occasions, an overall estimate of completion, as described above, is not feasible or desirable and it becomes necessary to consider the percentage completion of the individual cost elements; material, labour and overheads. The same principles are used but each cost element is treated separately and then the individual element costs per unit are added to give the cost of a complete unit. An example follows:

Example 5

Equivalent units and Cost Elements

In a period production and cost data were:

		£
Total costs	Material	12,555
	Labour	9,208
	Overheads	6,460
		28,223

Production was 2,800 complete units and 300 partly complete. The degree of completion of the cost elements of the 300 WIP was as follows:

Materials	80% complete
Labour	60% complete
Overheads	50% complete

Calculate the total equivalent production, cost per complete unit and value of the WIP

Solution

Cost element	Equivalent units in WIP	+	Fully complete units	=	Total equivalent production	Total costs £	Costs per unit £
Material	$300 \times 80\%$ =	240 +	2,800	=	3,040	12,555	4.13
Labour	$300 \times 60\%$ =	180 +	2,800	=	2,980	9,208	3.09
Overheads	$300 \times 50\%$ =	150 +	2,800	=	2,950	6,460	2.19
						£28,223	£9.41

Value of completed production = $2,800 \times £9.41$ = £26,348

∴ Value of WIP = £28,223 – 26,348 =   £1,875

The value of the WIP can be checked by multiplying each element's cost per unit by the number of equivalent units in the WIP, thus:

Cost element	Equivalent units in WIP	Cost per unit	Value of WIP
		£	£
Material	240	4.13	991
Labour	180	3.09	556
Overheads	150	2.19	328
			£1,875

Remember: Total cost = cost of completed units + cost of WIP

JOINT PRODUCTS DEFINED

A joint product is the term used when two or more products arise simultaneously during processing. Joint products each have a significant sales value in relation to each other and occur in numerous industries, for example; oil refining (where diesel fuel, petrol, paraffin, lubricants and other joint products arise), mining (different metal ores arise from the crushing process) and so on.

JOINT PRODUCT COSTING

Because joint products arise from the nature of the production process it follows that none of the products can be produced separately. The products become separately identifiable at a point known as the 'split off point'. Up to the split-off point all costs incurred are joint costs; after the split-off point, costs can be identified with individual products and are known as 'subsequent' or 'additional processing costs'. This is shown in Figure 6.2.

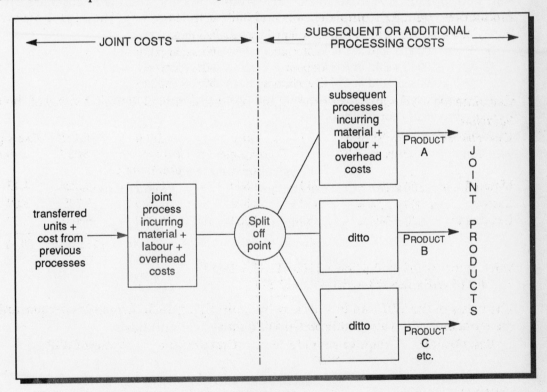

Figure 6.2

JOINT PRODUCT COSTING

Because subsequent processing costs are readily identifiable with a specific product they do not pose any particular costing problem. For product costing purposes the major problem in joint-product costing is how to divide up the joint costs, i.e. those prior to the split-off point, among the joint products in an acceptable manner.

DIVIDING UP JOINT COSTS

The two most common methods of dividing up joint costs are:

(a) The physical unit method:- The joint costs are shared between the joint products in proportion to the physical weight or volume of the production.

(b) The sales value method:- The joint costs are shared between the joint products in proportion to the relative sales value of the products. Both methods are illustrated in the following example.

Example 6

Joint Costs

Four joint products, A, B, C and D arise from a process. Total joint costs are £16,500 and outputs, selling prices and sales values are as follows:

A   200 kgs sold at £20 kg giving a sales value of £4,000
B   300 kgs sold at £14 kg giving a sales value of £4,200
C   500 kgs sold at £18 kg giving a sales value of £9,000
D   100 kgs sold at £30 kg giving a sales value of £3,000

Divide up the joint costs and calculate the profit percentage using

(a)   The physical unit method and
(b)   The sales value method.

Solution

Physical unit method

Product	Output	Cost calculation		Product costs
	kgs			£
A	200	200/1100 × £16,500	=	3,000
B	300	300/1100 × £16,500	=	4,500
C	500	500/1100 × £16,500	=	7,500
D	100	100/1100 × £16,500	=	1,500
	1,100			£16,500

Profit statement on physical unit basis

	A	B	C	D	Total
	£	£	£	£	£
Sales value	4,000	4,200	9,000	3,000	20,200
less Apportioned costs	3,000	4,500	7,500	1,500	16,500
Profit (Loss)	1,000	(300)	1,500	1,500	3,700
Profit (Loss) Percentage	25%	(7%)	16.7%	50%	18.3%

(The Profit/Loss percentage is calculated in relation to sales e.g. $A = \dfrac{£1,000}{£4,000} = 25\%$)

48

Sales value method

Product	Sales value	Cost calculation	Product costs
	£		£
A	4,000	4,000/20,200 × £16,500	3,267
B	4,200	4,200/20,200 × £16,500	3,431
C	9,000	9,000/20,200 × £16,500	7,351
D	3,000	3,000/20,200 × £16,500	2,451
	£20,200		16,500

Profit Statement on Sales Value basis

	A	B	C	D	Total
	£	£	£	£	£
Sales value	4,000	4,200	9,000	3,000	20,200
less Apportioned costs	3,267	3,431	7,351	2,451	16,500
Profit	733	769	1,649	549	3,700
Profit percentage	18.3%	18.3%	18.3%	18.3%	18.3%

Notes:

(a) It will be seen that the sales value basis produces the same profit percentage for each product unlike the physical unit method where varying profits (or losses) result.

(b) Neither of the two methods is more correct than the other. They are merely two different methods or conventions which produce different results from each other.

(c) The apportioned costs, by either method, can be used for Stock Valuation or for profit calculations but they are not a suitable basis for decision making. This latter point is developed later in the manual.

BY-PRODUCT

Joint products are the main required outputs of a process but on occasions there are other, small value, incidental products. These are known as by-products. For example, in the timber trade, sawdust, bark, off-cuts would be classed as by-products as they arise during processing and have a low value in relation to the main products such as planks, joists and so on.

Any income received from the by-products is deducted from the total process cost before the joint costs are divided amongst the joint products.

KEY POINT SUMMARY

- Service costing can be used either for services provided for sale or for internal services
- A problem is defining a suitable cost unit and composite units are often used
- Process costing is used where a series of processes produce identical units
- All costs are collected by the process cost centre and averaged over the units produced
- Normal process loss is the expected loss. Where losses differ from those expected, abnormal losses or gains may arise
- Equivalent units are the number of fully complete units that are equivalent to the partly finished units
- Joint products arise when two or more main products are produced simultaneously
- Joint costs may be spread either on the physical unit basis or by the sales value method
- Apportioned joint costs are used for stock valuations and profit calculations. They are not appropriate for decision making
- By-products are low value outputs, which arise incidentally during processing.

REVIEW EXERCISES

1. A process has a normal wastage of 15% which can be sold as scrap at £1 per kilo. In a period the following data were recorded

    Input 540 kgs at £4 per kilo

    Labour and overheads were £2,900.

    What is the cost per kilo of good production assuming losses were at normal levels?

2. What is the position assuming the same data as question 1 except that actual good production was 450 kilos?

3. Three joint products arise from a process which has a total joint cost of £62,500. The outputs and selling prices are:

Product	Output (tonnes)	Selling price per tonne £
X	500	90
Y	1,000	35
Z	300	25

    Apportion the joint costs using
    - (a) the physical unit method, and
    - (b) the sales value method.

SECTION 1 ASSESSMENT

COST ANALYSIS AND COST ASCERTAINMENT

MULTIPLE CHOICE QUESTIONS

1. Direct costs are costs that:
   (a) Are directly charged to a department
   (b) Can be directly identified with a product or service
   (c) Are directly under the control of a manager
   (d) Are incurred directly the factory is open.

2. Prime cost includes:
   (a) Direct materials plus total overheads
   (b) All direct costs plus factory overheads
   (c) Direct labour, direct materials and direct expenses
   (d) Direct labour plus factory overheads.

3. A cost centre is:
   (a) A unit of production or service
   (b) Any location or department which incurs costs
   (c) Part of the overhead system by which costs are gathered together
   (d) A location which controls direct costs.

4. Cost apportionment is done so that
   (a) Common costs are shared among cost centres in proportion to the benefit received
   (b) Each cost unit gathers overheads as it passes through a cost centre
   (c) Costs may be controlled
   (d) Whole items of cost are charged to cost centres.

5. Product costing is mainly concerned with
   (a) Controlling production costs
   (b) Finding the total of production costs
   (c) Analysing cost behaviour
   (d) Finding the cost of sales and valuing stock.

6. The First in First Out (FIFO) materials pricing system charges issues at:
   (a) The price of the oldest batch in stock
   (b) The price of the most recent batch in stock
   (c) The price of the first component or material used in a period
   (d) The average price of goods in stock.

7. The Last In First Out (LIFO) system
   (a) Values stocks at current values
   (b) Tends to produce realistic product costs
   (c) Makes cost comparisons between jobs easier
   (d) Understates product costs in times of rising prices.

8. Using the Average Price issuing system
   (a) Exaggerates price fluctuations
   (b) Makes cost control easier
   (c) The issue price is recalculated after each receipt
   (d) Always values stocks at the price of the oldest batch in stock.

9. Wages paid using differential piecework
   (a) Are classified as overheads
   (b) Increase as production rises
   (c) Decrease when production rises
   (d) Remain the same regardless of output.

10. A firm uses direct labour hours as a basis for overhead absorption. If large fluctuations in labour hours are experienced
   (a) This is a reason to use predetermined overhead rates
   (b) This will mean that overheads will be under or over absorbed for the year
   (c) Different amounts of overhead will be charged to jobs with the same labour hours
   (d) It will be better to use a machine hour rate.

11. A predetermined overhead rate using machine hours as a basis:
   (a) Is calculated by dividing actual overheads by budgeted machine hours
   (b) Results in the over absorption of overhead
   (c) Is inferior to a rate based on labour hours
   (d) Results in charging similar overheads to jobs with similar hours.

12. A firm recovers overheads on labour hours which were budgeted at 3,500 with overheads of £43,750. Actual results were 3,620 hours with overheads of £44,535
   (a) Overheads were under absorbed by £785
   (b) Overheads were over absorbed by £715
   (c) Overheads were over absorbed by £1,500
   (d) Overheads were under absorbed by £715.

13. A firm that has under absorbed overhead at the end of the period:
   (a) Has been working inefficiently
   (b) Would be better not using predetermined rates
   (c) Incorrectly budgeted the absorption base and/or the amount of overheads
   (d) Has overspent on overheads.

14. Which of the following firms would be most likely to use job costing?
   (a) A paint manufacturer
   (b) A sugar refinery
   (c) A firm of architects
   (d) A car manufacturers.

The following data are the basis of the next 3 questions. A firm makes special switchgear to customers requirements and uses job costing. The data for a period are:

	Job No		
	X100	Y252	Z641
Opening WIP	£6,200	21,000	0
Material added in period	£15,250	0	9,000
Labour for period	£9,000	7,000	8,000

The overheads for the period were exactly as budgeted, £60,000.

15. What overhead would be added to Job No X100 for the period?
    (a) £20,000
    (b) £22,500
    (c) £9,000
    (d) £24,000.

16. Job No. Y252 was completed in the period and consisted of 30 identical switch units. The firm adds 25% on to total costs to calculate the selling price. What is the price of a switch unit?
    (a) £1,167
    (b) £2,292
    (c) £1,896
    (d) £1,517.

17. Jobs X100 and Z641 are the only incomplete jobs. What is the value of closing WIP?
    (a) £89,950
    (b) £47,450
    (c) £112,437
    (d) £41,250.

18. The costing associated with a typical site based contract:
    (a) Means that more costs can be identified as direct
    (b) Requires some estimate to be made of interim profits
    (c) Means that the contract account will be credited with materials unused at the end of the contract
    (d) Includes all of these.

19. Which of the following firms are most likely to use process costing?
    (a) A car manufacturer
    (b) A sugar refinery
    (c) A builder
    (d) A departmental store.

20. Using process costing the amount of cost transferred to Finished Goods stock is the cost of:
    (a) The equivalent production for the period
    (b) The units started and completed during the period
    (c) The units completed during the period
    (d) The units in the opening Finished Goods stock.

21. Let O = units in opening WIP, C = units in closing WIP,S = units started in production. Then U = units completed and
    (a) $U = O + S - C$
    (b) $U = O + C - S$
    (c) $U = O - C - S$
    (d) $U = O + S + C$.

22. A process department began with no opening stocks. A total of 8,500 units was transferred in at a cost of £93,500. The cost of raw materials added was £3.50 per unit and labour costs were £5 per unit. If 6,750 units were completed and transferred out the total cost transferred out was:
    (a) £165,750
    (b) £93,500
    (c) £131,625
    (d) £74,250.

23. Apportioning joint costs over joint products on either the physical unit or sales value basis is useful for
    (a) No purposes as the methods are conventions only
    (b) Decision making
    (c) Stock valuation and decision making
    (d) Stock valuation.

The following data are to be used for questions 24 and 25. A process produces three products R, S and T. Total joint costs were £17,000 and outputs and selling prices were:

    R   250 kgs sold at £22 per kg
    S   550 kgs sold at £19 per kg
    T   450 kgs sold at £25 per kg.

24. Apportioning the joint costs on the physical unit basis gives:
    (a) R = £3,400   S = £7,480   T = £6,120
    (b) R = £3,438   S = £6,531   T = £7,031
    (c) R = £5,667   S = £5,667   T = £5,666
    (d) R = £5,667   S = £4,894   T = £6,439.

55

25. Apportioning the joint costs on the sales value basis gives:
    (a) R = £3,400   S = £7,480   T = £6,120
    (b) R = £3,438   S = £6,531   T = £7,031
    (c) R = £5,667   S = £5,667   T = £5,666
    (d) R = £5,667   S = £4,894   T = £6,439.

QUESTIONS WITH ANSWERS

A1. (a) Describe briefly THREE methods of pricing material issues to work-in-progress frequently used in cost accounting.

    (b) State the effect in times of inflation of each of the methods you have described in (a) above on:

        (i) The valuation of stocks;

        (ii) The cost of products made;

        (iii) The profit earned.

    (c) Explain why the pricing methods you have given in answer to (a) above may be unsuitable for use when prices (or estimates) are being prepared for work to be undertaken to customer's special requirements.

RSA Cost Accounting Stage II

A2. Nixan (Retail) Ltd sells only one model of portable colour television set and on 1 January 1989 held a stock of twenty sets which had cost £80 each.

Details of purchases and sales for the first three months of 1989 are as follows:

| | Details of Purchases | | Sales for each month | |
Date	Sets Received	Cost price per set £	Sets sold	Selling price per set £
10 January	20	81		
17 "	60	70		
31 "	30	82	50	140
7 February	50	85		
20 "	30	85		
28 "	20	94	100	140
10 March	60	90		
31 "	40	97	150	150

The physical stock checks at the end of January and February agreed with the recorded quantity shown on the stock record but a similar check on 31 March revealed a deficit of two sets, presumed stolen.

For updating stock records and monthly accounting routes, all issues during a month are priced on the last day of each monthly period.

Variable selling costs are incurred at the rate of 10% on sales and fixed costs amount to £4,000 per month.

Required

(a) Calculate the month end stock valuations for January and February which would arise from pricing out monthly issues on each of the following methods:

    (i)   FIFO

    (ii) LIFO

    (iii) Weighted average

(b) Prepare a detailed Profit and Loss Account for the month of March using the weighted average basis.

LCCI Cost Accounting

A3. A small business has recently started up in precision engineering, using expensive machinery to produce components made to specific orders. Prices are being quoted on the basis of estimated total factory cost for each job plus a mark up of 100% to cover all administration/selling costs and profit.

The production budget for the current year includes the following data:

Total factory overheads	£500,000
Direct material usage	£1,000,000
Direct labour (at £4 per hour)	£200,000
Machine hours	100,000

The estimated costs and times for Job 456 are as follows:

Direct material	£1,000
Direct labour hours (at £4.50 per hour)	60
Machine hours	72

Required:

(a) Calculate four possible price quotations for Job 456, using a different basis for factory overhead absorption in each case. Show details of your calculations which should be to the nearest £.

(b) State which basis should be used in these circumstances and give reasons for your choice.

LCCI Cost Accounting

A4. A machine shop has the machine capacity to produce 2,400 components each week. Each machine requires one operator, a 40 hour week is in operation and 2 grades of operator are employed. Each component is machined in four successive operations according to the following schedule:

	Operations			
	1	2	3	4
Machining time (in minutes)	20	30	10	15
Grade of Operator	A	A	B	B
Hourly Wage Rate	£4	£4	£3.20	£3.20

Required:

Prepare a statement in columnar form showing (i) for each operation and (ii) in total:

(a) The number of operators required

(b) The expected weekly payroll cost

(c) The labour cost per component (to 2 decimal places of £).

LCCI Cost Accounting

A5. A furniture making business manufactures quality furniture to customers' orders. It has three production departments and two service departments. Budgeted overhead costs for the coming year are as follows:

	Total £
Rent and Rates	12,800
Machine insurance	6,000
Telephone charges	3,200
Depreciation	18,000
Production Supervisor's salaries	24,000
Heating & Lighting	6,400
	70,400

The three production departments – A, B and C, and the two service departments – X and Y are housed in the new premises, the details of which, together with other statistics and information is given below.

	Departments				
	A	B	C	X	Y
Floor area occupied (sq metres)	3,000	1,800	600	600	400
Machine value (£'000s)	24	10	8	4	2
Direct labour hrs budgeted	3,200	1,800	1,000		
Labour rates per hour	£3.80	£3.50	£3.40	£3.00	£3.00
Allocated Overheads:					
Specific to each department (£'000s)	2.8	1.7	1.2	0.8	0.6
Service Department X's costs apportioned	50%	25%	25%		
Service Department Y's costs apportioned	20%	30%	50%		

Required:

(a) Prepare a statement showing the overhead cost budgeted for each department, showing the basis of apportionment used. Calculate also suitable overhead absorption rates.

(b) Two pieces of furniture are to be manufactured for customers.

Direct costs are as follows:

	JOB 123	JOB 124
Direct material	£154	£108
Direct labour	20 hours Dept.A	16 hours Dept.A
	12 hours Dept.B	10 hours Dept.B
	10 hours Dept.C	14 hours Dept.C

Calculate the total costs of each job.

(c) If the firm quotes prices to customers that reflect a required profit of 25% on selling price, calculate the quoted selling price for each job.

(d) If material costs are a significant part of total costs in a manufacturing company, describe a system of material control that might be used in order to effectively control costs, paying particular attention to the stock control aspect.

AAT Cost Accounting & Budgeting

A6. B.Limited uses raw material C in the manufacture of its products. There is given below information extracted from the raw material stores ledger account for material C.

March 1987	Receipts units	price per unit £	Issues units	amount
		£		
2	34	28.0		
4			18	504
9	16	29.0		
14			20	570
17	24	27.0		
19			22	
21	28	29.0		
23			32	
25	30	30.5		
28			26	
30	42	32.0		

You are required to:

(a) State the method of pricing used in the stores ledger;

(b) Prepare a ruling of a stores ledger account and record in it all the transactions for the month given above using the method you have stated in your answer to (a) above;

(c) State the value of the stock at 31st March 1987 using one other commonly used method of pricing.

RSA Cost Accounting Stage II

A7. (a)   A firm's computer department charges for the services which it provides to user departments.

The computer department has three main divisions of work:

(i)   development of systems and programs to be run on the computer

(ii)   data preparation

(iii)   computer operations

The budget for the department for the following year and the apportionments amongst its divisions of work is as follows:

	Budget	Development	Data Preparation	Computer Operations
	£	%	%	%
Salaries	200,000	30	25	45
Compilation & Testing	60,000	100		
Maintenance	20,000		10	90
Materials	10,000	10	20	70
Power	10,000		25	75
Office costs	10,000	20	20	60

Other information:

(i)   The estimated number of staff hours of work which will be chargeable by the development division is 12,000 hours.

(ii)   The estimated number of key depressions on terminals for data preparation is 24,300,000.

(iii)   The estimated number of hours of computer operation available is 7,000 hours. Because of downtime it is practice to recover costs over 'usable' hours which are estimated to be 60% of total available hours.

A user department has two jobs which require the services of the computer department, details of which are as follows:

	Job 1234	Job 5678
Development work	400 hours	20 hours
Data preparation		80,000 key depressions
Computer operations		5 hours

Required:

(a)   (i)   Prepare a table which shows total cost for each division of the computer department.

(ii)   Calculate the costs which would be charged to Job 1234 and Job 5678.

(b)   (i)   Explain what you understand by the following terms:

Cost unit

Cost centre

(ii)   Use the information in the question above to give TWO examples of each term, and give TWO OTHER examples of each term.

(c)   The following information gives details of the gross pay calculated for a production worker:

	£
Basic pay for normal hours worked:	
40 hours at £5 per hour	200
Overtime:	
5 hours at time and a half	37.50
Group bonus payment	4.00
Gross wages for the week	241.50

Although paid for 40 hours in normal time, the worker was in fact unable to work for 6 hours because of machine breakdowns.

Required:

Analyse the total of £241.50 into direct and indirect costs. Give reasons for your answers.

AAT Cost Accounting & Budgeting

A8. (i)   Define:

(a)   Cost Unit

(b)   Cost centre

(ii)   State which cost unit would be applicable to each of the following:

(a)   Brick making

(b)   Oil refining

(c)   A boiler house providing steam

(d)   A works canteen

(e)   Coal mining

(f)   Heavy goods transport

(g)   A School/College

(h)   A professional Accountant in private practice.

LCCI Cost Accounting

A9. (a)   Describe the benefits which cost accounting provides for an organisation. N.B. You may refer to your own experience in answering this question.

(b)   The following information is provided for a 30 day period for the Rooms Department of a hotel:

	Rooms with twin beds	Single rooms
Number of rooms in hotel	260	70
Number of rooms available to let	240	40
Average number of rooms occupied daily	200	30

Number of guests in period	6,450
Average length of stay	2 days
Total revenue in period	£774,000
Number of employees	200
Payroll costs for the period	£100,000
Items laundered in the period	15,000
Cost of cleaning supplies in period	£5,000
Total cost of laundering	£22,500
Listed daily rate for twin bedded room	£110
Listed daily rate for single room	£70

The hotel calculates a number of statistics, including the following:

Room occupancy	total number of rooms occupied as a percentage of rooms available to be let.
Bed occupancy	total number of beds occupied as a percentage of beds available.
Average guest rate	total revenue divided by number of guests.
Revenue utilisation	actual revenue as a percentage of maximum revenue from available rooms.
Average cost per occupied	bed total cost divided by number of beds occupied.

Required:

Prepare a table which contains the following statistics, calculated to 1 decimal place:
Room occupancy (%)
Bed occupancy (%)
Average guest rate (£)
Revenue utilisation (%)
Cost of cleaning supplies per occupied room per day (£)
Average cost per occupied bed per day (£)

(c) Explain what you understand by the following terms:
Cost unit
Cost centre

(d) Identify One Cost Centre which might exist in a hotel, excluding the Rooms Department. For the cost centre identified give an appropriate Cost Unit.

AAT Cost Accounting & Budgeting

QUESTIONS WITHOUT ANSWERS

B1. (a) Distinguish briefly between job costing and batch costing.

(b) The following information is available for Job 4321, which is being produced at the request of a customer:

	Dept. A	Dept. B	Dept. C
Materials consumed	£4,000	£1,000	£1,500
Direct labour: wage rate per hour	£3	£4	£5
Direct labour hours	300	200	400

In accordance with company policy the following are chargeable to jobs:

Fixed production overhead	£5 per direct labour hour
Fixed administration overhead	80% total production cost
Profit mark-up	20% margin on selling price

Required:

(i) Calculate the total cost and selling price of Job 4321.

(ii) Assume that shortly after the Job is completed the original customer goes bankrupt and the Job is not delivered. The only other possible customer is prepared to pay £9,000.

Briefly indicate, with reasons, whether you would accept the offer of £9,000.

(c) The following information is available for Z company:

	Division A		Division B	
	Year 1 £'000	Year 2 £'000	Year 1 £'000	Year 2 £'000
Stocks				
Value at end of year	300	400	440	480
Average stock value	280	336	390	390
Value of issues during year	689	695	2,000	2,106
Holding costs	40	46.5	108	105
Debtors				
Value at end of year	657	552	1,068	1,246
Turnover	4,000	4,200	6,000	6,500

Note: all sales are on credit.

The company uses a number of performance indicators:

Indicator	*Method of calculation*
Operating efficiency %	Holding cost/value of issues
Activity efficiency %	Average stock value/turnover
Turnover rate (times)	Value of issues/average stock value

In addition, the company finds that debtors turnover (in days) is useful.

Required:

(i) Calculate the indicators and debtors turnover for each year to 1 decimal place.

(ii) Comment briefly on your findings.

AAT Cost Accounting & Budgeting

B2. D Limited has two employees: Kay and Lee, making product E. During week ended 28th March, 1987 both employees each worked 40 hours. Kay's rate of pay was £3.20 per hour and he produced 180 units of product E. Lee's rate of pay was £2.75 per hour and he produced 150 units. Under all the bases of payment given below each employee is guaranteed a wage based on his respective hourly rate.

Overhead is absorbed into product costs at a rate of £4 for each hour worked.

You are required to calculate:

(a) The gross wage for each employee under each of the following bases of payment:

    (i) Daywork;

    (ii) Piecework at a rate of £0.75 per unit;

    (iii) Bonus scheme with bonus paid at £2.40 for each hour produced in excess of time taken, with time allowed at 15 minutes per unit;

    (iv) Differential piecework on the following basis:

for production in a 40 hour week,

For the first 100 units or less	£0.60 per unit
For the next 50 units	£0.90 per unit
For all units in excess of 150 units	£1.20 per unit

(b) The labour plus overhead cost per unit for each of the employees on each of the bases of payment you have calculated in answer to (a) above. Cost per unit should be shown to the nearest penny.

RSA Cost Accounting Stage II

B3. (a) Explain what you understand by the following terms, and briefly state the principal features of each:

Stock control
Store keeping

(b) Receipts and issues of Material X for the month of August are as follows:

	Receipts units	Total value £	Issues units
1st August	2,000	4,000	
2nd August	3,000	6,600	
3rd August	2,000	6,000	
4th August			3,000
5th August	3,000	7,500	
6th August			6,000

There were no opening stocks of Material X.

Required:

Using a FIFO method of valuation, show the price charged to each issue, and the closing stock valuation at 6th August. Assume that records are maintained using a perpetual inventory system.

(c) Assume that you discover that the actual number of units of an item in stock represents 1.5 times the maximum level set for that item. Briefly explain what you might do.

AAT Cost Accounting & Budgeting

B4. The total valuation of the opening work in progress in Process 2 was £2,500. This was based on the existence of 300 units which were only 80% complete so far as labour was concerned and 60% complete for overheads.

The following information is available concerning the current period:

	Units	£
Transferred from Process 1	4,000	20,000
Labour costs incurred		7,820
Overhead costs absorbed		11,760
Transferred to finished stock		3,600

Losses do not normally occur in Process 2, but, during the current period, a machine fault resulted in 200 units being scrapped at a stage when only 50% of the conversion costs had been incurred.

Closing work in progress consisted of 500 units, which were considered to be 90% complete for labour and 80% complete for overheads.

Required:

Produce detailed workings to calculate each of the following for the current period:

    (i)   The total cost of the units transferred to finished stock

    (ii) The total cost of the abnormal loss

    (iii) The total valuation of the closing work in progress.

LCCI Cost Accounting

B5. K Limited makes two products: L and M, has three production departments: N, P and Q and two service departments: R and S. The standard prime cost per unit of the two products are as follows:

		Product L			Product M		
		hours	£	£	hours	£	£
Direct material		89				77	
Direct labour:							
Department	N	8	16		6	12	
	P	12	24		10	20	
	Q	15	30		14	28	
				70			60
Total				£159			£137

The following information was taken from the budget for the month of March 1988:

Production:	Product:	L	300 units
		M	500 units

Overhead:			£
Production department	N		13,620
	P		26,720
	Q		24,660
Service department:	R		8,400
	S		14,400
Total			£87,800

The service departments are apportioned to the production departments on the following bases:

		Service department	
		R	**S**
		%	%
Production department:	N	20	25
	P	40	30
	Q	40	45

Using the information given above you are required to calculate:

(a) the budgeted overhead absorption rate on a direct labour hour basis for each of the three production departments;

(b) the sales price per unit of each of the products assuming a profit of 25% on total production cost is needed.

RSA Cost Accounting

B6. Stukk Chemicals Ltd. manufactures a special adhesive in Process A, employing direct workers paid at £4.25 per hour and absorbing overhead at the rate of £10 per direct labour hour. At the end of this process, it is normal to produce a by-product at the rate of 6% of total input. This by-product is then processed and packed in Process B at a cost of £1.20 per kg, after which it is sold for £1.70 per kg. Process A account is credited with the net realisable value of the by-product. An additional normal loss at the rate of 4% of total input is expected in Process A in the form of a poisonous waste which requires special treatment, at a cost of £7 per kg, before it can be disposed of with safety. There is no opening or closing work in progress in either process.

Data is available for last month as follows:

Input –	Material X	18,000 kg	– at £3 per kg
	Material Y	12,000 kg	– at £1.50 per kg
Direct labour hours worked		– 2,000	
By-product produced		– 1,800 kg	
Adhesive produced		– 26,300 kg	

Required:

(i) Prepare process A's account in detail for last month, clearly indicating the cost per kg of the adhesive. Show details of any supporting calculations.

(ii) Calculate the relevant total abnormal gain or loss which will appear in the Profit and Loss Account for last month.

LCCI Cost Accounting

B7. For profit determination and stock valuation purposes, it is conventional to apportion common costs incurred prior to split off between joint products. A process produces three joint products X, Y and Z, and the following data applies:

			Sales
			£
X	400 kilos @ £12.50	=	5,000
Y	300 kilos @ £20	=	6,000
Z	200 kilos @ £25	=	5,000
			16,000

Total joint costs amount to £11,000

Required:

(a) prepare statements to show gross profit per production on:
  (i) A physical units basis
  (ii) A sales value basis.
(b) Calculate gross profit percentages for each method commenting briefly upon their meaning
(c) Distinguish between joint products and by-products
(d) State how you would deal with by-products in a costing system.

LCCI Management Accounting

B8. VG Double Glazing Ltd employs sales representatives who own their own cars and who use them on company business in return for reimbursement of expenses at an agreed rate per mile travelled on company business. Records show that, after allowing for holidays, sickness and time spent at Head Office, each car is used for business on an average of 150 days in the year covering an average of 100 miles per day.

The following details have been agreed:

(a) Petrol costs £1.68 per gallon and average engine performance is 28 miles to the gallon.
(b) Oil is changed every 3,000 miles, costing £8.00 per change.
(c) Each car is serviced every 10,000 miles, costing £70.00 per service.
(d) Tyres are changed every 30,000 miles, costing £100 per set at each renewal.
(e) Each representative is to be allowed three-quarters of the following annual costs in the mileage rate calculation:

	£
Depreciation	1,400
Insurance	200
Licence	100
Garage costs	240

Required:

Calculate an appropriate rate per mile for use in the above situation, presented in detail to show clearly the allowance per mile for each of the five considerations, (a) to (e) as above.

LCCI Cost Accounting

B9. A factory has three production cost centres and four service cost centres. Budgets are being prepared for the next period and the allotment of overheads has reached the following stage:

| | Production cost | | | | Service cost centres | | |
	X	Y	Z	Stores	Personnel	Heating	Power
Budgeted overhead (£'000)	442.8	171.6	61.6	36	32	20	40

The following information is also available:

	X	Y	Z
Kilowatt-hours (thousands)	800	100	100
Average number of employees	480	160	160
Value of stores issued (£'000)	120	40	20
Floor areas (000 square metres)	80	8	32
Machine hours (thousands)	240	–	–
Direct labour hours (thousands)	–	140	80

Required:

(a) Using appropriate bases, apportion the service centre costs to the production cost centres and arrive at the final total budgeted overhead for each.

(b) Calculate overhead absorption rates.

LCCI Cost Accounting

ASSIGNMENT 1
BETA ENGINEERING LTD.

An assignment dealing with job costing in a jobbing engineering company and various methods of absorbing overheads.

BACKGROUND

Beta Engineering are manufacturers of small metal fabrications. All items are made to order and quantities range from a single fabrication up to batches of 1000. Some fabrications require a substantial amount of machining or welding, others are largely hand made using simple hand tools. Because of the varying applications for the fabrications, the materials used vary widely; including special purpose alloy and stainless steels, non-ferrous metals and ordinary mild steel.

Sara Hall has recently commenced work at Beta Engineering as a Cost Clerk and is given the task of calculating the cost of each job. This is done by using the Estimate Sheet, prepared at the Quotation stage, and adjusting this for the actual materials used so as to find the actual job cost. The amount of material used is found from the Stores Issue notes.

Extracts from the Estimate Sheet for 50 stainless steel fuse holders and the subsequent Job Costs are shown below:

Estimate Sheet

			£
Labour:	500 hours @ £4	=	2,000
Materials:	150 kgs @ £8 kg	=	1,200
Overheads:	400 % of materials	=	4,800
=	Total cost		8,000
+	20% profit		1,600
=	Selling price for batch		9,600

When this batch was made Sara totalled the Issue Notes and found that 173 Kgs of material had been used and accordingly prepared the following Job Cost:

Job Cost

		£
Labour:	(as estimate)	2,000
Materials:	173 Kgs @ £8	1,384
Overheads:	400% of materials	5,536
=	Total cost	8,920
	Selling price	9,600
	Actual Profit	£680

After only a few weeks of doing this work, Sara had serious misgivings about the system used which seem to have numerous problems.

STUDENT ACTIVITIES

(a) Prepare a report to the Managing Director criticising the present system of Job Costing.

Your report must include specific comments on the method used for absorbing overheads, the problems that might arise using the present method of calculating Job Costs, and a recommendation for a better method of absorbing overheads.

(b) Outline the features you would expect to find in a good Job Costing system for a firm such as Beta Engineering.

(c) Design a more appropriate Job Cost form.

For activities (b) and (c) you should, wherever possible, find out about the systems and forms used by actual firms in your locality.

OBJECTIVES

The student should show an understanding of:

Product and Job Costing
Overhead absorption
Form design
Report writing

ASSIGNMENT 2

CHALLENGE LADDERS LTD.

An assignment dealing with cost analysis and product costing.

Challenge Ladders have made builder's multi-section ladders for many years and have a good reputation. Alan Betts has just been appointed as the new Managing Director and wishes to diversify the product range in order to increase sales. One of the ideas being considered is a range of Loft Ladders to be marketed under the 'Rizeup' brand label in 4 standard sizes. This will require considerable investment and an important meeting has been planned with the company's bankers to discuss the whole project.

Alan Betts wishes to be well prepared and sends for you to help him with the details. Certain information has already been prepared but he thinks that more analysis is required and that some re-arrangement would make the data more understandable.

The existing information is as follows:

Planned sales and production data in first quarter.

Ladder size	Selling Price per unit £	Production units	Sales units
1	150	800	500
2	130	700	450
3	100	500	400
4	75	500	350

Expected Direct costs per unit (£)

			Direct wages	
Size	Materials £	Dept. A £	Dept. B £	Dept. C £
1	18	7	5	8
2	16	5	4	3
3	13	4	2	3
4	12	4	2	3

Planned total costs for the quarter

			£
Material purchases			43,000
Production overheads:			
– Allocated	Dept. A	4,800	
	Dept. B	7,500	
	Dept. C	3,900	16,200
Apportioned overheads			21,600
Administration & selling overheads		29,600	

It is the practice of the company to

(a) Apportion production overheads on departmental direct wages

(b) Value finished goods stock at prime cost plus production overheads

(c) Charge Administration and Selling overheads to products on the basis of full production cost of goods sold.

Work-in-progress is considered so small that it can be ignored.

STUDENT ACTIVITIES

Prepare the following extra information for the Managing Director, supported by any explanations thought necessary.

(a) Direct Wages by product and by department

(b) Material cost by product

(c) Departmental overhead absorption rates

(d) Total production cost by product

(e) Value of closing stock of raw materials

(f) Value of closing stock of finished goods, by product

(g) Sales by product

(h) Production cost of goods sold by product

(i) Profit and Loss account analysed by product.

OBJECTIVES

The student should show an understanding of the following topics and demonstrate skills in calculation and layout.

(a) Cost classification

(b) Cost allocation

(c) Cost apportionment

(d) Overhead absorption

(e) Stock valuation

(f) Product costing.

Section 2
Planning and Control

The emphasis of the book now changes from the detailed recording of past events to the provision of information to management to help them manage better. Management need not only data about what happened yesterday but also information about what is happening today and guidance about what may happen tomorrow.

The next six chapters deal with the provision of information for planning and control. Planning and control are key aspects of a manager's job and cost and management accounting can provide much useful, and sometimes vital, information to assist management. However, two points need to be kept in mind whilst studying this section. To plan and control effectively management need many types of information not just that concerning financial matters. They may need information about sales, quality, productivity, personnel, training, supplies and so on. Secondly, management work with and through people and so the motivation, behaviour and attitudes of people are all important. A predominantly quantitative or financial approach to managerial problems is unlikely to produce the best results.

7 PLANNING, CONTROL AND COST BEHAVIOUR

OBJECTIVES

After you have studied this chapter you will

- Understand the principles of planning and control
- Be able to distinguish between long and short term planning
- Know why the study of cost behaviour is important
- Understand the distinction between fixed, variable and semi-variable costs
- Be able to find the fixed and variable elements of a cost using the high/low techniques
- Know how to use a scattergraph to find fixed and variable costs.

PLANNING AND CONTROL

Before considering how accounting information can assist management to plan and to control it is useful to examine, in outline, what is meant by planning and control. Planning and control are closely related management tasks and, in practice, are effectively inseparable.

Planning is the managerial process of deciding in advance *what* is to be done and *how* it is to be done. Planning is done on both a formal and informal basis and the planning process uses information of various types from internal and external sources.

Planning can cover the short term and the long term and the planning process can be summarised as *Aims* and *Means*:

AIMS – These are the goals or results or objectives which should be achieved. These should be stated in some measurable way rather than by vague generalisations.

MEANS – This is the selection of specific actions and activities to achieve the stated objectives. (Note that the activities also include control activities).

Control is an important management task, especially for middle and lower management, and can be defined as the process of ensuring that operations proceed according to plan.

Remember, planning must precede control for it is meaningless to consider any form of control activity without a clear idea of what is to be achieved i.e. the target or plan. In organisations, control is exercised mainly by the use of information in the form of *feedback loops*, which are depicted in Figure 7.1.

Control, especially at the lower levels of management can be summarised as

Measure, Compare and *Adjust*.

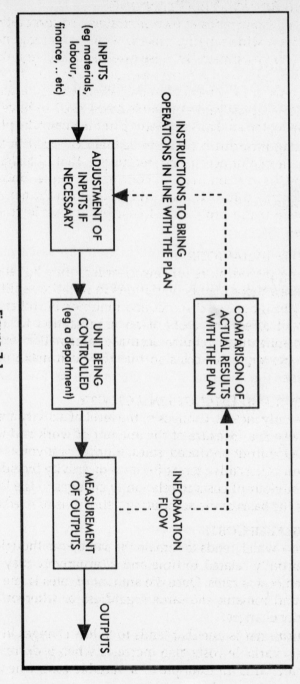

Figure 7.1

INFORMATION FEEDBACK LOOPS FOR CONTROL

LONG TERM AND SHORT TERM PLANNING

Long term planning (sometimes known as strategic or corporate planning) involves senior management and is a wide ranging process which uses judgement, information and forecasts from many sources, especially those external to the organisation. Long term planning covers periods from, say, two or three years and upwards, depending on the nature of the business. The details of long term planning are outside the scope of this book but it has been mentioned to emphasise that organisations need to have the discipline and framework of a long term plan so that short term planning can take place.

Short term planning is normally taken to be that dealing with the year ahead. Within this time period one particular accounting technique, that of *budgeting*, is probably the most widely used short term planning and control technique. Budgeting, with its associated technique of budgetary control,is dealt with in detail in the next three chapters but it is first necessary to consider the problems of cost behaviour for these lie at the heart of the budgeting process.

WHY STUDY COST BEHAVIOUR

In the forthcoming period more (or fewer) orders may be received, production may increase (or decrease), there may be variations in inflation, shift working may be contemplated, there may be industrial disputes and innumerable other changes could occur. All of these changes will affect the costs of an organisation to a greater or lesser degree. Consequently, management require accurate information from the accounting system about the likely behaviour of costs so that they can make better plans and take more informed decisions.

COST BEHAVIOUR AND CHANGES IN ACTIVITY

Although not the only factors, changes in the level of activity are major influences on costs. The level of activity is a measure of the amount of work and is expressed in many ways e.g., hours worked, output produced, sales, number of invoices typed, number of enquiries handled and so on. Alternative terms for level of activity include; volume, throughput and capacity. The behaviour of costs in relation to changes in the level of activity is so important that it forms the basis of the accounting definitions of fixed and variable costs.

FIXED AND VARIABLE COSTS

A *fixed cost* is a cost which tends to remain the same even though the activity level changes. A fixed cost is usually related to time and alternatively may be called a *period cost*. An example of a fixed cost is rates. Once the amount of rates is known, the amount is fixed for the year ahead and remains the same regardless of whether sales, output or any other measure of activity changes.

In contrast, a *variable cost* is one that tends to follow changes in the level of activity. When activity increases, variable costs also increase; when it decreases variable costs also decrease. Direct material is an example of a variable cost; when more units are produced, direct material costs increase in proportion.

Fixed and variable costs are shown in Figure 7.2.

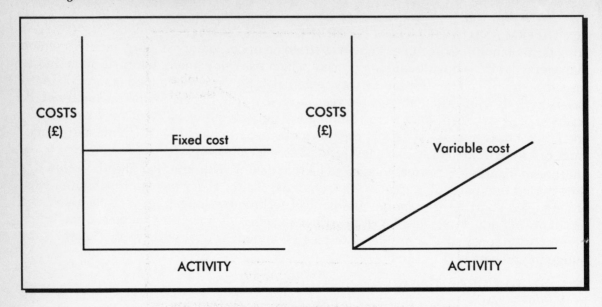

Figure 7.2

FIXED AND VARIABLE COSTS

Note that the diagrams and the definitions given above only apply in the short term and, in the case of the variable costs, assume a direct or linear relationship between cost and activity. For example, if activity increases by 20% then variable costs also increase by 20%. In the longer term, conditions and cost relationships do change and a variable cost which is assumed to behave linearly is not always an accurate representation.

Nevertheless, unless there are clear indications to the contrary, students are advised to assume that a cost described as fixed will remain the same when activity changes and that a variable cost will vary linearly, i.e. in direct proportion with activity changes.

Examples of fixed costs are; rent, rates, most types of insurance, salaries, depreciation and so on.

Examples of costs which are frequently variable in nature are; raw materials, royalties, sales commissions, carriage and packing charges and so on. Note that in many examination questions, direct wages are assumed to be variable although in practice, wages tend not to vary directly with output.

SEMI-VARIABLE COSTS

These are costs which have both fixed and variable elements and thus are only partly affected by changes in activity. A typical example would be telephone costs containing a fixed element, the standing charge, and a variable element, the cost of calls made.

These type of costs may alternatively be called *semi-fixed* or *mixed costs* and can be shown graphically, as in Figure 7.3

76

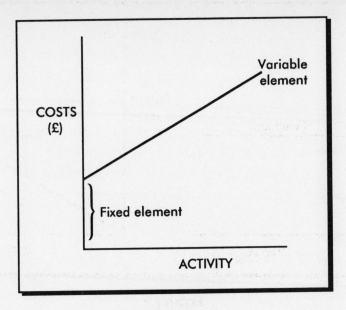

Figure 7.3

SEMI-VARIABLE COST

Example 1.

Fixed, Variable & Semi-Variable Costs

Analysis of a department's costs has produced the following data:

Expense	Type of cost	Cost characteristics
Rates	Fixed	£1,650 per month
Salaries	Fixed	£7,800 per month
Materials	Variable	£2 per unit
Labour	Variable	£18.50 per 10 units
Maintenance	Semi-variable	£1,600 per month plus £35 per 100 units
Electricity	Semi-variable	£150 per month plus £12 per 100 units

What are the expected costs in a month when production is planned for

(a) 2,000 units

(b) 2,400 units?

Solution

Expense		2,000 units		2,400 units
		£		£
Rates		1,650		1,650
Salaries		7,800		7,800
Materials	(2,000 × £2)	4,000	(2,400 × £2)	4,800
Labour	(200 × £18.50)	3,700	(240 × £18.50)	4,440
Maintenance	(£1,600+20 × £35)	2,300	(1,600+24 × £35)	2,440
Electricity	(£150+20 × £12)	390	(150+24 × £12)	438
Cost estimates:		£19,740		£21,568

CLASSIFYING COSTS

By studying records of past cost variations against activity it is possible to classify a cost as fixed or variable or semi-variable according to its behaviour. In general, pure fixed costs i.e. those that remain unchanged, and pure variable costs i.e. those that change in direct proportion to activity changes, pose few problems. It is semi-variable costs which cause most difficulties as their fixed and variable elements need to be estimated before cost predictions can be made. In practice, most costs are semi-variable in nature so finding the cost characteristics is a recurring problem.

FINDING THE FIXED AND VARIABLE ELEMENTS

In Example 1 the fixed and variable components of the semi-variable costs were given but in practice these have to be estimated and there are a number of ways this can be done. Some of the methods use statistical techniques outside the scope of this book but two useful approaches; the scattergraph and the high/low method, are described below.

HIGH/LOW METHOD

This is a simple approximate technique which uses the highest and lowest values contained in a set of data and, arithmetically or graphically, finds the rate of cost change and hence the variable costs. The variable costs are then used to estimate the fixed element of the costs.

Example 2

High/Low Method

Records have been kept of maintenance expenditure at various activity levels, expressed in machine hours.

Machine hours	Costs (£)
502	2,591
471	2,208 *
563	2,411
542	2,316
593	2,405
494	2,280
601	2,663 *
585	2,602
567	2,398
480	2,300

* It will be seen that the high/low cost points are

> 471 hours at a cost of £2,208
>
> 601 hours at a cost of £2,663

This is a range of 130 hours (601-471) and £455 (£2,663-2,208).

From this the rate of cost change, i.e. the variable element of cost, can be found thus:

$$\frac{£455}{130} = £3.5 \text{ per hour}$$

From this rate of variable cost the fixed cost can be deduced:

Cost at 471 hours	=	£2,208
less variable element		
(471 × £3.5)		1,648
∴ Fixed costs		£560

Maintenance costs are semi-variable and can be summarised as containing a fixed element of £560 plus a variable element of £3.50 for every machine hour worked.

(The above values could also be found by plotting the hours and costs on a graph).

The high/low method only produces approximate results and if the extreme values are unrepresentative the calculated variable and fixed costs will be inaccurate.

SCATTERGRAPH

This is a simple method where past data of costs and activity are plotted on a graph and then, by judgement, a line is drawn representing the average cost level. This line is known as the 'line of best fit'.

The data in Example 2, costs against machine hours, have been plotted on Figure 7.4, together with a possible line of best fit.

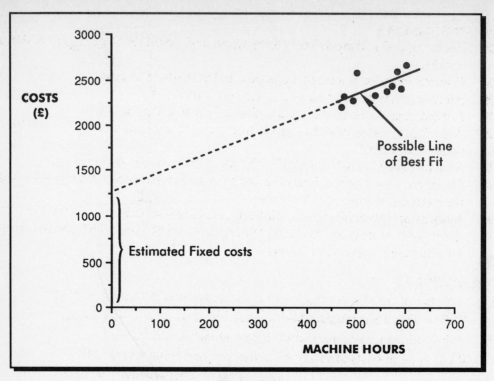

Figure 7.4
SCATTERGRAPH OF COSTS AND HOURS

Notes on Figure 7.4

(a)   Each cost and activity has been plotted individually as a cross.

(b)   Using judgement a line of best fit has been drawn. It is a solid line within the known values and where it has been extended it is shown as a dotted line. As judgements will, of course, vary between persons so will the lines of best fit.

(c)   Based on the graph the fixed cost estimate is £1,250 and the variable cost is represented by the slope of the line. At zero activity the cost is £1,250 and at 600 hours the cost is £2,650.

$$\text{Variable costs per hour} = \frac{£2,650 - 1,250}{600} = £2.33$$

(d)   Using the high/low technique maintenance costs were calculated as £560 fixed plus £3.5 per hour variable. Using a scattergraph with the line of best fit shown costs were estimated at £1,250 fixed and £2.33 per hour variable. These estimates differ but this is not surprising and, in practice, further investigation and analysis would take place to improve accuracy.

(e)   Instead of using estimation, the line of best fit can be found using the statistical technique of least squares. This process is sometimes known as regression analysis.

KEY POINT SUMMARY
- Planning is deciding what is to be done and how it is to be done i.e. Aims and Means
- Control ensures that operations proceed according to plan
- All changes in the future will cause cost variations
- A fixed cost is one that does not alter when activity changes
- A variable cost is one that tends to follow changes in activity. Linearity is usually assumed
- A semi-variable cost contains both fixed and variable elements
- The high/low method finds the variable and fixed elements of a cost using the extreme values
- A scattergraph is formed by plotting costs against activity
- A line of best fit is the assumed average cost level from which the fixed and variable elements can be found.

REVIEW EXERCISES
1. How can planning and control be summarised? How is control achieved?
2. (a) Define: Fixed Variable and Semi-variable costs.

   (b) Values of four costs are shown below at two activity levels.
   What type of costs are they and what are their characteristics?

	Cost 10,000 units £	Cost at activity level: 15,000 units £
L	27,500	41,250
M	13,750	18,750
N	50,000	72,500
O	31,250	31,250

3. Records have been kept for distribution costs at various activity levels, expressed in Sales Value, as follows:

Sales value	Distribution costs
£154,000	£17,790
£216,500	£18,650
£187,000	£18,420
£149,500	£15,950
£209,600	£17,300
£163,900	£16,550

   Using the High/Low method, find the Fixed and Variable components of the Distribution Costs.

   What would you expect Distribution Costs to be if sales were £230,000?

8 | INTRODUCTION TO BUDGETING

OBJECTIVES

After you have studied this chapter you will

- ■ Understand what budgeting is and be able to define a budget
- ■ Know what a limiting factor is and be able to give examples
- ■ Know, in outline, how budgets are prepared
- ■ Understand the inter-relationships between budgets
- ■ Realise the importance of the behavioural aspects of budgeting.

BUDGETS AND BUDGETING

Budgeting is a short-term planning and control technique which is widely used in industry, commerce and government. The budgeting process produces budgets for the forthcoming accounting period, usually a year sub-divided into months. A budget is a financial and/or quantitative expression of a plan of action. Thus a plan is made, for example, produce 10,000 units, then a budget is devised showing the types and amounts of expenditure necessary to produce 10,000 units.

Ideally, budgeting should take place within the framework of a long term plan.

BENEFITS OF BUDGETING

These can be summarised as follows:

Co-ordination: budgets are prepared for all the departments and functions (i.e. sales, purchasing etc.) of the organisation. Each budget dovetails and inter-relates to other budgets thus helping to ensure the co-ordination of activities throughout the organisation.

Communication: budgeting is an important way of communicating the organisations policies and objectives between the levels of management. Each manager who has responsibility for fulfilling a part of the overall plan is involved in budgeting thus communication up and down and across the management structure is improved.

Management By Exception: budgeting makes it necessary to clarify the responsibilities of each manager who has a budget. This together, with an agreed budget, makes possible management by exception i.e. where a subordinate is given a clearly defined role with the authority to carry out the tasks required. When activities are not proceeding to plan (as expressed in the budget) the variations are reported to a higher level. Thus higher management need only concentrate on exceptions to the plan.

Control: the process of comparing actual results with the budget and reporting variations, known as budgetary control, helps to control expenditure and imposes a financial discipline on the organisation.

Motivation: the involvement of lower and middle management in budgeting and the resulting establishment of clear targets has been found to be a motivating factor. People respond positively when their opinions are sought and they know where the firm is going.

Budgeting, and a related technique known as Standard Costing which is dealt with later, are known in America as *responsibility accounting*. This is an appropriate name because it focuses attention on a key aspect of the techniques whereby a named manager is given the responsibility for a task together with the necessary funds to fulfil that task.

The benefits of budgeting do not automatically arise, they have to be worked for. If the manager responsible for a budget does not participate in budget preparation most benefits will not be achieved. Imposed budgets and unwilling managers make a bad system.

LIMITING FACTOR

During the budgeting process it will become apparent that there is a factor which limits the activities of the organisation. This is known as a limiting factor and its effect on all budgets must be carefully assessed. In a normal commercial company the typical limiting factor is sales demand i.e. the company cannot profitably sell all it could produce or supply. This means that it is usual to commence budgeting with the sales budget so that all other budgets reflect the influence of the limiting factor. If sales were the limiting factor and the sales budget was for, say, 12,500 units it would clearly be essential that the Production Budget reflected this, after allowing for any stocks.

Of course, the limiting factor need not be sales. It might be lack of finance or space, lack of machine time or of skilled labour and so on. At any time there will be a limiting factor otherwise the firm could expand infinitely, but from time to time the limiting factor might change.

Note: The limiting factor can also be called, the key factor or the principal budget factor.

PREPARING BUDGETS

The preparation of budgets may take weeks or months and in many organisations budgeting is done on a rolling basis, i.e. budgeting is a regular, continuous activity. A *budget committee* is formed, usually serviced by the Management Accountant, consisting of people from various parts of the organisation. The committee's task is to oversee the preparation and administration of the budget and to improve planning and control within the organisation.

It is usual for a *budget manual* to be issued. This manual does not contain the current budgets but sets out such matters as:

- What budgets should be prepared and who is responsible for each budget
- Details of how to prepare the budgets, including a budget timetable
- An outline of the inter-relationships between the budgets
- Samples of forms used in budgeting, and so on.

All budgets produced must be co-ordinated with each other and contribute towards the final summary budget known as the *Master Budget*. This comprises the budgeted operating statement and balance sheet of the organisation. (An operating statement is akin to a Profit and Loss account and shows the results for a period and a balance sheet shows the assets and liabilities at the end of the period).

The budget preparation process is summarised on Figure 8.1

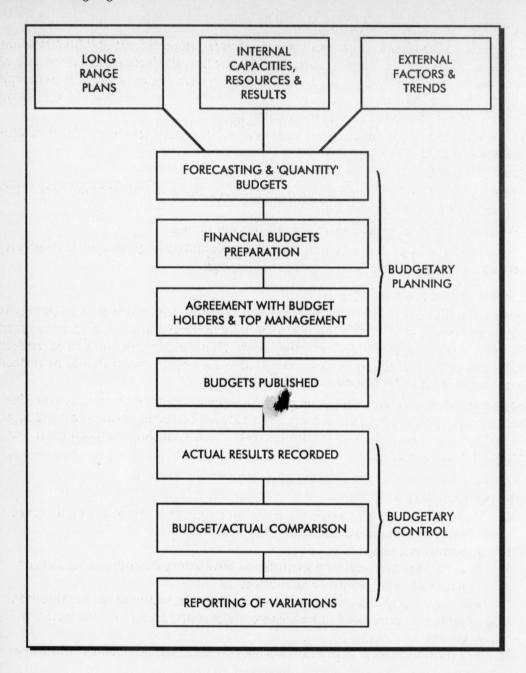

Figure 8.1

OUTLINE OF BUDGETING

BUDGET INTER-RELATIONSHIPS

A key objective of budgeting is to ensure that activities, departments and functions are co-ordinated with each other. Thus it is vital to consider how the budgets influence and interact with each other. The budget relationships within each organisation will be unique to that particular organisation and it is always necessary to consider the linkages between budgets as well as the contents of individual budgets.

As an example, the major budgets and their inter-relationships for a typical manufacturing company are shown in Figure 8.2.

Notes on Figure 8.2

(a) The diagram is only a summary and, in practice, there would be many more budgets especially for control purposes.

(b) See how all the budgets contribute to the master budget.

(c) Because of the importance of cash flow, the cash budget is given special attention and is dealt with in Chapter 10.

HUMAN FACTORS IN BUDGETING

It is important that the attitudes, aspirations and feelings of everyone associated with budgeting should be considered. This applies especially to those managers who are responsible for keeping expenditures within budgeted levels. They must be encouraged to participate in each stage of the budgeting process, suggestions for improvement should be welcomed and co-operative attitudes fostered.

If budgets are seen as threatening or as p   of a top management policing system then the system is unlikely to be effective. Some accountants see budgeting purely as a technical exercise but this is not how managers with budgets see it. Their human reactions to budgeting must be fully considered.

KEY POINT SUMMARY

- Budgeting is a short-term planning and control technique which works within the framework of longer term plans
- A budget is a financial expression of a plan
- The benefits of budgeting include; co-ordination, communication, exception management, control and motivation
- A limiting factor is something which limits the activities of the organisation
- A budget committee is responsible for preparing and administering the budgeting system
- A master budget comprises a budgeted operating statement and balance sheet
- It is essential to consider the linkages and inter-relationships between budgets
- The human factors in budgeting are all important.

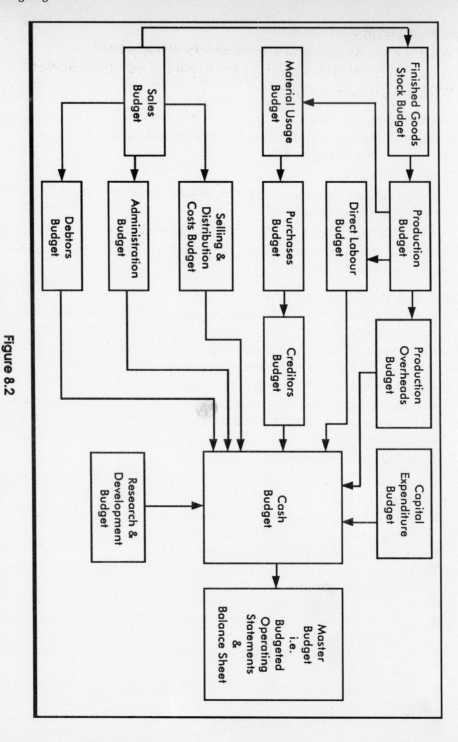

Figure 8.2

TYPICAL BUDGETS & RELATIONSHIPS IN A MANUFACTURING COMPANY

REVIEW EXERCISES

1. What is a budget and what are the benefits of budgeting?
2. What is a limiting factor and why is it important that it is identified?
3. What is the master budget?

9 FLEXIBLE BUDGETING AND BUDGETARY CONTROL

OBJECTIVES

After you have studied this chapter you will

- ■ Realise the importance of flexible budgets for control purposes
- ■ Be able to prepare a flexible budget
- ■ Be able to define and calculate budget variances
- ■ Know how budgetary control is operated
- ■ Be able to design a suitable budgetary control report.

FIXED BUDGETS

The budgets described in the previous chapter were *fixed budgets*. This means that they were prepared to suit one estimated volume of sales or production and that no plans were made for the possibility that actual volumes of production or sales may be different from budgeted levels. A fixed budget is a single budget with no analysis of cost i.e. no adjustment is possible.

FLEXIBLE BUDGETS

A *flexible budget* is one designed so that the permitted cost levels can be adjusted to suit the level of activity actually attained. This is done by recognising the existence of fixed, variable and semi-variable costs so that the budget may be 'flexed' or adjusted to correspond with actual activity. The basis of flexing a budget is an understanding of cost behaviour, described in Chapter 7.

Flexible budgets are useful for planning and are essential elements of the control part of budgeting, known as budgetary control, for the following reasons:

- – All budgets are based on estimates so actual volumes of sales and production cannot be expected to conform exactly to the estimates in the fixed budget
- – To provide useful control information, *actual costs* for the actual activity level should be compared with the *expected costs* for that level of activity, i.e. the flexible budget.

In summary:

Actual Costs for Actual Activity should be compared with *Budgeted Costs for Actual Activity*.

It is meaningless to compare actual costs levels for the production of, say, 8,000 units with a budget for the production of 7,000 units. Like must be compared with like.

The following example illustrates the main principles of flexible budgeting.

Example 1

Uni-product Ltd make a single product and has an average monthly production of 12,000 units, although production varies widely. The necessary cost analysis has been done and the following budget has been prepared.

Cost budget for average production of 12,000 units

Cost	Cost behaviour	Budget £
Direct labour.	Variable (£2 per unit)	24,000
Direct material.	Variable (£3.5 per unit)	42,000
Production overheads	Semi-variable (£10,000 fixed + £2 per unit)	34,000
Admin. overheads	Fixed	27,000
	Total budgeted cost	£127,000

(a) Prepare budgets for 10,000 and 14,000 units

(b) In a month, actual production was 12,800 units and actual costs were

	£
Labour	28,200
Material	43,500
Production overheads	34,800
Admin. overheads	27,300

Find the cost variations from budget

Solution

(a) The budget as given needs to be flexed to produce cost budgets for 10,000 and 14,000 units, having regard to the types of cost and their behaviour

	Flexed budget for 10,000 units £	Original budget 12,000 units £	Flexed budget for 14,000 units £
Labour (£2 per unit)	20,000	24,000	28,000
Material (£3.5 per unit)	35,000	42,000	49,000
Production overheads (£10,000 + £2 per unit)	30,000	34,000	38,000
Admin. Overheads	27,000	27,000	27,000
Total	£112,000	£127,000	£142,000

(b) As previously stated, actual costs for a given production level must be compared with a budget for that level. In this case a budget for 12,800 units must be prepared by the usual flexible budgeting procedure.

89

Cost	Flexed budget for 12,800 units	Actual costs for 12,800 units	Cost Differences
	£	£	£
Labour	25,600	28,200	– 2,600
Materials	44,800	43,500	+ 1,300
Production overheads	35,600	34,800	+ 800
Admin.overheads	27,000	27,300	– 300
Total	£133,000	£133,800	– 800

Notes:

(a) The cost differences are called 'variances'.

(b) A negative variance indicates an overspend compared with budget, a positive variance an underspend.

(c) Although the budget and actual totals are quite close, this masks substantial variances, especially for labour and material. These would be investigated.

(d) Comparison of the actual costs for 12,800 units with the original budget for 12,000 units would have been meaningless. The budget had to be flexed first.

(e) The accuracy of a flexed budget is entirely dependent on the accuracy of the original cost behaviour analysis.

FLEXIBLE BUDGETING AND CONTRIBUTION

It will be apparent by now that the underlying principle of flexible budgeting is the separation of costs into fixed and variable. This separation makes it possible to present budgets and results in a way that shows more information to management. Instead of just showing a final profit figure, the amount of *contribution* can also be shown.

Contribution is calculated thus:

Sales *less* variable costs = Contribution

Fixed costs are then deducted from the contribution to arrive at the final profit. The separation of fixed and variable costs in the collection, recording and presentation of information is known as *marginal costing*.

This is illustrated below:

Example 2

Assume that the units in Example 1 are sold at £11 each. Re-present the flexed budget for 14,000 units using the marginal costing approach showing contribution and profit, and contrast this with the total cost method.

Solution
Flexed budget for 14,000 units using the Marginal cost approach

	£	£
Sales (14,000 × £11)		154,000
less Variable costs		
Labour	28,000	
Materials	49,000	
Variable production overheads		
(14,000 × £2)	28,000	105,000
= Contribution		49,000
less Fixed costs		
Fixed production overheads	10,000	
Admin. overheads	27,000	37,000
= Profit		£12,000

Flexed budget for 14,000 units using the Total cost approach

	£	£
Sales		154,000
less Costs		
Labour	28,000	
Materials	49,000	
Production overheads	38,000	
Admin. overheads	27,000	142,000
= Profit		£12,000

Notes:
(a) The marginal cost approach separates out the fixed and variable costs whereas the total cost method does not. Naturally, both methods give the same final profit.
(b) The marginal cost method enables the amount of contribution to be calculated. This can be very useful to management. Contribution and marginal costing are explored in more detail later in the manual.

Because of the extra information provided it is usual for flexible budgets to be presented in marginal cost form.

BUDGETARY CONTROL
This is the process of comparing actual costs with budgeted costs on a regular basis, usually monthly. Variances are calculated and reports, showing budget, actual and variances (if any), are produced for every manager responsible for a budget and, in summary form, for higher management. In order to show realistic cost allowances, flexible budgeting must be used.

The aim of budgetary control is to highlight variations from the plan so that corrective action can be taken to bring operations back into line with the plan or, if circumstances have changed drastically, to make adjustments to the plan.

CONTROLLABLE AND NON-CONTROLLABLE COSTS

Budgetary control reports for a manager should show only those cost items for which he is accountable and which are under his control. These are known as *controllable costs*.

Costs over which the manager has no control are known as *non-controllable* and would not normally appear on a manager's budgetary control report. It is important to note that *all* costs are controllable by someone in the organisation and part of the development of a proper budgeting system is the detailed clarification of responsibilities for all levels of management. A proper budgetary control system forms a hierarchy of control. Each level of reporting should be inter-related with the levels which are above and below the one concerned. In this way each manager is kept informed of his own performance and of the progress of budget holders junior to him for whom he is responsible.

Remember, the primary objective of budgetary control is not merely the production of regular reports. The purpose of the reports is to serve as a trigger for corrective action to put right any problems shown up.

BUDGETARY CONTROL REPORTS

A budgetary control report is an important part of the control process. Its purpose is to initiate effective action so its design, content and timing must be carefully considered.

The key items which should be shown are:
(a) The budgeted costs and revenues for the period and year to date (YTD)
(b) The actual costs and revenues for the period and YTD
(c) The variances between (a) and (b) together with the trends in the variances
(d) An indication of whether the variance is of sufficient size to be considered significant.

Budgetary control reports are often very detailed and show the above items for each of the costs for which the manager is responsible. A typical budgetary control report is shown in Figure 9.1 opposite. The budgeted figures would be found using a flexible budget.

It will be apparent that variances are important figures and the following example illustrates the development of a flexible budget and the resulting variance calculations.

Example 3
Flexible budgets have been prepared for two output levels as follows:

Production and sales (units)	5,000	7,000
	£	£
Sales Revenue (£6 per unit)	30,000	42,000
Direct materials	7,500	10,500
Direct labour	5,000	7,000
Maintenance	2,500	3,000
Depreciation	3,000	3,000
Total costs	18,000	23,500
Profit	12,000	18,500

BUDGETARY CONTROL REPORT NO ....

BUDGET CENTRE _____

BUDGET HOLDER _____

REPORT RELATIONSHIP   UP ____   DOWN ____

ACCOUNTING PERIOD _____

DATE PREPARED _____

BUDGETED ACTIVITY LEVEL _____

ACTUAL ACTIVITY LEVEL _____

BUDGETED ITEM		CURRENT PERIOD			YEAR TO DATE			TREND OF VARIANCE	SIGNIFICANT? (Yes/No)	COMMENTS
CODE	DESCRIPTION	BUDGET	ACTUAL	VARIANCE	BUDGET	ACTUAL	VARIANCE			

Figure 9.1

TYPICAL BUDGETARY CONTROL REPORT

93

Actual production and sales were 6,200 units and actual revenues and costs were

	£
Sales revenue	37,820
Direct materials	9,300
Direct labour	7,440
Variable maintenance costs	1,600
Fixed maintenance costs	1,400
Depreciation	3,000
Total costs	£22,740
Profit	£15,080

Prepare a flexible budget for 6,200 units and show all variances indicating which variances are significant. In this instance a variance is significant if it is greater than ± 5% of budget. A marginal cost format is required.

Solution

First it is necessary to find the types of cost and their behaviour patterns. This can be done quite easily when it is realised that the cost differences between the two budgets (at 5,000 and 7,000 units) are caused by variable cost changes only; the fixed costs remaining unchanged. The table below shows the calculations for the cost changes arising from a change of 2,000 units i.e. 7,000 – 5,000.

	Budgeted cost		Cost	Difference	Type of	See
	5,000 units	7,000 units	Difference	+ 2,000 i.e.variable element	cost	note
	£	£	£	£		
Materials	7,500	10,500	3,000	1.5	Fully variable	
Labour	5,000	7,000	2,000	1	Fully variable	1
Maintenance	2,500	3,000	500	0.25	Semi-variable (25p unit variable + £1,250 fixed)	2
Depreciation	3,000	3,000	–	–	Fixed	3

Note 1

Both materials and labour are fully variable, because if the variable element per unit is multiplied by either output level, the total equals the budgeted cost at the given output e.g. Materials: 5,000 × £1.5 = £7,500 i.e. the budgeted cost.

Note 2

A similar calculation to Note 1 shows that there is a fixed element in the total maintenance cost, i.e. £2,500 – 5,000 × 0.25 = £1,250 i.e. the fixed element.

Note 3

As there is no change in the budgeted cost at the two output levels it is wholly fixed.

The derived cost characteristics can now be used in the normal way to produce a flexed budget for 6,200 units against which the actual costs and revenues can be compared and the variances calculated.

	Flexed budget for 6,200 units	Actual results for 6,200 units	Variances
	£	£	£
Sales (£6 per unit)	37,200	37,820	+ 620
less Variable costs			
Materials (£1.5 per unit)	9,300	9,300	0
Labour (£1 per unit)	6,200	7,440	–1240 *
Var.Maintenance (25p per unit)	1,550	1,600	- 50
Total variable costs	17,050	18,340	
= Contribution	20,150	19,480	
less Fixed costs			
Maintenance	1,250	1,400	–150 *
Depreciation	3,000	3,000	
Total fixed	4,250	4,400	
= Profit	15,900	15,080	- 820

* Significant variances

The labour variance is $(\frac{1,240}{6,200} \times 100\%) = 20\%$ over budget

The fixed maintenance cost variance is $(\frac{150}{1,250} \times 100\%) = 12\%$ over budget

Note that even though the sales variance is much larger (£620) it is only 2% approx different from budget and is therefore not deemed significant in this case.

The reasons for the significant variances would be investigated so that appropriate action can be taken to cure the problems, if possible.

KEY POINT SUMMARY

- A flexible budget is one designed so that the permitted cost levels can be adjusted to suit the actual activity
- The basis of flexible budgeting is an understanding of cost behaviour
- Flexible budgets are essential for control purposes
- To prepare flexible budgets, costs must be separated into variable, semi-variable and fixed

- Cost differences between budget and actual are known as variances
- Contribution is sales minus variable cost
- Marginal costing is where fixed and variable costs are separated in the collection, recording, and presentation of information
- A key part of budgetary control is the regular production of reports related to responsibilities, showing budget, actual and variance for each cost.

REVIEW EXERCISES

1. Distinguish between fixed and flexible budgets.
2. The following cost budget was prepared for a production level of 15,000 units for Department X.

	Budget £
Prime cost (variable) 15,000 × £4	60,000
Production overheads (semi-variable)	
(£20,000 + £1.50 per unit)	42,500
General overheads (fixed)	35,000
Total	£137,000

Prepare budgets for 13,000 and 17,000 units.

3. In a month output for Department X mentioned in 2 above, was 16,100 units and actual costs were:

	£
Prime costs	62,790
Production overheads	47,370
General overheads	36,300
Total	£146,460

Find the cost variations from budget.

10 CASH BUDGETING

OBJECTIVES

After you have studied this chapter you will

- Know what a cash budget is and why it is important
- Understand the contents of a typical cash budget
- Be able to construct a cash budget
- Know that profit for a period does not equal the cash flow for the period
- Be able to reconcile cash flow and profit.

WHAT IS A CASH BUDGET?

A cash budget is a detailed statement of the expected receipts and payments of cash during the next year. The annual cash budget is divided into shorter time periods (or control periods); quarterly, monthly or even weekly to suit the requirements of the organisation.

The cash budget is one of the most important budgets and receives close attention in every organisation. It is vital that there is always sufficient cash to pay wages and salaries, buy materials and so on. The cash budget shows the expected cash position for each of the periods ahead. This enables the organisation to assess whether operations can continue as planned, whether they need to be curtailed, whether there is the need to approach the bank for a loan and so on.

It is important to realise that the cash flow for a period does not equal the profit for a period. This means it is quite possible for a profitable company to have a shortage of cash. This is explained later in the chapter, after cash budgets have been dealt with.

CONTENTS OF CASH BUDGETS

A cash budget must include every type of cash outflow and cash receipt. In addition to the *amounts*, the *timings* of all receipts and payments must be forecast.

Examples of typical receipts and payments follow:

Typical receipts include:

cash sales

receipts from debtors (i.e. arising from credit sales)

sales of fixed assets

receipts of interest or dividends

issue of new shares

any other fees, royalty or incomes.

Typical payments include:

cash purchases

payments to creditors for stock and material purchases on credit

wage, salary and bonus payments

payments for overhead and expense items

purchase of fixed assets

payments of dividends, interest and tax.

Note: A fixed asset is an asset bought for use within the business. For example, a greengrocer might buy a van to make deliveries. This would be a fixed asset as opposed to the purchase of, say, cabbages for re-sale which are termed *current assets*. Expenditure on fixed assets is known as *capital expenditure*.

FORMAT FOR CASH BUDGETS

Figure 10.1 shows a typical format for a cash budget.

CASH BUDGET

	Period 1	Period 2	Period 3	Period 4
Receipts:	£	£	£	£
OPENING CASH BALANCE b/f	ZZZ	AAA	BBB	CCC
+ Receipts from Debtors + Sales of Capital Items + Any Loans Received + Proceeds from Share Issues + Any other Cash Receipts				
= TOTAL CASH AVAILABLE				
Payments:				
- Payments to Creditors - Wages and Salaries - Loan Repayments - Capital Expenditure - Dividends and Taxation - Any other payments				
= TOTAL CASH PAYMENTS				
= CLOSING CASH BALANCE c/f	AAA	BBB	CCC	

Figure 10.1

FORMAT FOR A CASH BUDGET

Note how the closing balance of cash for one period becomes the opening balance for the next and that it is always necessary to know the opening cash balance.

An example follows.

Example 1

Cash Budget

The opening cash balance, on 1st June, is £25,000. Budgeted sales, all on credit, are as follows:

	£
May	65,000
June	95,000
July	105,000
August	85,000

Analysis of records shows that debtors settle according to the following patterns:

70% in the month of sale
25% the month following

(The balance being bad debts i.e. the cash is never received)

All purchases are for cash and budgeted purchases are:

	£
June	65,000
July	80,000
August	55,000

Wages are £8,000 per month and overheads are £17,000 per month (including £4,000 depreciation) settled monthly. Tax of £20,500 has to be paid in July and the organisation will receive a loan repayment of £12,500 in August.

Prepare cash budgets for June, July and August.

Solution
Workings:
The cash receipts from sales are

	June cash receipts
From May sales (65,000 × 25%)	£16,250
From June sales (95,000 × 70%)	66,500
	82,750

	July cash receipts
From June sales (95,000 × 25%)	£23,750
From July sales (105,000 × 70%)	73,500
	97,250

	August cash receipts
From July sales (105,000 × 25%)	£26,250
From August sales (85,000 × 70%)	59,500
	85,750

Cash Budget

	June £	July £	August £
Opening balance	25,000	21,750	– 2,500
+ Receipts from sales	82,750	97,250	85,750
+ Loan repayment			12,500
= Total cash available	107,750	119,000	95,750
– Purchases	65,000	80,000	55,000
– Wages	8,000	8,000	8,000
– Overheads (less depreciation)	13,000	13,000	13,000
– Tax	20,500		
= Total payments	86,000	121,500	76,000
Closing Balance	21,750	– 2,500	19,750

Notes:

(a) Depreciation is an accounting expense but is not a cash flow. Accordingly, only those overheads which create a cash flow should appear in the budget i.e. Total Overheads, £17,000 *less* depreciation of £4,000 = £13,000 cash flow.

(b) The budget shows that planned activities result in a cash deficiency of £2,500 in July. The organisation thus has advance notice of this problem and has time to take action. This may be to obtain their bank's agreement to run an overdraft for the month or to delay some expenditure for a month or so.

(c) It is normal to have to make various preliminary calculations, as in this example, before the finalised cash budget can be prepared.

PROFITS AND CASH FLOWS

As previously stated, profit for a period does not equal the cash flow for that period, except by coincidence. Profit (or loss) is found by using a number of accounting rules or conventions. The profit or loss is calculated in an account called the Profit and Loss Account (P & L account) which, in summary form, is shown below:

Profit & Loss Account for period

	Sales
less	*Cost of sales*
=	Gross Profit (or loss)
less	*Expenses*
=	Net Profit (or loss)

Sales, cost of sales and expenses in a period are not the same as cash receipts and payments for a variety of reasons, including:

- Most sales and purchases are made on credit. A sale is included in the P & L account when the invoice is sent to the customer but the cash may not be received until a later period. Credit purchases create a similar problem over timing.

- Some expenses in the P & L account are not cash costs but are costs derived from accounting conventions e.g. depreciation, loss or profit on sale of fixed assets and so on.

- Some types of cash income or cash payments may not appear in the P & L account e.g. proceeds from a new issue of shares or a loan, payment of dividends and so on.

- Changes in working capital (e.g. stocks, creditors, debtors and cash balance) affect cash flow but not the P & L account.

- Purchases of fixed assets affect the P & L account only indirectly (through depreciation) but have immediate and often substantial cash flow effects.

A comprehensive example follows:

Example 2

Motor Spares Ltd supply parts and tools to garages. Goods are sold at cost plus 25%.

	Budgeted sales £	Labour costs £	Expenses £
August	85,000	5,000	7,500
September	110,000	6,000	8,500
October	180,000	8,500	11,000
November	130,000	8,000	10,500

Goods for resale and expenses are bought on credit and creditors are paid the following month. The expenses include a monthly depreciation charge of £3,000. Labour is paid monthly. It is company policy to have sufficient stock in hand at the end of each month to meet sales demand in the next half month.

40% of the sales are for cash and 60% on credit. Cash from credit sales is received the next month.

The company is buying a new delivery van in October for £15,000 cash and has to pay tax of £8,500 in September. The opening cash balance at 1st September is £30,000.

Required:

(a) Profit and Loss accounts for September and October, and in total

(b) Cash budgets for September and October

(c) Reconcile the profit and cash flow for September and October.

Solution

(a)

	Profit and Loss Accounts			
	Sept.	Oct.	Total	
	£	£	£	
Sales	110,000	180,000	290,000	
less cost of sales	88,000	144,000	232,000	Note 1
= Gross Profit	22,000	36,000	58,000	
less Labour	6,000	8,500	14,500	
Expenses	8,500	11,000	19,500	Note 2
= Net Profit	7,500	16,500	24,000	

Note 1. As stated, the selling price is cost + 25%. This means that the cost of sales is 80% of sales value.

e.g.   Sept. Sales = £110,000.   Cost of sales = £110,000 × 80% = £88,000

If the mark up was cost + 33⅓% the cost of sales would 75% of sales value. If the mark up was cost + 50%, the cost of sales would be 66⅔% of sales value and so on).

Note 2. For the P & L accounts, the expenses must include the depreciation charge.

(b)   Workings for cash budget

Sales

September cash receipts

	£
From August sales (85,000 × .6)	51,000
From Sept. sales (110,000 × .4)	44,000
	95,000

October cash receipts

	£
From Sept. sales (110,000 × .6)	66,000
From Oct. sales (180,000 × .4)	72,000
	138,000

Purchases

The goods required for the budgeted sales can be found by taking, as previously explained, 80% of the sales value, i.e.

	Sales × 80%	=	Required purchases
August	£85,000		£68,000
September	110,000		88,000
October	180,000		144,000
November	130,000		104,000

Each month, because of their stock policy, the firm buys 50% of the goods required for the current month's sales plus the goods required for 50% of the next month's sales. All purchases are on credit, settled a month in arrears.

The cash payments arising from purchases can be summarised thus:

	September cash flows i.e. August's purchases £	October cash flows i.e. September's purchases £
For August sales		
(50% × 68,000)	34,000	
For September sales		
(50% × 88,000)	44,000	44,000
For October sales		
(50% × 144,000)		72,000
	78,000	116,000

Expenses

Expenses less depreciation, which is not a cash cost, are paid a month in arrears.

September cash flow	=	August expenses – depreciation
	=	7,500 – 3,000
	=	4,500
October cash flow	=	September expenses – depreciation
	=	8,500 – 3,000
	=	5,500

Cash Budget

	September £	October £
Opening balance	30,000	28,000
+ receipts from sales	95,000	138,000
Total cash available	125,000	166,000
– Purchases	78,000	116,000
– Expenses (less depreciation)	4,500	5,500
– Labour	6,000	8,500
– Tax	8,500	
– Van		15,000
Total cash payments	97,000	145,000
= Closing balance	28,000	21,000

Thus the next cash flow effect over the two months is a *reduction of £9,000* in the cash balance, from £30,000 to £21,000.

This should be contrasted with the profit for the period of £24,000 from part (a).

The cash, profit and working capital changes are now reconciled.

(c)   Profit and cash flow reconciliation for September and October

		£
Profit for period		24,000
+ adjustment for item not causing cash flow		
Depreciation (2 × £3,000)		6,000
Total source of funds		0,000

	£	
Funds used for van purchase	15,000	
Taxation	8,500	23,500
Net surplus of funds		6,500

Accounted for by changes in working capital

See note		£
1	Stocks – Increase of	8,000
2	Debtors – Increase of	57,000
3	Creditors – Increase of	(49,500)
4	Cash – Decrease of	(9,000)
	= Net increase in working capital	6,500

Note 1

	£
Stocks at 1st Sept. (August's forward purchases)	44,000
Stocks at 31st Oct. *	52,000
= Stock increase	8,000

* Stocks at 31st October are October's forward purchases, i.e. 50% × £104,000 = £52,000

Note 2

	£
Debtors at 1st Sept. (60% of August sales)	51,000
Debtors at 31st Oct. (60% of October sales)	108,000
= Increase in Debtors	57,000

Note 3

Creditors at 1st Sept.:

	£	
– Expenses (August's less depreciation)	4,500	
– Purchases (from part (b))	78,000	82,500

Creditors at 31st Oct.:

	£	
– Expenses (October's less depreciation)	8,000	
– Purchases (from part (b))	124,000	132,000
= Increase in Creditors		49,500

Note that an increase in creditors reduces the working capital.

Note 4

This is the net decrease in cash i.e. £30,000 – 21,000 =   £9,000

KEY POINT SUMMARY

- A cash budget is a summary of the expected receipts and payments of cash
- Both the amounts and timings of cash flows must be estimated
- The closing cash balance of one period becomes the opening balance of the next
- Profits (or losses) are found from the Profit and Loss Account (P & L account)
- Gross Profit is the difference between Sales and Cost of Sales. Net Profit is Gross Profit less expenses
- Profit is derived using rules and conventions. Normally it does not equal the cash flow
- Profit for the period can be reconciled to the cash movement for the period, having regard to working capital changes.

REVIEW EXERCISES

1. What are the typical contents of a cash budget? Why are cash budgets prepared?
2. A company has a cash balance of £27,000 at the beginning of March and you are required to prepare a cash budget for March, April and May having regard to the following information.

   Creditors give 1 month credit

   Salaries are paid in the current month

   Fixed costs are paid one month in arrears and include a charge for depreciation of £5,000 per month.

   Credit sales are settled as follows: 40% in month of sale, 45% in next month and 12% in the following month. The balance represents bad debts.

Month	Cash Sales £	Credit Sales £	Purchases £	Salaries £	Fixed Overheads £
Jan		74,000	55,200	9,000	30,000
Feb		82,000	61,200	9,000	30,000
March	20,000	80,000	60,000	9,500	30,000
April	22,000	90,000	69,000	9,500	32,000
May	25,000	100,000	75,000	10,000	32,000

11 | STANDARD COSTING

OBJECTIVES

After you have studied this chapter you will

- ■ Know how a standard cost is derived and what standard costing is
- ■ Understand a standard cost card
- ■ Be able to describe the problems and advantages of standard costing
- ■ Understand the purpose of variance analysis
- ■ Be able to show the relationship between common variances
- ■ Be able to calculate basic labour, material and overhead variances and interpret them.

STANDARD COST

A standard cost is the planned cost for a unit of production. It is prepared in advance and it is an estimate of what production costs are expected to be having regard to:

(a) Expected prices of labour, materials and expenses

(b) Expected labour times and amounts of material usage

(c) Expected overhead costs and level of activity (i.e. as the budget)

A standard cost is *not* an average of past costs; it is a target cost for a future period taking into account what conditions are expected to be like.

STANDARD COSTING

Standard costing is a system of accounting based on standard costs. Standard costs are prepared, actual costs are recorded and the differences (i.e. variances) between actual and standard are analysed in order to help management control operations. It will be seen that standard costing and budgetary control are based on similar principles but they differ in scope. Budgets are concerned with totals; they lay down cost limits for functions, departments and the organisation as a whole. In contrast standards are a unit concept. They are more detailed and apply to particular products, to individual operations or processes. Standard costing is best suited to repetitive manufacturing processes.

THE STANDARD COST CARD

After detailed technical studies, analyses of rates and prices, and so on, standard costs are prepared and recorded on a standard cost card or on a computer file. It is common practice for the standard cost card to include only factory costs although a full standard costing system would include, administration and marketing overheads, selling prices and so on.

An example of a standard cost card follows.

Standard Cost Card – Product XY 596

	£	£
Direct materials:		
Material A – 10.5kg @ £6.5 per kg	68.25	
Material B – 3.2kg @ £37.8 per kg	120.96	189.21
Direct labour		
Grade K – 22 hrs @ £4.5 per hour	90.00	
Grade L – 14 hrs @ £5.75 per hour	80.50	179.50
Standard Prime cost		368.71
Variable production overheads*		
36 hours @ £1.5 per hour		54.00
Standard variable production cost		422.71
Fixed production overheads*		
36 hours @ £8.00 per hour		288.00
Standard total production cost		£710.71

* Both variable and fixed production overheads are absorbed on total labour hours i.e. 22 + 14 = 36. The overhead absorption rates of £1.5 and £8 are found from the budgeted overheads for the period.

PROBLEMS IN STANDARD COSTING

Standard costing is a detailed process with a number of possible problems, including:
(a) Difficulties of forecasting rates of pay, material prices, inflation and so on
(b) Problems of deciding what efficiency levels will apply, what material qualities will be used, and so on
(c) Changes in prices, rates, methods and so on which make the standard cost less appropriate
(d) Possible behavioural problems e.g. resentment, antagonism to system, fear of being blamed and so on.

ADVANTAGES OF STANDARD COSTING

If standard costing is properly used for the right type of application there can be a number of advantages including:
(a) Useful control information is provided by the standard: actual comparison and the resulting analysis of variances
(b) The technical analysis necessary to set standards may lead to better methods, greater efficiency and lower costs
(c) Cost consciousness is stimulated
(d) The variances enable 'management by exception' to be practised
(e) Standard costs simplify record keeping and stock valuation because standards are used throughout the system
(f) Motivation may be increased because of the existence of clear targets.

VARIANCE ANALYSIS

A variance is the difference between standard cost and actual cost. Variance analysis subdivides the difference between total standard cost and total actual cost into the detailed differences (relating to material, labour, overheads and so on) which make up the total difference.

The purpose of variance analysis is to provide practical pointers to the causes of off-standard performance so that management can improve operations and increase efficiency. The only criterion for the calculation of a variance is usefulness; if it is not useful for management purposes, it should not be produced. Ideally, variances should be in sufficient detail so that responsibility for a specific variance can be assigned to a particular individual, although this ideal is not always achievable in practice.

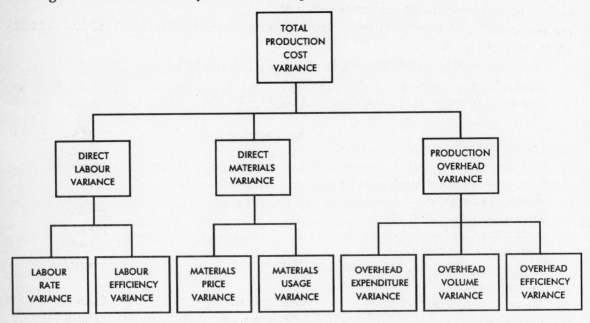

Figure 11.1

TYPICAL COST VARIANCES AND RELATIONSHIPS

RELATIONSHIP OF VARIANCES

Variances are related to each other and Figure 11.1 above shows some typical cost variances which are generally found useful. However it should be emphasised that many other variances exist and the chart only shows variances relating to product costs and does not cover variances for administration overheads nor for sales.

The chart should be studied carefully together with the following notes.

Notes on Figure 11.1

(a) Each variance shown in described and exemplified in the following paragraphs.

(b) The chart is arithmetically consistent i.e. the linked variances equals the senior variance shown.

(c) In general, variances show the differences due to *price* or *rate* and the differences due to *usage*. As examples, the Direct Material variance can be sub-divided into a Price Variance and a Usage Variance; the Direct Labour Variance into a Rate Variance and an Efficiency Variance and so on.

THE VARIANCES DESCRIBED

In the following paragraphs each variance shown on Figure 11.1 is explained and a formula provided together with a worked example.

The worked examples are all based on the following details for Part No. Y252 and the budget and actual results.

Data for Examples. Figure 11.2

Standard cost card (extract)
Standard Production cost per unit   Part No. Y252

		£
Direct materials	15kgs @ £3.50kg	52.50
Direct labour	20hrs @ £6	120.00
Standard Prime cost		172.50

Budget for period (extract)

Production fixed overheads	£25,530
Production variable overheads	£18,630
Budgeted labour hours	4,600
Budgeted standard hours of production (SHP)	4,600

Actual Results

Materials purchased and used	3,712 kgs cost	£12,620
Labour paid	4,790 hours, cost	£29,524
Actual production	248 units (or 4,960 SHP)	
Actual overheads		£44,600

Note: Standard Hours of Production (SHP) are a measure of work content. Each unit of Part No. Y252 is equivalent to 20 SHP and it will be seen from the planning budget that each labour hour is expected to produce 1 SHP. During actual production, of course, labour efficiency may vary causing more or less SHP's to be produced than actual labour hours. SHP's are widely used in budgeting and standard costing as they enable different types of production to be combined using their SHP's.

PRINCIPLES OF VARIANCE CALCULATIONS

Before considering the individual variances it is worthwhile emphasising some general principles:

(a) Price variances are always extracted first. Thereafter the standard price is used for all calculations. Depending on the type of cost, Price Variances may be called Rate or Expenditure variances.

(b) The basis of virtually all variances is the following comparison:

Actual Cost of Actual Quantity is compared with the *Standard Cost of Actual Quantity:*

(c) As previously mentioned under budgeting, a *minus* variance is where the actual price/usage is *greater than* Standard and a *plus* variance is where the actual price/usage is *less than* standard. (Alternative names are *adverse* and *favourable* variances, usually abbreviated to *adv* and *fav*).

(d) As with budgeting, if a variance is sufficiently large it would be thoroughly investigated so that management can take appropriate action.

Remember variances are the triggers for actions not an end in themselves.

LABOUR VARIANCES

The three labour variances can be defined thus:

Direct Labour Variance
– the difference between actual labour cost and the standard labour cost of the production achieved.

This variance can be sub-divided into the Rate Variance (i.e. the 'price' variance) and the Efficiency Variance (i.e. the 'usage' variance).

Direct Labour Rate Variance
– the difference between actual and standard hour rate for the total hours worked.

Direct Labour Efficiency Variance
– the difference between the actual hours worked and the standard hours for the actual production achieved, valued at the standard labour rate.

Formulae

Labour Total Variance:
(Standard labour hours produced × standard rate) –
(Actual hours × Actual rate)

Labour Rate Variance:
(Standard rate – Actual rate) × Actual hours or
(Standard rate × Actual hours) – (Actual rate × Actual hours)

Labour Efficiency Variance:
(Standard hours produced – Actual hours) × Standard rate

Notes:

Rate + Efficiency Variances = Total Variance and (Actual hours × Actual rate) = Actual wages paid.

Example 1

Calculate the labour variances for the data in Figure 11.2 and interpret

Solution:

Rate Variance

(Standard rate × Actual hours) – (Actual rate × Actual hours)

$$= \quad (\text{£}6 \times 4,790) - \text{£}29,524$$
$$= \quad \text{£}27,740 - \text{£}29,524 \qquad = \quad \underline{\text{£}784 \text{ ADV}}$$

Efficiency Variance

(SHP – Actual hours) × Standard Rate

$$= \quad (4,960 - 4,790) \times \text{£}6 \qquad = \quad \underline{\text{£}1,020 \text{ FAV}}$$

Rate + Efficiency = Total variance

$$= \quad -784 + 1,020 \qquad = \quad \underline{\text{£}236 \text{ FAV}}$$

Proof of total variance

(SHP × Standard rate) – (Actual hours × Actual rate)

$$= \quad (4,960 \times \text{£}6) - \text{£}29,524$$
$$= \quad \text{£}29,760 - 29,524 \qquad = \quad \underline{\text{£}236 \text{ FAV}}$$

Interpretation

Rate variance.

Payments above standard rate have caused costs to be £784 over standard. This may be due to paying the right grade of worker above standard rates or using a higher grade of worker than planned.

Efficiency.

During 4,790 actual hours 4,960 standard hours were produced. An obvious gain in efficiency resulting in a large favourable variance. Because both variances are large they would be investigated in order to find the reason for paying above standard rates and if possible to be able to capitalise on the more efficient production methods used.

MATERIAL VARIANCES

The material variances can be defined thus:

Direct Materials Variance.

The difference between the standard material cost for the actual production and the actual cost.

The total variance can be sub-divided as follows:

Direct Materials Price Variance

The difference between the standard price and actual purchase price for the actual quantity of material.

(Note that this variance can be calculated at the time of purchase or the time of usage. As price variations are deemed to be the responsibility of the buyer, calculation at the time of purchase is more usual).

Direct Materials Usage Variance

The difference between the actual quantity used and the standard quantity for the actual production achieved, valued at standard price.

Formulae

Materials Total Variance:

(Standard quantity × Standard Price) – (Actual Quantity × Actual Price)

Materials Price Variance:

(Standard Price – Actual Price) × Actual Quantity or

(Standard Price × Actual Quantity) – (Actual Price × Actual Quantity)

Materials Usage Variance:

(Standard quantity for actual production – Actual quantity) × Standard Price

Notes:

Price + Usage Variances = Total Variance

(Actual Quantity × Actual Price) = Purchase cost

Example 2

Calculate the material variances for the data in Figure 11.2 and interpret

Solution

Price variance

(Standard Price × Actual Quantity) – (Actual Price × Actual Quantity)

(£3.50 × 3,712) – £12,620

= £12,992 – 12,620 = £372 FAV

Usage variance

(Standard quantity for Actual production – Actual quantity) × Standard price

= ((248 × 15) – 3,712) × £3.50

= (3,720 – 3,712) × £3.50 = £28 FAV

Price + Usage = Total Variance

£372 + 28 = £400 FAV

Proof of total variance

(Standard quantity × Standard Price) – (Actual quantity × Actual price)

((248 × 15) × £3.50) – £12,620

= £13,020 – 12,620 = £400 FAV

Interpretation

There is a large favourable Price variance of £372 which should be investigated. Price variances arise from paying higher or lower prices than standard, gaining or losing quantity discounts or buying a different quality of material.

Usage variances arise from greater or lower yields or rates of scrap than planned, or gains or losses arising from non-standard material. In this case the variance is very small in relation to material expenditure so it would appear that usage is very much as planned.

Not all variances are investigated – only those deemed significant are worth pursuing in depth.

OVERHEAD VARIANCES

It will be recalled that overheads are absorbed into production by using predetermined Overhead Absorption Rates (OAR) calculated from the budget. Overheads can be absorbed using production units or labour hours but when standard costing is used, absorption based on the standard hours of production (SHP) is most commonly used. Thus:

$$\text{Total overheads absorbed} = \text{OAR} \times \text{SHP}$$

The overhead variances can be defined thus:

Production overhead total variance:

The difference between the standard overhead for actual production and the actual overheads.

The total variance can be sub-divided as follows

Overhead expenditure variance:
The difference between budgeted and actual expenditure

Overhead volume variance:
The difference between standard overheads for actual hours and the flexed budget for actual hours.
(This variance measures the fixed overhead difference between absorbing overheads using a total OAR and flexing a budget).

Overhead efficiency variance:
The difference between the standard overheads for production achieved (measured in SHP) and the standard overheads for the actual hours taken (measured in labour hours).
(This variance measures the overhead effects of working above or below standard efficiency).

Formulae

Total Overhead Variance:

SHP × OAR – Actual Overheads

Overhead Expenditure Variance:

Actual total overhead – Budgeted total overheads

Overhead Volume Variance:

Budgeted total overheads – Actual hours × OAR

Overhead Efficiency Variance:

(SHP – Actual hours) × OAR

Notes:

Expenditure + Volume + Efficiency variances = Total variance. Budgeted total over-heads are found by 'flexing' the budget using the actual hours worked.

Example 3

Calculate the overhead variances for the data in Figure 11.2 and interpret

Solution:

It is necessary first to calculate the OAR from the budgeted figures

Total budgeted overheads	=	Fixed + Variable
	=	£25,530 + 18,630
	=	£44,160

| Budgeted labour hours and SHP | = | 4,600 |

$$OAR = \frac{£44,160}{4,600} = £9.6 \text{ per hour}$$

Overhead Expenditure Variance

(actual overheads – Budgeted overheads)

£44,600 – 44,929.50 = £329.50 FAV

Note: The budgeted overheads is found by the usual process of flexing a budget i.e.

Fixed overheads + Actual hours × Variable OAR

$$= \quad £25,530 + (4,790 \times \frac{£18,630}{4,600}) \quad = \quad £44,929.50$$

Overhead Volume Variance

Budgeted total overheads – Actual hours × OAR

| = | £44,929.50 – (4,790 × £9.6) | |
| = | £44,929.50 – 45,984 | = £1,054.50 FAV |

Overhead Efficiency Variance

(SHP – Actual hours) × OAR

(4,960 – 4,790) × £9.6   = £1,632 FAV

Expenditure + Volume + Efficiency   = Total Variance

     = £329.50 + 1,054.50 + 1,632   = £3,016 FAV

Proof:

Total Overhead Variance

(SHP × OAR) – Actual overheads

(4,790 × £9.6) – £44,600

     = £47,616 – 44,600   = £3,016 FAV

Interpretation

Overhead variances are somewhat more complex than material and labour variances, mainly because of the conventions of overhead absorption.

The Expenditure variance shows the difference between actual overheads and the budgeted allowance. In this example, actual spending is £329.50 less than the allowance when 4,790 hours are worked.

When activity is greater or less than budget, the volume variance shows the under or over recovery of the fixed element of the OAR. When activity is greater than budget (as in this Example) there is over-recovery of fixed overheads resulting in a favourable variance. When activity is less than budget, an adverse variance will result. An alternative way of calculating the volume variance which demonstrates this point is:-

$$(\text{Actual hours} - \text{Budgeted hours}) \times \text{Fixed OAR}$$

$$= (4,790 - 4,600) \times \frac{£25,530}{4,600}$$

$$= 190 \times £5.55 \quad = \quad £1,054.50 \text{ FAV}$$

The Efficiency variance shows the overhead effect of working above or below standard efficiency. In this example, 4,960 standard hours were produced in 4790 actual labour hours which is above standard efficiency result in a favourable variance of £1,632.

Example 4

In conclusion, calculate the Total Production Cost Variance and reconcile with the material, labour and overhead variances already calculated.

Solution

The Total Production Cost Variance is the difference between the Actual cost of Actual Production and the Standard cost of Actual Production.

Standard Cost, 1 unit Y252

	£
(from Figure 11.2) Prime Cost	172.50
+ overheads 20 hours × £9.6	192.00
= Standard Total Cost per unit	364.50

Total variance = Actual costs – Standard cost of Production

     = £(12,620 + 29,524 + 44,600) – 248 × £364.60

     = £86,744 – £90,396   = £3,652 FAV

i.e. actual costs were lower than standard

Proof: Labour variance + Material variance + Overhead Variance

=   Total variance

=   £236 + 400 + 3,016   =   £3,652 FAV

EXTENSIONS OF VARIANCE ANALYSIS

This chapter has introduced variance analysis but it must be realised that many more variances could be produced, if thought useful.

More detailed material, labour and overhead variances could be calculated plus those for sales. However, all variances follow a similar pattern so it is essential that the basics as covered in this chapter are thoroughly understood.

KEY POINT SUMMARY

- A standard cost is a target cost for a future period. It is not an average of past costs
- Standard costing is an important control technique best suited to repetitive manufacturing operations
- Detailed standards for each product are recorded on a standard cost card
- Problems in standard costing include; forecasting difficulties, changes in prices and methods, and possible behavioural difficulties
- The advantages of standard costing include; cost control, simplification of record keeping, enhanced motivation
- Variance analysis sub-divides the total difference between actual and standard into differences relating to material, labour and overheads
- Price variances are always calculated first; thereafter standard price is used
- The basis of virtually all variances is the following comparison: *Actual* cost of *Actual* Quantity c.f. *Standard* cost of *Actual Quantity*
- A total variance can be sub-divided into a variance for; Price, Rate or Expenditure and a variance for Efficiency or Usage
- The variances which should be calculated are those which are useful to management.

REVIEW EXERCISES

1.   How is a standard cost derived?
2.   What is variance analysis and why is it carried out?
3.   What are the key principles of all variance calculations?
4.   Calculate the labour variances for the following data and interpret.

Standard labour per unit

=   16 × £6.50   =   £104

Actual production	2,186 units
Actual labour hours	35,792
Actual wages paid	£229,069

SECTION 2 ASSESSMENT

PLANNING AND CONTROL

MULTIPLE CHOICE QUESTIONS

1. If the total expenditure on Cost type X was expressed as a cost per unit of the product, X would be classified as variable if:
   (a) The cost per unit changed with the level of activity
   (b) The cost per unit was affected by inflation
   (c) The cost per unit remained constant with changes in the level of activity
   (d) The total expenditure on X remained the same.

2. Using the high/low method what is the value of the variable cost based on the following data?

Cost	Units
£12,650	6,000
9,200	4,520
8,800	3,500
11,750	5,200

   (a) £1 per unit
   (b) £2.11 per unit
   (c) £2.51 per unit
   (d) £1.54 per unit.

3. From the data in (2) what is the fixed element of the cost?
   (a) £3,410
   (b) £8,800
   (c) £6,650
   (d) It cannot be calculated.

4. Information feedback is
   (a) Used to calculate the profit for the period
   (b) Used to monitor the efficiency of labour
   (c) Part of the control system
   (d) To enable managers to keep abreast of business developments.

5. A fixed budget is:
   (a) One containing only fixed cost items
   (b) Designed for one activity level
   (c) One where costs are analysed into fixed and variable elements
   (d) One where the expenditure levels are fixed by senior management.

6. A flexible budget is:
   (a) The only suitable budget for control purposes
   (b) A budget analysed to fixed and variable elements
   (c) Designed to show the appropriate expenditure for the actual production level
   (d) All of the above.

7. The total budgeted expenditure for 17,000 units was £58,500 and for 17,500 units £59,875. This means that fixed costs were estimated to be:
   (a) £11,750
   (b) £1,375
   (c) £58,500
   (d) £23,500.

8. A firm exactly met its budgeted output of 42,500 litres but the total expenditure of £196,200 was £12,000 over budget. Analysis showed that fixed costs of £35,500 were exactly as budgeted. What was the budgeted variable cost per litre?
   (a) £0.83
   (b) £3.50
   (c) £4.62
   (d) £1.12.

9. A cash budget
   (a) Shows the expected cash shortages or surpluses in the periods ahead
   (b) Is the authorisation for a manager to spend cash
   (c) Always exactly equals the firm's cash balance
   (d) Cannot be prepared without an authorisation from a bank.

10. Depreciation is not included in cash budgets because:
    (a) It is not paid until the end of an asset's life
    (b) It cannot be known accurately until the end of an asset's life
    (c) It is not a cash flow
    (d) The same amount is charged each year so it cancels out.

11. Management by exception means that
    (a) Management are able to concentrate on items not proceeding according to plan
    (b) More attention can be given to things which happen infrequently
    (c) Only exceptionally bad performances are reported
    (d) Only exceptionally good performances are reported.

12. Budgeting and Standard Costing
    (a) Are based on similar principles
    (b) Together make up 'Responsibility Accounting'
    (c) Compare actual expenditure to target expenditure
    (d) Are all of the above.

13. A standard hour:
    (a) Is one where operatives work for 60 minutes
    (b) Is the number of hours worked above normal time
    (c) Is a measure of work content
    (d) Is any hour in which standard labour rates are paid.

14. A standard cost is
    (a) The cost that will produce maximum profit
    (b) A target cost for the period ahead
    (c) The average cost of production in the last period
    (d) Always greater than actual cost.

15. In a period 5,220 hours were worked at a total cost of £22,185. The Labour Rate Variance was £1,566 (ADV) and the Labour Efficiency Variance was £711 (FAV). How many standard hours were produced?
    (a) 5,200
    (b) 5,400
    (c) 5,588
    (d) 5,421

The following data are to be used for the next two questions.

The standard Material content of Part No. Y252 is 27 kgs at £5.75 per kg. In a period 486 units of Part No. Y252 were produced and actual material usage was 13,132 kgs at a cost of £74,852.

16. What was the Material Price Variance?
    (a) £155 (FAV)
    (b) £657 (ADV)
    (c) £575 (FAV)
    (d) £657 (FAV).

17. What was the Material Usage Variance?
    (a) £295 (ADV)
    (b) £57.5 (ADV)
    (c) £57.5 (FAV)
    (d) £295 (FAV).

The following information is to be used for the next two questions.

The standard labour content of Part No. X55 is 18 hours at £6.50 per hour. In a period 942 units were made and £110,524 wages were paid for 16,746 hours work.

18. What was the Labour Rate Variance?
    (a) £1,675 (ADV)
    (b) £1,675 (FAV)
    (c) £117 (ADV)
    (d) £117 (FAV).

19. What was the Labour Efficiency Variance?
    (a) £1,365 (ADV)
    (b) £1,675 (ADV)
    (c) £1,657 (FAV)
    (d) £1,365 (FAV).

The data below are to be used for the next four questions.

Budget for Period, Dept. XXX

Fixed overheads	£27,495
Variable overheads	£31,850
Labour hours	6,500
Standard hours of production	6,500

Actual for period

Fixed overheads	£29,800
Variable overheads	£31,850
Labour hours	6,450
Standard hours produced	6,550

20. What is the overhead expenditure variance?
  (a) £2,550 (FAV)
  (b) £2,305 (ADV)
  (c) £2,550 (ADV)
  (d) £2,305 (FAV).

21. What is the overhead volume variance?
  (a) £456 (ADV)
  (b) £212 (ADV)
  (c) £212 (FAV)
  (d) £456 (FAV).

22. What is the overhead efficiency variance?
  (a) £913 (FAV)
  (b) £456 (FAV)
  (c) £913 (ADV)
  (d) £456 (ADV).

23. What is the Total Overhead Variance?
  (a) £2,550 (ADV)
  (b) £2,550 (FAV)
  (c) £2,305 (ADV)
  (d) £1,849 (ADV).

The following information is to be used for the next two questions.

Output	12,000 units	15,000 units
	£	£
Production cost	46,500	52,500
Administration cost	38,000	38,000

24. If 13,500 units were sold at £7.50 each what is the contribution for the firm?
    (a) £101,250
    (b) £74,250
    (c) £27,000
    (d) £84,500.

25. What are the fixed costs of the firm?
    (a) £60,500
    (b) £38,000
    (c) £52,500
    (d) £46,500.

QUESTIONS WITH ANSWERS

A1. Company Z is preparing budgets for the coming year. 120,000 labour hours will be 100% level of expected productive time, but a flexible budget at 90%, 110% and 120% is required so that cost allowances can be set for these possible levels.

Budgeted Cost Details

1.   Fixed Cost per annum

	£
Depreciation	22,000
Staff salaries	43,000
Insurances	9,000
Rent & Rates	12,000

2.   Variable Costs

Power	30p per direct labour hour
Consumables	5p direct labour hour
Direct labour	£3.50 per direct labour hour

3.   Semi-Variable Costs

Analysis of past records, adjusted to eliminate the effect on inflation shows the following:

	Direct labour hours	Total Semi-variable cost
Last year 1988	110,000	£330,000
1987	100,000	£305,000
1986	90,000	£280,000
1985	87,000	£272,500
1984	105,000	£317,500
1983	80,000	£255,000

122

Required:

A cost budget at 100% and flexed to show cost allowances at 90%, 110% and 120% of expected level.

AAT Cost Accounting & Budgeting (part question)

A2. Kanflexus Ltd uses flexible budgets and standard costing in its control systems. The overhead costs of Machine Shop A can be analysed into four distinct behavioural groups. Extracts from the approved monthly flexible budget are as follows:

Activity Level

in 000 machine hours	50	55	60	65	70	75	80	85	90

Overhead Costs

in £									
Group 1	50,000	(a)	50,000	(b)	(c)	(d)	50,000	(e)	50,000
Group 2	(f)	69,250	71,000	(g)	74,500	(h)	(i)	(j)	81,500
Group 3	(k)	46,750	51,000	(l)	(m)	(n)	68,000	(o)	(p)
Group 4	24,000	(q)	28,000	28,000	32,000	32,000	(r)	36,000	40,000

The standard overhead absorption rate is based on a normal activity level of 85,000 hours per month and the flexed budget allowance used in variance analysis is based on the actual hours worked during the month.

During last month, 68,600 actual machine hours were worked in Shop A producing output equivalent to 72,200 standard hours. The total overhead incurred by Shop A for the month was £216,450.

Required:

(i)   In your answer book, calculate the missing figures, as indicated by (a) to (r) in the tabular flexible budget.
(ii) Give a concise description of the cost behavioural characteristic of each group.
(iii) Calculate the following variances for last month:
   (a) Overhead total variance
   (b) Overhead expenditure variance
   (c) Overhead volume variance
   (d) Overhead efficiency variance.

LCCI Cost Accounting

A3. E Ltd. has two production departments: F and G and makes two products: H and J. The standard direct labour cost/unit of each product is based on the following data:

Dept.	Grade of labour	Standard rate per hour £	Standard hours Product H	Standard hours Product J
F	1	2.50	2	12
	2	3.00	4	6
G	1	2.50	8	–
	3	2.30	10	–

Actual data for the four weeks ended 26th March 1988 were as follows:

Production: Product H   200 units
                        J   300 units

| | Department F | | Department G | |
Grade of labour	Actual hours worked	Actual wages £	Actual hours worked	Actual wages £
1	4,028	10,200	1,610	3,960
2	2,570	7,750	–	–
3	–	–	1,980	4,540

Using the information given above you are required to:
(a) Calculate the standard direct labour cost of:
   (i) One unit of each product;
   (ii) The total products made;
(b) Ascertain for each department the direct labour total variance;
(c) Analyse the variances in (b) above into:
   (i) Direct labour rate variance;
   (ii) Direct labour efficiency variance.

RSA Cost Accounting

A4. Taman Bhd produces three grades of potting compost, trade name 'Compo', by mixing three material ingredients, G, R and O, in different proportions. Budgeted cost prices of these materials are G – $0.40 per kg, R – $0.20 per kg, and O – $0.80 per kg.

There is a normal loss of 4% of total input to the mixing and filling process, at the end of which all grades of Compo emerge in sealed plastic sacks, each containing 48 kg of compost. Direct workers are paid $12 per hour and are expected to mix and fill thirty sacks per hour. An absorption rate of 400% on direct wages cost is necessary, to recover the budgeted production overheads.

Stocks at 1 May 1989 are expected to be:

| Materials (in kg) | | | Finished Compo (in sacks) | | |
G	R	O	No.1	No.2	No.3
155,000	182,500	142,500	5,000	5,500	7,500

The company plans to have decreased all stocks of raw materials by 20% at 30 April 1990 and to have increased all stocks of Compo by 60% at the same date.

Other details are as follows:

	Compo No.1	Compo No.2	Compo No.3
Standard mixes (as % of total input)			
G	50%	30%	10%
R	40%	50%	60%
O	10%	20%	30%
Sales budget (in sacks) for the year ended 30 April 1990	50,000	40,000	60,000

124

Required:
Prepare the following budgets for the year ending 30 April 1990:
(i)   Production
(ii) Material purchases
(iii) Production cost

LCCI Cost Accounting

A5. XY Products makes only two products, X and Y, both of which require operations in Department 3 where it budgets to employ twenty direct workers paid at a standard rate of £3.50 per labour hour. Other budgeted data for Department 3 is as follows:

	Product X	Product Y
Standard time per unit	35 minutes	40 minutes
Budgeted weekly output	720 units	570 units

The wage analysis for last week indicated that 760 hours were worked at a cost of £2,926.

Recorded output for that week was 672 units of X and 615 units of Y, with no opening or closing work in progress.

Required:
(a) calculate the following variances for Department 3 for last week:
   (i)   Total labour cost
   (ii) Labour rate
   (iii) Labour efficiency
(b) Suggest two possible reasons for each of the variances in (a) (i) and (ii) above.

LCCI Cost Accounting

A6. The following budgeted Profit and Loss Account has been prepared for Company B for the first six months of the coming year.

	Jan £	Feb £	Mar £	April £	May £	June £
Sales	22,000	24,000	25,000	29,000	18,000	23,000
Less costs						
Materials	8,000	9,000	9,500	10,000	6,000	8,500
Labour	3,900	4,000	4,200	4,700	3,700	4,100
Overheads	4,600	4,700	4,900	5,200	3,800	4,500
	16,500	17,700	18,600	19,900	13,500	17,100
Profit	5,500	6,300	6,400	9,100	4,500	5,900

The material cost above is arrived at as follows:

Opening stock	3,000	5,000	3,000	2,500	3,500	1,500
Purchases	10,000	7,000	9,000	11,000	4,000	11,000
	13,000	12,000	12,000	13,500	7,500	12,500
Closing stock	5,000	3,000	2,500	3,500	1,500	4,000
	8,000	9,000	9,500	10,000	6,000	8,500

Notes:

(i)   All materials are paid for one month after delivery. December purchases £9,000.

(ii) Customers are expected to pay two months after sale. Sales for the previous November were £18,000 and for December £19,000.

(iii) Labour costs are paid in the month wages are earned.

(iv) Included in the overhead figure is £1,000 per month for depreciation – all other overhead costs are paid for in the month the cost is incurred.

(v)   Capital Expenditure is planned for March of £7,500 and June £27,200.

(vi) A tax payment is due in January of £8,000.

(vii) The expected cash balance at the beginning of January is £2,000.

Required:

(i)   A cash budget for the first six months of the coming year.

(ii) Discuss the action the firm should take in view of the cash budget you have prepared.

AAT Cost Accounting & Budgeting (part question)

A7. In Department X work is done on a wide variety of products and a standard time has been set for every operation with the participation of both direct workers and management. Standard direct labour costs are based on these times priced at the budgeted rate of £4 per direct labour hour.

The total factory overhead budget for the department contains both variable and fixed elements which, based on a normal monthly budgeted output equivalent to 24,000 hours, are absorbed into standard product costs using these absorption rates:

Variable   – £1.25 per standard hour
Fixed   – £3.75 per standard hour

The following data relates to the actual performance in Department X during last month:

Output in standard hours	–	25,200
Actual hours	–	24,600
Actual wages paid	–	£102,350
Total overhead costs	–	£132,650

Required:

Calculate the total direct labour variance and the total factory overhead variance for the month, with detailed sub-variance analysis of each.

LCCI Cost Accounting

QUESTIONS WITHOUT ANSWERS

B1. Assume that the actual results for HL Company for the year included the following:

Sales of product X	250,000 units	£18,750,000
Direct materials:		
consumption of component BW		1,000,000 kilos
total cost		£2,500,000
Direct labour:		
total hours		900,000
total cost		£10,500,000

Required:

(i) Calculate the following variances: total material variance; total labour variance; material usage; material price; labour rate; labour efficiency.

(ii) Suggest *two* possible reasons for an adverse (unfavourable) material usage variance.

Suggest *two* possible reasons for a favourable labour rate variance.

AAT Cost Accounting & Budgeting (part question)

B2. A system of budgetary control is being introduced in a manufacturing company and a budget committee has been set up under the chairmanship of the chief executive. At the first meeting, it was decided to appoint a budget officer and also to develop a budget manual.

Required:

(i) List the main duties of a budget officer.

(ii) Briefly explain the general purpose of using a budget manual and list examples of the type of information it would contain.

LCCI Cost Accounting

B3. Dajini Plastics Ltd produce a wide range of plastic products. The following are the standards that apply to their largest industrial bucket:

Direct materials
   1 handle $0.25
   Plastic 1.25 lbs at $0.60 per lb

Direct labour
   0.2 hours at $5.00 per hour

Overhead

Variable	$0.50 per bucket
Fixed	$1.00 per bucket

The budgeted monthly volume of buckets is 8,000.

The actual results for the month of May were:

Materials used

        10,050 handles at $0.26 each

        12,000 lbs plastic at $0.59 per lb

Labour

        2,400 hours at $5.10 per hour

Overhead incurred

Variable overhead	$4,400
Fixed overhead	$7,500

10,000 buckets were produced in the month.

Required:

(i) State the standard cost of the bucket

(ii) Calculate 7 variances for the month of May

(iii) Give two illustrations of how the labour efficiency variance may have arisen.

LCCI Management Accounting

B4. The increasing use of advanced manufacturing technology is causing the amount charged for depreciation of plant and machinery to be a significantly higher proportion of total manufacturing costs. Depreciation charges normally relate to the original cost of the asset and most systems include the use of a detailed plant register.

Required:

(i) State why depreciation is included as part of manufacturing costs and what exactly is achieved by the normal provision of depreciation for an item of plant and machinery.

(ii) State how you would normally classify depreciation in terms of cost behaviour.

(iii) List ten items of information that you would expect to find on the plant register record for each asset.

LCCI Cost Accounting

B5. The following draft budgeted Profit and Loss Account has been prepared for Company X for the coming year.

	£'000s	£'000s
Sales		8,000
Direct Materials	2,400	
Direct Labour	2,000	
Variable Overhead	800	
Fixed Overhead	1,800	7,000
Profit		1,000

There has been a proposal from the sales department to reduce unit selling prices by 10% as this is expected to increase the volume sold by 25%. The above budgeted figures *exclude* possible cost increases that are now thought likely.

These are:
(i) Material prices may increase by 10%.
(ii) Labour rates may increase by 6%.
(iii) Fixed overheads may increase by £200,000 because a recent change in the law requiring new safety equipment.

Required:

(a) Re-draft the budget after considering this proposal and the possible cost increases outlined above.

(b) Discuss the factors the firm should consider before accepting this proposal to reduce selling prices in order to increase sales volume.

(c) Calculate the contribution to sales ratio:
   (i) In the original draft budget
   (ii) If the sales department's plans are implemented *and* the possible cost increases take place.

(d) Briefly explain and give examples of the types of expenditure that might be included under the headings of:
   (i) Variable overhead
   (ii) Fixed overhead
   (iii) Semi-variable overhead.

Show by simple charts the behaviour of costs under each heading with cost on the vertical axis and volume on the horizontal axis.

AAT Cost Accounting & Budgeting

B6. LNE Electronics Bhd makes and sells a range of electric kettles. These are marketed as models L, N and E, the current monthly budget being 1,000, 1,750 and 2,000 units respectively. All models require manufacturing operations in three production departments as indicated in the following extracts from standard specifications:

Dept.	Standard rate per direct labour hour	Standard times in minutes per unit		
		Model L	Model N	Model E
1	$14.00	72	48	36
2	$12.00	60	24	24
3	$15.20	30	15	18

There is no opening or closing work in progress in any production department. The cost department has recorded the following actual data for last month:

	Model L	Model N	Model E
Finished output (units)	900	1,800	2,100

	Dept. 1	Dept. 2	Dept. 3
Direct wages incurred	$52,800	$32,160	$25,300
Efficiency ratio	105%	100%	90%

Required:

(i) Explain the term 'standard hour', clearly indicating how and for what purpose it is used.

(ii) From the data given, calculate, for each department:

    (a) The direct labour rate variance

    (b) The direct labour efficiency variance.

LCCI Cost Accounting

B7. (a) Define the following terms:

    (i) Functional budget;

    (ii) Master budget.

(b) Give *three* examples of functional budgets.

(c) Describe briefly the major sections of a master budget.

(d) Give two examples of a 'principal budget factor' and state how each of your examples should be taken into consideration when preparing the budgets given in (a) above.

RSA Cost Accounting Stage II

B8. The following report was presented to the management of Langford Ltd:

Quarter 1

	£
Planned sales 10,000 units	840,000
Standard cost of sales	640,000
Standard profit	200,000

Variances	A	F
	£	£
Sales margin quantity	16,000	
Sales margin price		9,200
Material price		12,300
Material usage	10,200	
Labour rate	6,500	
Labour efficiency	8,000	
	40,700	21,500

Standards for 1 unit of this product are:

Materials	– 2 coils at £17 per coil
Labour	– 2 hours at £4 per hour

Actual production achieved in the quarter – 12,000 units.

Required:

(i) Calculate:

    (a) The quantity of units sold

    (b) The actual selling price per unit

    (c) The quantity of coils used

    (d) The price paid per coil for material

    (e) The time taken for production

    (f) The actual labour hour rate.

(ii) For this report to be useful to the management of Langford Ltd, it must satisfy certain conditions. Discuss two such conditions.

LCCI Management Accounting

B9. (a) Explain the following terms:

    Continuous or rolling budget
    Budget manual
    Budget committee
    Master budget

(b) On 1 January 1988 a company has an opening bank balance of £20,000. There were also debtors in respect of sales in November and December 1987.

The budget for the next 3 months include the following sales data:

January	£60,000
February	£80,000
March	£100,000

20% of each months sales are for cash. Of the credit sales, 60% are paid for in the month after the sale, and 30% paid for in the following month. On average 10% of credit sales are not recovered.

Sales in November	£50,000
Sales in December	£70,000

Required:

    (i) Calculate the debtors figure at 1 January 1988

    (ii) Prepare that part of the cash budget relating to income for each month January to March

    (iii) Briefly explain the advantages of preparing cash forecasts for say three to six months ahead of the current month or period.

(c) The following information is available for the preparation of the overhead budget for a production department:

100% activity	50,000 direct labour hours
indirect labour cost	£1 per direct labour hour
consumable materials	£0.5 per direct labour hour
fixed costs	£30,000

In addition there are semi-variable costs. Information gathered from previous years has revealed the following relationship:

	level of activity	
	65%	90%
semi-variable costs	£15,600	£19,600

Required:

Prepare a budget flexed at the following activity levels:

    (i)   70%

    (ii) 85%.

AAT Cost Accounting & Budgeting

ASSIGNMENT 3

DOLLBEE ELECTRONICS PLC

An assignment including the behavioural aspects of budgeting and the problems caused by preparing budget statements on incorrect principles.

Dollbee Electronics are manufacturers of high quality audio amplifiers and loudspeakers. The company has recently been taken over by Electronics International Inc. (EII) a multi-national company operating on all continents. Hyram K. Cross of EII has been sent to review the budgeting and reporting systems used by Dollbee and finds that monthly budgets are prepared for each department. He asks to see the last budget statement for a typical department and is shown the statement for the Loudspeaker Department; whose manager is Jack Bell.

The budget statement for the last period was:

Budget Statement for period .....
Department: Loudspeaker Department
Actual Results: 12,500 units produced with 35,350 labour hours

	Actual Results £'000s	Budgeted Results £'000s	Budget Variances £'000s
Direct Materials	252	240	– 12
Direct Labour	123	120	– 3
Variable Prod.Overhead	79	72	– 7
Fixed Prod.Overhead	59	56	– 3
Variable Admin.Overhead	41	40	– 1
Fixed Admin.Overhead	50	48	– 2
Total costs	604	576	– 28
Sales value of Production	775	744	+ 31
Profit	171	168	+ 3

Hyram found that the budget was based on 12,000 units with a standard labour content of 2.85 hours and went to Jack Bell to find out his reactions to the budget and what use he makes of the budgeting system.

To Hyram's surprise, Jack Bell was not enthusiastic about the system and thought it of little value to a departmental manager. Jack said, 'It was introduced about a year ago by consultants who only spent about 10 minutes with me, then the budgeting system was introduced without any explanation. Frankly I think they put in a ready made system developed elsewhere. It doesn't seem to help me to run my department. For example, last month's statement showed a positive variance on profit yet I know costs have risen, though nothing like as much as the statement shows, so I would have expected to be down on budgeted profit yet according to this I am £3,000 up! It just doesn't make sense so I tend to ignore it altogether'.

After leaving Jack Bell, Hyram visited several other departments and had similar reactions from the departmental managers. Hyram decided, as a matter of urgency, to try to make the budgeting system more useful and more acceptable to the departmental managers.

STUDENT ACTIVITIES

(a) Criticise the approach of the consultants who installed.

(b) Find out what behavioural objectives should, ideally be fulfilled by budgetary control systems. Do you think that the system outlined meets these objectives?

(c) Criticise the way the budget statement has been prepared.

(d) Redraft the statement in a more informative manner and give an explanation of your reasoning.

OBJECTIVES

The student should show an understanding of the following topics:

> Budgeting and budget preparation
> Behavioural aspects of budgeting
> Budgeting objectives
> Control aspects of budgeting
> Cost behaviour
> Variance calculation.

ASSIGNMENT 4
PURPOSE PACKING LTD.

Purpose Packing Ltd are manufacturers of special purpose racks and containers, mainly for the transport of machined components. On one of their production lines they make a gear wheel carrier out of wood and plastic. The quantities made are large and the Factory Director, John Forbes, thinks it would be worthwhile considering the possibility of installing a standard costing system. Before making a final decision it has been decided that the Accounting Department should prepare some information about current operations.

The following information is available:

Gear Wheel carrier expected unit costs

Direct materials	2 kgs wood @ £3.2 kg
	½ kg plastic @ £5.8 kg
Direct labour	
Preparation	1.4 hours @ £4.8 per hour
Assembly	½ hour @ £3.25 per hour

Budgeted total overheads for the period

	£	Labour hours
Preparation Dept.	135,000	11,000
Assembly Dept.	80,000	6,000

(Fixed overheads contained in the above are Preparation £45,000 and Assembly £35,000)

During the last period actual results were:

Output in units	8,150	
Wood usage	16,050 kgs costing	£52,965
Plastic usage	4,890 kgs costing	£27,300
Labour:		
Preparation	11,820 hours costing	£59,100
Assembly	4,300 hours costing	£15,487
Actual overheads:		
Preparation		£140,100
Assembly		£76,500

STUDENT ACTIVITIES

(a) Prepare a standard cost card for a gear wheel carrier showing Prime Cost and Total Production Cost.

(b) Calculate the following variances for the period

- Direct materials variance sub–divided into Price and Usage for each material.

- Direct labour variance sub–divided into Rate and Efficiency for each type of labour.

- Total overhead variance for each department sub–divided into Expenditure, Volume and Efficiency.

(c) Comment on the possible reasons for any variances found.

(d) Calculate the under/over absorption of overheads for each department for the period.

(e) Comment on whether you think the manufacture of the gear wheel carriers is a suitable application of standard costing.

Section 3
Decision Making and Performance Appraisal

Decision making is a vital part of every manager's job. If decision making is to be more than just inspired guess work then the decision maker needs information about the options being considered. There are numerous sources and types of information; some comes from within the organisation, some from outside. Depending on the decision, information may be required on sales, personnel, resources, productivity and so on. Whatever else is needed, information on the financial aspects of the problem is invariably required. Accordingly the next section of the book deals with some of the more important ways in which the cost and management accounting system can assist management with information for decision making.

The section concludes with an outline of the problems of performance appraisal and how cost and management accounting can assist. Systematic performance appraisal is especially important in organisations that have operating divisions with managers responsible for costs, profits and achieving a satisfactory return on the capital invested in the division. In such circumstances, senior management need appropriate information about the performance of operating management.

12 DECISION MAKING AND RELEVANT INFORMATION

OBJECTIVES

After you have studied this chapter you will
- Be able to define decision making
- Understand the stages in decision making
- Know what information is relevant for decision making
- Be able to calculate relevant costs and revenues
- Understand the problems caused by uncertainty
- Be able to define and use expected values in decision making.

WHAT IS DECISION MAKING?

Decision making means making a *choice* between *alternatives* in pursuit of an *objective*. Decision making relates to the *future*; nothing can be done now that will alter the past. As the future cannot be known with certainty, decision making must cope with the effects of uncertainty.

The emphasis of this book is on decision making by managers in organisations, what may be termed rational decision making. Although many other factors are involved in these types of decisions (for example personal, psychological, and social considerations) quantitative and financial information plays a crucial part, especially that relating to costs and revenues. It is vital however, that the information supplied is *relevant* for the decision being considered. What is relevant information is dealt with later in the chapter.

In summary, decision making:
- Means making choices between future, uncertain alternatives
- Needs clear objectives to be specified
- Needs relevant information

THE DECISION PROCESS

The decision process can be sub-divided into stages although in practice the divisions between the stages may be blurred. The stages are:

(a) Definition of objectives

The objectives should be specific and quantified wherever possible; e.g. maximise profit or contribution, minimise cost, reduce delivery time and so on

(b) Consider possible alternatives

The various ways that the objective(s) can be achieved should be listed. Ideally, all possible options should be included

(c) Evaluate alternatives

The financial and quantitative implications of each of the alternatives should be compared. It is at this stage that the 'relevant' information mentioned earlier would be used, especially that relating to the costs and revenues of each alternative. In addition the risk and uncertainties of the options should be assessed, if possible

(d) Choose the best option

Having regard to the analysis outlined above and the specified objectives the best option(s) is chosen. This may be the one that produces the maximum profit or contribution or one that is the best compromise between profit and risk. In practice of course, decision making is rarely as clear cut as indicated. There are competing claims for limited resources, there are political and personal pressures, there is risk and uncertainty and so on.

RELEVANT COSTS AND REVENUES

The importance of relevancy has already been stressed and it is now time to consider what are relevant costs and revenues. In summary, relevant costs and revenues are:

(a) *Future costs and revenues*

Decision making is concerned with the future so it is *expected future costs and revenues* which are important to the decision maker. This means that the records of past costs and revenues contained in the accounting system are of value only insofar as they provide a guide to future values. Costs which have already been spent, known as *sunk costs*, are irrelevant for decision making. Fortunately, past cost levels are often a good guide to future levels but they cannot be accepted uncritically. It is how costs behave tomorrow that is important for decision making; not how they behaved yesterday.

(b) *Changes in costs and revenues*

Only costs and revenues which alter as a result of a decision are relevant. If a cost or revenue remains the same for all the options being considered it can be ignored; only the differences are relevant. These types of cost and revenues are known as *differential* costs and revenues. They are costs which may be avoided or revenues foregone, if the particular alternative is not adopted.

Some examples follow illustrating relevant costs.

RELEVANT COST EXAMPLES

Example 1

A contract has been offered which will utilise an existing machine which is suitable only for such contracts. The machine cost £40,000 four years ago and has been depreciated on a straight line basis. It has a current book value of £24,000. The machine could be sold now for £28,000 or for £22,000 after completion of the contract.

The contract uses three types of material:

Material	Units In stock	Contract requirements	Purchase price of stock £	Current buying-in price £	Current Resale price £
A	1,700	1,300	4.80	5.30	5.00
B	2,400	3,600	3.75	3.30	2.50
C	1,200	400	2.20	3.10	2.40

137

A is in regular use within the firm. B could be sold if not used for the contract. There are no other uses for C which has been deemed to be obsolete.

What are the relevant costs to use in the contract decision for the machine and the three materials?

Solution

Machine costs.

The original purchase price is a sunk cost and is not relevant.

The depreciation details given relate to accounting conventions and are not relevant.

The relevant cost is the reduction in resale value over the contract life i.e.

£28,000 – 22,000 = £6,000

Materials.

Material A

Although there is sufficient in stock, the use of 1,300 units for the contract would necessitate the need for replenishment at the current buying in price.

$$\text{relevant cost} = 1,300 \times £5.30 = £6,890$$

Material B

If the contract was not accepted, 2,400 units of B could be sold at £2.50 per unit. The balance of 1,200 required would need to be bought at the current buying in price.

$$\begin{aligned}
\text{relevant cost} = 2,400 \times £2.50 &= £6,000 \\
+ 1,200 \times £3.30 &= \underline{3,960} \\
&\ \underline{9,960}
\end{aligned}$$

Material C

If 400 units were used on the contract they could not be sold so the relevant cost is the current resale price of £2.40

$$\text{relevant cost} = 400 \times £2.40 = £960$$

Note: It will be seen that the recorded historical cost, which is the 'cost' using normal accounting conventions is not the relevant value in any of the circumstances considered.

Example 2

A firm is considering whether to continue work on an existing contract or to terminate it now and pay an agreed penalty of £70,000 to the client. This is being considered because the penalty is less than the anticipated contract loss.

The following summary has been prepared:-

	£
Expenditure to date	130,000
Estimated future costs to completion in 1 year's time	

	£	£
Material	60,000	
Staffing	30,000	
Overheads	60,000	150,000
Estimated total cost		280,000
Contract value		200,000
Estimated loss on contract		£80,000

The following information is also available

Material

Contracts have been exchanged for the purchase of the £60,000 material. This is special purpose material which has no alternative use. If not used on this contract it will incur disposal costs of £10,000

Staffing

Two specialists are employed on the contract each at £12,500 p.a. If the contract was terminated now they would each receive £7,000 redundancy pay. The other £5,000 staffing cost is the allocated cost for a supervisor who is also in charge of several other contracts.

Overheads

The £60,000 comprises £20,000 specific to the contract and £40,000 general fixed overheads allocated to the contract.

Required

Prepare relevant financial information so that the firm can decide whether or not to abandon the contract.

Solution

Relevant Benefits of continuation   Notes

	£	
Contract price	200,000	
Penalty saved	70,000	1
Material disposal costs saved	10,000	2
	280,000	

Relevant Costs of continuation   Notes

	£	
Staff	11,000	3
Overheads	20,000	4
	31,000	

∴ net benefit from continuation
= £280,000 − 31,000 = £249,000

Contract should be continued to completion.

Notes:

1. If the contract is continued the firm will not have to pay the penalty of £70,000. This is therefore a benefit of continuation.

2. Similarly, if the material is used on the contract, the £10,000 disposal costs will be saved. Note that the cost of £60,000 for the material will be incurred whether or not the contract continues so is not a relevant cost for the decision being considered.

3. The staff will cost £25,000 if the contract is continued but their redundancy pay will be saved. (£25,000 – 14,000 = £11,000.)

    The £5,000 allocated cost is not relevant as the supervisor will continue to be paid whether or not the contract continues.

4. The £20,000 overheads specific to the contract are avoidable and therefore relevant. The allocated fixed costs are not relevant.

5. The expenditure to date of £130,000 is a sunk cost and is not relevant for the decision.

6. To prove the net benefit of £249,000 from continuation, the statement below shows the opposing position i.e. if the contract is abandoned. This naturally produces a cost of £249,000.

Benefits from abandonment

	£
Staff salary savings	25,000
Overhead savings	20,000
Total savings	45,000

Costs of abandonment

	£
Penalty	70,000
Material disposal costs	10,000
Redundancy payments	14,000
Loss of contract value	200,000
Total costs	£294,000

∴ cost of abandonment:

$$+\,45{,}000 - 294{,}000 = \quad -£249{,}000$$

RISK AND UNCERTAINTY IN DECISION MAKING

If the future was known with certainty then forecasts could be made which would be exactly achieved. This would greatly assist decision making but life is not as simple as that. Uncertainty does exist and actual results rarely turn out exactly as anticipated.

There is no technique which enables us to forecast the future perfectly. All we can do is to help the decision maker by indicating some of the uncertainties which exist and by producing information which shows the variabilities expected. There are numerous techniques which can be used. Some use advanced mathematical and statistical methods outside the scope of this book but one commonly used technique, that of expected value, is described below.

EXPECTED VALUE

Expected value is a simple way of bringing some of the effects of uncertainty into the appraisal process. Expected value is the average value of an event which has several possible outcomes. The expected value or average is found by multiplying the value of each outcome by its probability. The probability of an outcome (probability could also be called the likelihood or chance of the outcome occurring) is based on the judgement of the people concerned.

For example, assume that it is required to forecast the sales for next month. The Sales Manager thinks that there is a 40% (or .4) chance that sales will be 10,000 units and a 60% (or .6) chance that they will be 13,000 units. What is the expected value of sales?

$$\text{Expected sales value} = (10,000 \times .4) + (13,000 \times .6)$$
$$= \underline{11,800 \text{ units}}$$

Thus, the use of expected value enables the variabilities and their likelihoods, that is the uncertainties, to be incorporated into the information. Where several alternatives are being considered each of which has several outcomes the usual decision rule is to choose the option with the highest expected value.

Example 3

Expected value

Three options are being considered each of which has several possible outcomes. The values and probabilities have been estimated as follows

Option A		Option B		Option C	
Outcomes		Outcomes		Outcomes	
Probability	Profit £	Probability	Profit £	Probability	Profit £
0.3	8,000	0.2	4,000	0.3	2,500
0.7	11,000	0.3	7,000	0.4	9,000
		0.4	10,000	0.3	15,000
		0.1	14,000		

Required
Calculated the expected values of the three options and recommend which should be accepted.

Solution

Expected values

Option A

$$(0.3 \times 8,000) + (0.7 \times 11,000) \qquad = \qquad £10,100$$

Option B

$$(0.2 \times 4,000) + (0.3 \times 7,000) + (0.4 \times 10,000) + (0.1 \times 14,000) \qquad = \qquad £8,300$$

Option C

$$(0.3 \times 2,500) + (0.4 \times 9,000) + (0.3 \times 15,000) \qquad = \qquad £8,850$$

Thus, on the basis of Expected Value, Option A would be preferred and the options would be ranked ACB

Notes

(a) In each case it will be seen that the probabilities total 1 (or 100%). This shows that all outcomes have been included.

(b) The number of outcomes can vary as shown in the example but a commonly encountered situation is that shown for Option C where there are three outcomes; often termed Optimistic, Most Likely and Pessimistic.

SHORT TERM AND LONG TERM DECISION MAKING

The principles of decision making and of relevant costs and revenues apply equally to short and long term decision making.

Short term decision making deals with problems concerning the immediate period ahead say, up to 1 year hence. Problems covering periods longer than a year would normally be classed as long term.

The major difference between the two is that for long run decisions, usually called investment decisions, the time value of money has to be considered. Investment decisions are dealt with later in the book. Short run decision making is dealt with in the chapters immediately following.

KEY POINT SUMMARY

■ Decision making is making a choice between alternatives in pursuit of of objective

■ Decision making relates to the future, which is always uncertain

■ The decision process is; define objectives, consider alternatives, evaluate alternatives, choose best option

■ Relevant costs and revenues are; future costs and revenues which change as a result of the decision

■ Sunk costs and costs which are common to all options, are irrelevant for decision making

- Risk and Uncertainty are always present in decision making
- Uncertainty means that multiple outcomes are possible
- Expected value is the average value of an event which has several possible outcomes
- Expected value is probability × value.

REVIEW EXERCISES

1. Into what stages can the decision process be divided?
2. What are relevant costs and revenues for decision making?
3. Calculate the expected values of the options given below.
   Which should be accepted?

Option X		Option Y		Option Z	
Outcomes		Outcomes		Outcomes	
Probability	Profit £	Probability	Profit £	Probability	Profit £
0.4	10,000	0.2	3,000	0.3	- 1,000
0.6	15,000	0.7	13,000	0.4	15,000
		0.1	22,000	0.3	25,000

13 MARGINAL COSTING

OBJECTIVES

After you have studied this chapter you will

- ■ Understand the importance of marginal costing in decision making
- ■ Be able to define a key factor
- ■ Know the importance of maximising contribution per unit of the limiting factor
- ■ Be able to use marginal costing in decision making
- ■ Understand the distinction between marginal costing and total costing for routine reporting
- ■ Be able to calculate stock valuations using marginal and total costing approaches.

SHORT RUN DECISION MAKING AND MARGINAL COSTING

This chapter deals with the important short run decision making technique known as marginal costing. This was introduced previously and it will be recalled that the key features of marginal costing are; the separation of costs into fixed and variable and the calculation of contribution. Contribution is sales less variable costs.

The importance of marginal costing for this type of decision making is that, in the short run, fixed costs remain the same and the only costs that alter (and thus the only ones which are relevant) are the variable costs. Accordingly the selection of the option which maximises contribution is usually the correct decision.

Note: Variable costs may alternatively be called marginal costs.

KEY FACTOR

Sometimes known as the limiting factor or principal budget factor. This was mentioned previously when dealing with budgeting and it will be recalled that the key factor is a binding constraint upon the organisation i.e. the factor which prevents indefinite expansion or unlimited profits. It may be sales, availability of skilled labour, space, supplies of material or finance. Where a single key factor can be identified, then the general objective of maximising contribution can be achieved by selecting the option which *maximises the contribution per unit of the key factor.*

EXAMPLES OF DECISION MAKING USING MARGINAL COSTING

Several typical problems using marginal costing are illustrated below. Once the general principles are understood they can be applied in any other similar circumstances.

The steps in analysing such problems are:

(a) If necessary, separate out fixed and variable costs.

(b) Check that fixed costs are expected to stay the same.

(c) Calculate the revenue, marginal cost and contribution of each of the alternatives.

(d) Check to see if there will be a key factor which will be binding. If so, calculate the contribution per unit of the key factor.

(e) Finally, select the alternative which maximises contribution.

Example 1

SPECIAL ORDER DECISION

(Typically these decisions are required when a firm has spare capacity and is offered a special order, below normal prices, which will take up the unused capacity.)

Morning Start Ltd. manufacture a breakfast cereal which they sell for 50p per packet. Current output is 200,000 packets per period which represents 80% of capacity. They have the opportunity to use the surplus capacity by selling their product at 30p per packet to a supermarket chain who will sell it as an 'own label' product.

Total costs for last period were £70,000 of which £20,000 were fixed. This represented a total cost of 35p per packet.

Should the supermarket order be accepted even though the selling price is below total cost?

What other factors should be considered?

Solution

The key point is that the price of 30p offered by the supermarket should be compared with the marginal cost of production, not with total cost (assuming fixed costs do not change).

The present position is

	£	
Sales (200,000 × 50p)	100,000	
less marginal cost	50,000	(i.e. 25p per packet)
= Contribution	50,000	
less Fixed cost 20,000		
= Profit	30,000	

The supermarket order would produce the following extra contribution

	£
Sales (40,000 × 30p)	12,000
less marginal cost (40,000 × 25p)	10,000
= Contribution	2,000

Thus, assuming that fixed costs remain the same the profit would increase from £30,000 to £32,000 so, on the figures above, the supermarket order looks worthwhile.

However, before a final decision is made several other factors need to be considered.

(a) Will the acceptance of one order at a lower price lead other customers to demand lower prices as well?

(b) Is this particular order the most profitable way of using the spare capacity?

(c) Will the supermarket order lock up capacity which could be used for future full price business?

(d) Is it absolutely certain that fixed costs will not alter?

(e) Will sales of the product in the supermarket's 'own label' form reduce the main branded sales?

Example 2

DROPPING A PRODUCT

(If a company has a range of products one of which is thought to be unprofitable it may consider dropping the 'loss-making' product. Exactly the same principles would be involved if it was a department, not a product).

A company makes three products, one of which shows a loss, and it is considering whether to drop the unprofitable product. The following statement has been prepared.

	Product A	Product B	Product C	Total
	£	£	£	£
Sales	90,000	160,000	145,000	395,000
Total costs	102,000	126,000	108,000	336,000
Profit (Loss)	(12,000)	34,000	37,000	59,000

The total costs are ⅔ variable ⅓ fixed.

Based on the above information should Product A be dropped? What other factors should be considered?

Solution

First calculate the fixed costs for the firm as a whole and the marginal or variable costs for each Product.

	Product A	Product B	Product C	Total
	£	£	£	£
Total costs (as given)	102,000	126,000	108,000	336,000
Fixed costs (⅓)	34,000	42,000	36,000	112,000
Variable costs (⅔)	68,000	84,000	72,000	224,000

It is a feature of the Marginal Costing approach that Fixed Costs are not spread over the individual products or departments but kept as a single total, in this case £112,000.

The original statement can now be rearranged in Marginal Costing form.

	Product A	Product B	Product C	Total
	£	£	£	£
Sales	90,000	160,000	145,000	395,000
less marginal costs	68,000	84,000	72,000	224,000
= Contribution	22,000	76,000	73,000	171,000
less Fixed costs				112,000
= Profit				59,000

Naturally, this presentation gives the same overall profit but, in addition, the contribution of each product is shown. It will be seen that Product A provides a contribution of £22,000 which means that the Product is worthwhile.

If Product A was dropped the position would be:

	£
Contribution Product B	76,000
Contribution Product C	73,000
	149,000
less Fixed costs	112,000
Profit	£37,000

Thus dropping Product A with an apparent loss of £12,000 reduces total profit by £22,000 which is, of course, the amount of contribution lost from Product A.

Other factors which need to be considered.

(a) The assumption above was that the fixed costs were general fixed costs which would remain if Product A was dropped. If some of the fixed costs were specific to Product A and would cease if the product was dropped then this would need to be taken into account.

(b) Although Product A produces some contribution, it is at a low rate compared to the other products. Other more profitable products should be considered.

Example 3

KEY FACTOR DECISION

(This is a problem where a firm has a choice between various products and there is a single binding constraint).

A company is able to produce four products and is planning its production mix for the next period. Estimated cost, sales, and production data are:

PRODUCT	L	M	N	O
	£	£	£	£
Selling price per unit	60	90	120	108
less variable costs				
Labour (at £6 per hour)	18	12	42	30
Material (at £3 per kg)	18	54	30	36
= Contribution per unit	24	24	48	42
Resources per unit				
Labour (hours)	3	2	7	5
Materials (kgs)	6	18	10	12
Maximum demand (units)	5,000	5,000	5,000	5,000

Based on the above information what is the most profitable production mix under the two following assumptions:

(a)   If labour hours are limited to 50,000 in a period, or

(b)   If material is limited to 110,000 kgs in a period.

Solution

It will be seen that all the products show a contribution so that there is a case for their production. However, because constraints exist, the products must be ranked in order of contribution per unit of the limiting factor so that overall contribution can be maximised. Accordingly, the contribution per unit of the inputs must be calculated.

PRODUCT	L	M	N	O
	£	£	£	£
Contribution per unit	24	24	48	42
Contribution per labour hour	8	12	6.85	8.5
Contribution per kg. of material	4	1.33	4.8	3.5

When labour hours are restricted to 50,000:

To make all products to the demand limits would need $(5,000 \times 3) + (5,000 \times 2) + (5,000 \times 7) + (5.000 \times 5) = 85,000$ hours. As there is a limit of 50,000 hours in a period the products should be ranked in order of attractiveness judged by contribution per labour hour i.e. M, O, L and N

Best production plan when labour is restricted

Produce	5000 units M using	10,000	labour hours	
	5000 units O using	25,000	labour hours	
	5000 units L using	15,000	labour hours	

and no units of N

which uses the total of   50,000   hours available

Thus if labour hours are restricted to 50,000 the maximum possible contribution is $(5,000 \times £24) = (5,000 \times £42) + (5,000 \times £24) = £450,000$.

No other plan will produce more total contribution when labour is limited.

When material is restricted to 110,000 kgs

Similar reasoning produces a ranking by contribution per kg of material of N, L, O, M which will be noted is the opposite to the ranking produced if labour was the constraint.

Best production plan when material is restricted

5,000 units of N using	50,000	kgs material
5,000 units of L using	30,000	kgs material
2,500 units of O using	30,000	kgs material
and no units of M		
which uses a total of	110,000	kgs of material

Thus if material is restricted to 110,000 kilograms the maximum possible contribution is $(5,000 \times £48) + (5,000 \times £24) + (2,500 \times £42) = £465,000$. No other plan will produce more contribution when material is limited.

Note: In general where no constraint is identified a reasonable decision rule is to choose the alternative which maximises contribution per £ of sales value.

MARGINAL COSTING AND DECISION MAKING – SUMMARY

The examples above are merely some indicative ones and marginal costing principles can be applied to many other types of short run decisions. Where fixed costs remain the same for all the alternatives being considered, and this should always be verified, then variable or marginal costs and the resulting contributions are the relevant factors.

The use of total costs, including a fixed element, can be misleading in decision making and it is usually more informative to separate fixed and variable costs and to show contribution.

MARGINAL COSTING AND THE ROUTINE ACCOUNTING SYSTEM

In addition to its use in decision making, marginal costing can also be used in the routine accounting system for calculating costs, valuing stocks and as a basis for the presentation of information. The alternative method is known as total costing (or absorption costing) and the two approaches are illustrated below.

Example 4

In a period 40,000 units of S were produced and sold. Costs and revenues were:

	£
Sales	200,000
Production costs	
– variable	70,000
– fixed	30,000
General overheads – fixed	50,000

Produce operating statements using total costing and marginal costing showing the results for the period.

Solution

Operating Statements

Total Costing Approach		Marginal Costing Approach	
	£		£
Sales	200,000	Sales	200,000
less Production cost of sales	100,000	*less* marginal cost	70,000
= Gross Profit	100,000	= Contribution	130,000
less General overheads	50,000	*less* Fixed costs	
		Production	30,000	
		General	50,000	80,000
= Net Profit	£50,000	= Net Profit	£50,000

Notes

(a) The key figure in the marginal statement is the contribution of £130,000. Note that this not the same as the Gross Profit in the Total approach because the production costs of £100,000 are a combination of fixed and variable elements.

(b) In this case the statements produce the same net profit. This is because there were no stocks but where stocks exist, differences arise. This is dealt with below.

STOCK VALUATIONS: MARGINAL AND TOTAL COSTING

Where there are stocks at the end of a period they are normally valued as follows:

Using Total Costing:

at production cost (i.e. including both fixed and variable costs)

Using Marginal Costing:

at marginal cost (i.e. no fixed costs are included)

The effect of these valuation methods is, that, using Total Costing, some of a period's fixed costs are transferred to the next period through the stock valuation. Using marginal costing *all* the fixed costs of a period are charged in that period as only variable costs are transferred in the stock valuation.

This is illustrated below.

Example 5

Assume the same data as Example 4 except that only 36,000 of the 40,000 units produced were sold, 4,000 units being carried forward to the next period.

Produce operating statements based on marginal costing and total costing principles.

Solution

Workings

Stock valuations:

Using total costing

$$\text{cost per unit} \quad = \quad \frac{\text{Production Cost}}{\text{No. of units produced}}$$

$$= \quad \frac{£100,000}{40,000} = £2.50$$

Closing stock value = 4,000 × £2.50 =   £10,000

Using marginal costing

$$\text{Cost per unit} \quad = \quad \frac{\text{Marginal Production Cost}}{\text{No. of units produced}}$$

$$= \quad \frac{£70,000}{40,000} = \underline{£1.75}$$

Closing stock value = 4,000 × £1.75 =   £7,000

The statements can now be prepared.

OPERATING STATEMENTS

Total Costing			Marginal Costing		
		£			£
Sales (36000 × £5)		180,000	Sales		180,000
less Production			*less* Marginal		
cost	£100,000		cost	£70,000	
– closing stock	10,000	90,000	– closing stock	7,000	63,000
= Gross Profit		90,000	= Contribution		117,000
less General overheads		50,000	less Fixed costs		
			Production	30,000	
			General	50,000	80,000
= Net Profit		£40,000	= Net Profit		£37,000

Notes:

(a) The difference in profits shown is entirely due to the difference in stock valuation.

(b) In effect, the total absorption approach transfers £3,000 of this period's fixed costs into next period and thus shows a £3,000 higher profit.

(c) All other things being equal the position would be reversed in the next period. Then, the results using the marginal costing approach would show the higher profit because they would not be carrying part of a previous period's fixed costs.

(d) Either technique could be used for routine internal reporting. However, because absorption costing is the recommended basis for external financial accounting, the total costing approach is probably more commonly used for internal purposes as well.

It must be stressed, however, that the use of marginal costing principles as an aid to *decision making* is universal and is very important.

KEY POINT SUMMARY
- Marginal costing is useful for short run decision making.
- In the short run, fixed costs are likely to remain unchanged and the relevant factors are variable (or marginal) costs and contribution.
- A key factor is a binding constraint which prevents indefinite expansion or unlimited profits.
- Where a key factor exists the best decision rule is to choose the option which maximises contribution per unit of the key factor.
- Marginal costing principles can be applied to numerous decisions. Examples include; special order acceptance, dropping a product or department and so on.
- Marginal costing can also be used for the routine internal accounting system. The important differences to a total absorption system is the separation of fixed and variable costs and the calculation of contribution.
- Marginal costing values stocks at variable cost. Absorption costing values them at total production cost.

REVIEW EXERCISES

1. (a) What is the key feature of using marginal costing for short-run decision making?
   (b) What is the decision rule where a key factor exists?

2. A firm has three departments, one of which shows a loss as shown in the statement below.
   Should Department M be closed? What assumptions have you made?

	Dept.M. £	Dept.N. £	Dept.O. £	Total £
Sales	280,000	415,000	146,000	841,000
Total costs	322,000	338,000	112,000	772,000
Profit (Loss)	(42,000)	77,000	34,000	69,000

   The total costs are 60% fixed, 40% variable.

3. In a period 20,000 kilos of sparko were produced. Costs, revenues and sales were as follows:

	£
Sales (18,000 kilos)	900,000
Production costs	
– variable	350,000
– fixed	220,000
General overheads-fixed	180,000

   There were no opening stocks.

   Produce separate operating statements using total costing and marginal costing, showing the results for the period. Explain any difference in profit for the period.

14 BREAK-EVEN ANALYSIS

OBJECTIVES
After you have studied this chapter you will
- ■ Understand break-even analysis and the principles upon which it is based
- ■ Know and be able to use a variety of break-even analysis formulae
- ■ Be able to draw a traditional break-even chart
- ■ Be able to draw a contribution break-even chart
- ■ Know the main limitations of break-even analysis.

BREAK-EVEN ANALYSIS
This is the term given to the study of the relationships between costs, volume, contribution and profit at various levels of activity. Break-even analysis (B-E analysis) uses the principles of marginal costing and, like marginal costing, is best suited to short run problems where existing cost patterns are likely to continue. B-E analysis can be carried out using simple formulae or graphs. Both are illustrated in this chapter.

Like marginal costing, B-E analysis has a number of restrictive assumptions but it can provide useful guidance to management seeking answers to a variety of questions. For example, what profit will be made if sales are 25,000 units? How many units need to be sold to break-even (i.e. the point of neither profit nor loss)? What sales are needed to produce a profit of £75,000? and so on.

B-E ANALYSIS BY FORMULA
Some typical B-E analysis formulae are given below and illustrated by examples.

$$\text{CS ratio} = \frac{\text{Contribution per unit}}{\text{Sales price per unit}} \%$$

(CS ratio means 'Contribution to sales' ratio)

$$\text{Break-even point (in units)} = \frac{\text{Fixed costs}}{\text{Contribution per unit}}$$

Break-even point (sales value)

$$= \frac{\text{Fixed costs}}{\text{Contribution per unit}} \times \text{Sales price per unit}$$

Level of sales to give a target profit (in units)

$$= \frac{\text{Fixed costs} + \text{Target profit}}{\text{contribution per unit}}$$

Level of sales to give a target price (sales value)

$$= \frac{\text{Fixed costs} + \text{Target Profit}}{\text{contribution per unit}} \times \text{Sales price per unit}$$

Note: The above formulae assume a single product firm or one with a constant sales mix.

Example 1

A firm makes a single product which sells for £7 per unit and has a marginal cost of £4 per unit. Fixed costs are £50,000 p.a.

Calculate

(a)   The CS ratio

(b)   The number of units required to break-even

(c)   The sales value required to break-even

(d)   The number of units that need to be sold to make £31,000 profit

(e)   The sales value required to make £31,000 profit.

Solution

$$\text{Contribution} = \text{Sales} - \text{Marginal cost}$$
$$= £7 - 4 = £3 \text{ per unit}$$

(a)   CS ratio $= \dfrac{£3}{7} = 0.43 \text{ or } 43\%$

(b)   Break-even point (units) $= \dfrac{£50,000}{3} = 16,667 \text{ units}$

(This means that when 16,667 units are sold the firm neither makes a profit nor a loss. At this level of sales the contribution exactly equals the fixed costs i.e. 16,667 units × £3 = £50,000)

(c)   Sales value to break-even $= 16,667 \times £7 = £116,669$

(d)   Units for £31,000 profit $= \dfrac{£50,000 + 31,000}{3}$

$$= 27,000 \text{ units}$$

(e)   Sales value for £31,000 profit $= 27,000 \times £7$

$$= £189,000$$

GRAPHICAL APPROACH TO B-E ANALYSIS

The graphical approach may be preferred when a simple overview is sufficient or when greater visual impact is required, such as in a report for management.

The basic chart is known as a *Break-Even Chart* and can be drawn in two ways. The first is known as the traditional approach and the other the contribution approach. Whatever method is used all costs must be separated into fixed and variable elements i.e. semi-variable costs must be analysed into their components.

TRADITIONAL BREAK-EVEN CHART

Assuming that fixed and variable costs have been separated, the chart is drawn as follows:

(a) Draw the axes

    – The horizontal, showing levels of activity expressed as units of output or percentages of total capacity.

    – The vertical, showing values in £'s or £'000s as appropriate, for costs and revenues.

    (As with all graphs, some experimentation with the scales is usually required to produce a reasonable looking graph).

(b) Draw the cost lines

    Fixed cost – This is a straight line parallel to the horizontal axis at the level of the fixed costs.

    Total cost – This starts from the fixed cost line and is a straight line sloping upwards at an angle depending on the proportion of variable costs in total costs.

(c) Draw the revenue line

    – This is a straight line from the point of origin sloping upward at an angle determined by the selling price.

Example 2

A company makes a single product with a total capacity of 35,000 units. Cost and sales data are as follows:

> Selling price £7 per unit
> Marginal cost £4 per unit
> Fixed costs £50,000

Draw a traditional break-even chart showing the profit at the expected production level of 27,000 units.

See Figure 14.1 on the following page.

NOTES ON FIGURE 14.1

(a) The 'margin of safety' shown on the graph is the term given to the difference between expected or normal production level and break- even point. In this case, 27,000 – 16,667 units = <u>10,333 units</u>

(b) The graph is based on the same data used for Example 1. Compare the answers produced by using the B-E formulae and the graph.

(c) On the traditional B-E chart plot fixed costs first *then* variable.

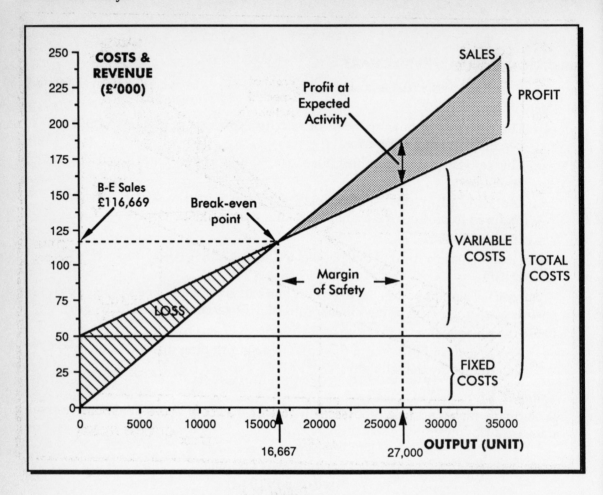

Figure 14.1

TRADITIONAL BREAK-EVEN CHART

CONTRIBUTION BREAK-EVEN CHART

This uses the same axes and data as that for the traditional chart. The only difference is that variable costs are drawn *before* fixed costs. This produces a 'wedge' depicting the contribution earned at different levels.

Example 3

Repeat Example 2 except that a Contribution break-even chart should be drawn
See Figure 14.2 opposite.

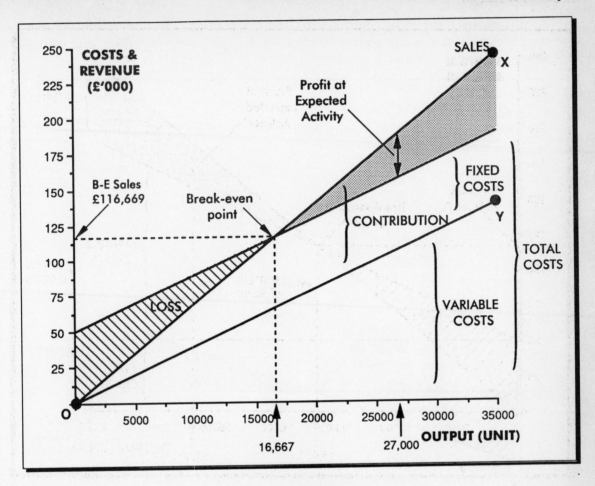

Figure 14.2

CONTRIBUTION BREAK-EVEN CHART

NOTES ON FIGURE 14.2

(a) It will be seen that the 'LOSS' and 'PROFIT' wedges are identical to the traditional chart and so is the break-even point and profit at the expected activity.

(b) Additional information is supplied by the 'CONTRIBUTION' wedge (X, O, Y). This clearly shows the surplus of sales over variable cost, i.e. the contribution gradually eating into the fixed costs as activity increases. After the break-even point, the extra contribution becomes profit because all the fixed costs have been met.

(c) On the contribution B-E chart, plot variable costs first *then* fixed.

An alternative form of the contribution chart is where the contribution line (i.e. sales – variable costs) is plotted against fixed costs. This is shown in Figure 14.3 using the same data as in Examples 1, 2 & 3.

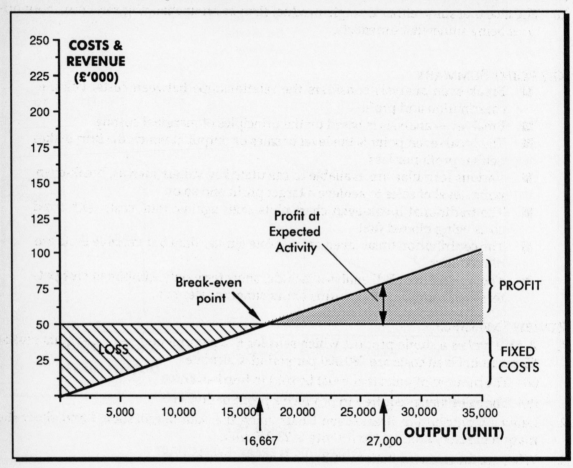

Figure 14.3

ALTERNATIVE FORM OF CONTRIBUTION BREAK-EVEN CHART

LIMITATIONS OF BREAK-EVEN ANALYSIS

The charts show the relationships between costs, volume and profit in a simplified and approximate manner. They are useful aids and can add to the attractiveness of a report but they do have a number of limitations which should not be forgotten.

(a) The charts are reasonable points to performance within reasonable activity ranges, say. ± 20% of normal activity. Outside these limits the results shown are not likely to be accurate.

(b) The simple cost patterns shown, i.e. linear or straight line variable costs and unchanging fixed costs, are unlikely to apply in practice.

(c) The charts show relationships which are essentially short-term.

(d) The charts assume either a single product firm or an unchanging sales mix; both options being somewhat unrealistic.

KEY POINT SUMMARY

■ Break-even analysis considers the relationships between costs, volume, contribution and profit

■ Break-even analysis is based on the principles of marginal costing

■ The break-even point is the level of sales or output at which the firm makes neither profit nor loss

■ Various formulae are available to calculate key values such as; break-even point, level of sales to achieve a target profit and so on

■ The traditional break-even chart plots sales against total costs with fixed costs being plotted first

■ The contribution break-even charts plots similar data but variable costs are plotted first

■ The limitation of B-E analysis include; short term only, simplified cost patterns, and single product firms or unchanging sales mix.

REVIEW EXERCISES

1. A firm makes a single product which sells for £12 per unit and has a marginal cost of £5 per unit. Fixed costs are £80,000 per period. Calculate

    (a) The number of units that must be sold to break-even

    (b) The sales value required to produce a profit of £100,000

2. Draw a Contribution Break-Even Chart using the data in Question 1 and show the margin of safety if budgeted activity is 23,000 units.

3. What are the main limitations of Break-Even analysis?

15 PRICING DECISIONS

OBJECTIVES
After you have studied this chapter you will
- Understand the importance and complexity of pricing decisions
- Realise that both costs and demand must be considered in pricing
- Be able to derive full cost plus prices
- Understand target return pricing
- Be able to use marginal price
- Know the reasons for setting transfer prices
- Be able to calculate transfer prices using full cost or variable cost
- Know the major problems associated with transfer pricing.

PRICING DECISIONS
Because of the direct relationship between the prices at which a firm sells its products and its profitability, pricing decisions are important. They are complex and judgement is invariably required because the required information is not always available.

A firm may have to make two types of pricing decisions. Those for sales external to the firm, that is, to its customers, and those relating to prices used for internal transfers between parts of the same organisation. This latter process is known as *transfer pricing* and is dealt with later in the chapter.

Pricing decisions for external sales are dealt with first.

SOME PRICING PROBLEMS
The pricing decision is a difficult one with numerous factors to be considered of which the following are examples:

The market in which the firm operates:

Are there many firms or just a few large ones? What is the extent of the competition? Is the firm the dominant one in the industry or one of the minnows?

The product

Is it well established or trying to break into the market? Is it up to date? Are there close substitutes?

The demand for the product

Is it known what quantities can be sold at various prices? Will demand fall if prices are increased or will it remain largely unaffected?

The economy

Is inflation rising or falling? Will the firm be working at full or below capacity? Are there any Government or EC regulations regarding price?

The cost structures of the firm and the product

What are the future expected marginal costs? Fixed costs?
and so on.

BACKGROUND TO PRICING DECISIONS

Ideally, prices should be set by recognising the interaction of costs and demand. Pricing is not simply a decision based on costs and cost changes; demand must also be considered. If the demand for a product was known, (i.e. the number that could be sold at various prices) together with the marginal cost of production, it is theoretically possible to set an ideal price. This is a price which maximises the profits of the firm. As would be expected, this theoretical ideal is difficult to achieve in practice mainly because the required information about demand is not available. Most firms can make a reasonable estimate of costs and likely cost changes but reliable demand information is much more difficult to obtain. However difficult the task may be it is nevertheless important to try to establish some form of information on demand. This could be done in various ways e.g. surveys, market research, test marketing and so on.

Studies of pricing methods used in practice have shown that firms frequently use some type of formula based on costs to arrive at a selling price. These are known as cost plus pricing systems.

COST PLUS PRICING SYSTEMS

There is a variety of these systems which have the general form:

$$PRICE = COST + \% \text{ MARK UP}$$

In general these systems are concerned with two questions – what is the relevant cost to include in the price? and – what is the 'profit' margin which must be added to the costs to arrive at the selling price?

Three cost plus systems are described below; full cost plus, target return pricing and marginal cost plus.

FULL COST PLUS

Typically, firms using full cost plus calculate the total production cost (including both fixed and variable costs) and add a mark up, say 30%, to arrive at the selling price.

Example 1

Walker Ltd. have developed a new product called Super and need to set a selling price. The budgeted production costs for an anticipated production level of 50,000 units are given below. The company uses a 40% mark up to arrive at the selling price.

Budgeted production costs per unit (assuming 50,000 production)

	£
Direct material	4.50
Direct labour	2.25
Production overheads	
variable	1.75
fixed	3.80
	£12.30

What is the recommended selling price?

Solution

Selling price   = full production cost + 40% of production cost

                    = £12.30 + 40% (£12.30)

                    = £17.22

Notes:

(a) The £17.22 selling price produced by the full cost formula is only a base figure and may be adjusted by management.

(b) If full cost plus pricing is used in a mechanical way, without regard to demand and other factors, then the firm will lack short term flexibility and may lose sales.

(c) The expected production cost of £12.30 will be correct only at the budgeted level of 50,000 units. Because of the effect of the fixed element of costs, production cost will vary with output level.

(d) Other variants exist of full cost plus pricing. A common one is to use total cost, i.e. production cost + administration and other overheads, instead of just production cost.

TARGET RETURN PRICING

Organisations frequently use the concept of *Return on Capital Employed* (ROCE) as a measure of performance. ROCE is calculated as follows:

$$\frac{\text{Profit}}{\text{Capital Employed}}\%$$

When ROCE is used management may aim for a target rate of ROCE and thus need to know what mark up on costs will be necessary to give the required ROCE percentage.

To use target return pricing it is necessary to

   – Decide upon a target rate of return on capital employed

   – Estimate the total costs for the year

   – Estimate the amount of capital employed.

These values can then be used in the following formula:

$$\text{Percentage mark upon cost} = \frac{\text{capital employed}}{\text{total annual costs}} \times \text{target rate of ROCE}$$

The percentage mark up on cost is then used to find the selling price in the usual cost plus way, i.e.

$$\text{PRICE} = \text{COST} + \% \text{ MARK UP}$$

Example 2

A firm wish to achieve a target return on capital employed of 20%. The capital employed is £4.2m and the estimated total production costs per year are £7m

(a)   What is the percentage mark up on cost to achieve 20% ROCE?

(b)   What is the selling price of a job with an estimated total production cost of £435?

Solution

(a)   Percentage mark up on cost $\quad = \dfrac{\text{capital employed}}{\text{Total annual costs}} \times \text{Target ROCE}$

$$= \dfrac{£4.2m}{£7m} \times 20\%$$

$$= \underline{12\%}$$

(b)   Selling price $\quad = \quad$ cost + % mark up on cost

$\qquad\qquad\qquad = \quad$ £435 + 12% (435)

$\qquad\qquad\qquad = \quad$ £487.2

Notes:

(a)   Target return pricing is based on full cost pricing but has the advantage of relating pricing to longer term financial objectives.

(b)   It suffers from similar disadvantages to full cost pricing and is essentially a long term pricing system and thus may lack short term flexibility.

(c)   Demand is not directly considered and there may be difficulties in determining the amount of capital employed, especially in a multi-product company.

(d)   Target return and full cost pricing systems enable the pricing decision to be delegated to lower management whilst keeping pricing policy under the control of senior management.

MARGINAL COST PLUS

This method of pricing sometimes known as the variable cost or contribution method is simply the application of marginal costing principles to pricing decisions. Using marginal pricing the firm sets prices so as to maximise contribution to fixed costs and profit.

A typical example of marginal pricing in practice is where hotels cater for full price business during the week and offer the spare capacity at weekends at some price above marginal cost, but less than normal price, thus gaining extra contribution and thereby increasing profits. It is not usual for a set percentage mark up to be used; rather the price is set as much above marginal cost as the market will bear.

As an example consider the data given in Example 1 for the new product, Super being made by Walker Ltd.

	Costs per unit of Super
	£
Direct material	4.50
Direct labour	2.25
Variable overheads	1.75
= marginal cost	8.50
Fixed overheads	3.80
Total cost	12.30

Clearly the firm would like to sell at as high a price as possible but if they were working below capacity and could not obtain full priced work then it may be worthwhile considering work which provides some contribution.

For example, if Walker Ltd. had unused capacity and were offered a contract which would utilise this spare capacity but with a selling price of £11.50 each, should they accept it?

The price of £11.50 produces £3 contribution (£11.50 – 8.50) and, although below total cost, is well above marginal cost and should be seriously considered by Walker Ltd. Naturally, they should try to obtain higher prices if at all possible but if all else fails the fact that the contract produces some contribution makes it worthwhile.

Marginal pricing can give short-term flexibility but must be used with caution. Care must be taken that there is not an undue proportion of low priced work. It must be emphasised that in the long run prices must cover all costs – both fixed and variable – plus a reasonable margin of profit.

TRANSFER PRICES

Many organisations are separated into operating divisions which supply goods or services to other divisions within the group. The divisions may supply goods or services exclusively to other internal divisions or they may sell some of their output on the open market. Where there are operating divisions, group management need to be able to assess the performance and profitability of each of the divisions. To do this it is necessary to consider the prices at which the internal transfers are made i.e. the transfer prices. Transfer prices are not true selling prices but are a device for valuing internal transfers. The transfer price should enable the transferring division to earn a return for its efforts and the receiving division to incur costs for the benefits received. In general, transfer pricing is an internal book-keeping exercise which does not effect the overall profitability of the firm. However, badly set transfer prices may cause divisional management to make decisions which do effect company profitability.

Ideally, transfer prices should be set which

(a) Ensure that the divisional management's desire to maximise divisional earnings does not conflict with the objectives of the company as a whole. The profitability and objectives of the organisation must take precedence over that of the divisions.

(b) Enable the performance of each of the divisions to be fairly assessed

(c)   Enable the divisions to act as independently as possible. The profits of one division should not be dependent on the actions of another division.

In practice it is extremely difficult to set prices which meet all these objectives. Some of the main methods used for setting transfer prices are given below together with the problems arising from their use.

MARKET VALUE TRANSFER PRICES.

If an external market price exists for transferred goods then using this as the transfer price means that

-    The transferring division will earn the same profit on transfers as on external sales. The receiving division will pay a commercial price for transferred goods and both divisions will have their profit measured in a fair way.

-    Because the divisions can sell or buy at the same price on the open market it is likely that decisions on transfer quantities between the divisions will not conflict with overall company objectives and profitability.

Thus, market based transfer prices would seem to be ideal but there are some difficulties.

(a)   Frequently there is no market for the product or service being considered. This is typically the case for specialised components, materials or services.

(b)   Internal transfers are often cheaper than external sales with savings in selling costs, delivery and other costs. Accordingly the buying division would expect a discount on the external market price.

(c)   Even if a market price exists it may be temporary and may fluctuate wildly, causing difficulties in setting a fair price to be used for transfers.

COST BASED PRICING

Cost based transfer pricing is commonly used because the conditions for setting ideal market prices do not always exist. A general problem with cost based systems is that the costs may contain inefficiencies of the selling division which could be passed on to the buying division. Accordingly it is common practice to use standard rather than actual costs so that the receiving department does not have to bear the burden of any cost inefficiencies.

The two main cost based methods are full cost and variable cost.

FULL COST TRANSFER PRICING

This system uses full standard cost as the transfer price (or full standard cost plus a mark-up). The price is used as the output value for the selling division and the input cost of the buying division.

For example, division T transfers components to division R at full standard cost plus 20%. Division R use the components in the manufacture of Product XX which is sold externally at full standard cost + 20%, as follows:

Division T	£	**Division R**	£
Variable costs per unit	6	Transfer price	12
Fixed costs per unit	4	Own variable costs per unit	24
		Fixed costs per unit	14
Total costs	10	Total costs	50
+ 20% mark up	2	+ 20% mark up	10
Transfer price	£12	Selling price	£60

Full cost (or cost plus) transfer pricing has a number of problems.

(a) The full cost, or cost plus, is likely to be treated as an input variable cost by the receiving division. If selling prices are based on costs, as in the example above, the prices may not produce the best results for the firm as a whole.

(b) The cost is only correct at one output level and when the transferring division is given a profit mark-up, as above, it is guaranteed a certain level of profit making genuine performance appraisal difficult.

VARIABLE COST TRANSFER PRICING

Using this system transfers would be made at the standard variable cost of the supplying division. In the example above the transfer price from Division T to Division R would be £6 per unit.

This method of transfer pricing is more likely to produce decisions on transfer quantities and external selling prices which correspond with the interests of the firm as a whole. However, as a transfer price based on variable cost results in a loss for the supplying division, divisional performance appraisal becomes meaningless.

KEY POINT SUMMARY

- Pricing problems are complex and many factors must be considered including; the market, demand, the product, costs and so on
- The ideal price is one which relates demand and costs
- Cost plus systems have the general form:
      Price = Cost + % mark up
- Cost plus systems include; full cost plus, target return pricing and marginal cost plus
- Full cost plus and target return pricing are long term systems which lack flexibility
- Marginal cost plus has more flexibility but needs to be used with discretion
- In the long run, prices must cover all costs plus a reasonable margin of profit
- Transfer prices are used for valuing internal transfers

■ Ideally, transfer prices should encourage decision making which benefits the whole organisation, enable performance to be assessed and allow independence

■ Transfer prices can be based on market prices or on costs.

REVIEW EXERCISES

1. What are some of the factors that may need to be considered in a pricing decision?

2. A firm is aiming for a Return on Capital Employed (ROCE) of 16%. There is £6m capital employed and the total annual production costs are £3.75m.

   (a) What percentage mark-up on cost should the firm use to set selling prices?

   (b) What is the recommended selling price for a job with a cost of £150,000?

3. What are the objectives which transfer prices should ideally achieve?

   If available, what is the best transfer price to use?

16 INVESTMENT APPRAISAL

OBJECTIVES

After you have studied this chapter you will

- Know the similarities and differences between short and long term decision making
- Understand the traditional investment appraisal techniques of accounting rate of return and payback
- Know the basis of discounted cash flow techniques
- Be able to use discount tables and calculate the Net Present Value of a project
- Know how to deal with Annuities
- Understand how to calculate the Internal Rate of Return and how to use it for project appraisal.

LONG RUN DECISION MAKING

So far the principles of short-run decision making have been explained but organisations also have to take decisions where a long term view is required. These are called capital expenditure decisions and they are dealt with by using investment appraisal techniques. Examples of capital expenditure decisions are; investment in a new factory, buying a new company or machine, launching a different product and so on.

There are a number of similarities between short and long-run decision making; for example the choice between alternatives, the need to consider future costs and revenues, the importance of changes in costs and revenues, the irrelevance of sunk costs and so on. However, an additional factor in long-run decision making is the need to take account of the time value of money. When a decision is concerned with costs and revenues arising over a number of years the sums cannot be compared directly, they must be reduced to equivalent values at a common date. This point is developed later in the chapter when discounting methods are dealt with.

Numerous investment appraisal techniques are available to assist with investment decisions but, however sophisticated they all compare the *returns expected* with the *investment required*.

The techniques covered in this chapter are the so called 'traditional' techniques and Discounted Cash Flow (DCF).

TRADITIONAL METHODS OF INVESTMENT APPRAISAL

Two traditional methods are dealt with; the Accounting Rate of Return (ARR) and Payback.

Accounting Rate of Return (ARR)

This method, also known as the Return on Capital Employed, expresses the average profits per year as a percentage of the investment required.

Example 1

Two investment projects are being considered, each with an initial investment of £50,000 and producing profits as follows.

Estimated Net Profits per year

		Project A	Project B
Year	1	£6,000	£8,000
	2	11,000	14,000
	3	9,000	8,000
	4	10,000	3,000
	5	4,000	2,000
Total		£40,000	£35,000

Calculate the ARR and recommend which project, if any, would be selected.

Solution

	Project A	Project B

Average profits p.a. $\quad \dfrac{£40,000}{5} = \underline{£8,000} \qquad \dfrac{£35,000}{5} = \underline{£7,000}$

ARR $\qquad = \dfrac{8,000}{50,000} = \underline{16\%} \qquad \dfrac{7,000}{50,000} = \underline{14\%}$

Thus, based on ARR, Project A would be preferred.

Problems with ARR

ARR is simple to calculate but has several disadvantages for investment decision making, as follows:

(a) Ignores the timing of inflows and outflows

(b) Uses profit as a measure of return. Profit is calculated using accounting conventions and is not equivalent to relevant cash inflows and outflows

(c) There is no universally accepted way of calculating ARR.

Payback

Payback is a widely used investment appraisal technique. Payback is the period, usually in years, which it takes for the cash inflows of an investment project to equal the initial cash outflow. The usual decision rule is to accept the project with the shortest payback period.

Example 2

Three projects are being considered and estimates of the cash flows are as follows:

	Project X		Project Y		Project Z	
Years	Annual Cash Flow	Cumulative Cash Flow	Annual Cash Flow	Cumulative Cash Flow	Annual Cash Flow	Cumulative Cash Flow
Now	− £5,000	− £5,000	− £5,000	− £5,000	− £5,000	− £5,000
1	+ 2,100	− 2,900	+ 400	− 4,600	+ 900	− 4,100
2	+ 1,800	− 1,100	+ 700	− 3,900	+ 800	− 3,300
3	+ 700	− 400	+ 1,800	− 2,100	+ 1,100	− 2,200
4	+ 400	−	+ 2,100	−	+ 1,000	− 1,200
5	−	−	−	−	+ 1,200	−
6	−	−	−	−	+ 950	+ 950

Payback periods	Project X	=	4 years
	Project Y	=	4 years
	Project Z	=	5 years

Note: Each project requires an initial investment now of £5,000 which is an outflow, denoted by a negative sign. The positive signs denote cash inflows after 1 year, 2 years and so on.

Features of Payback

(a) It is based on cash flows not profits and thus is more objective than ARR

(b) It is a measure of liquidity not of wealth. Judged on Payback alone, Projects X and Y would be preferred to Z even though Z carries on earning after the payback period

(c) Payback does consider the timing of cash flows but only in a crude manner. Projects X and Y are ranked equally yet there are clear timing differences

(d) Payback is simple and easily understood and is widely used either by itself or in conjunction with other investment appraisal techniques.

DISCOUNTED CASH FLOW (DCF)

All DCF methods use cash flows and automatically make allowance for the time value of money. As previously mentioned, accounting profits are based on conventions and are less objective than cash flows so that cash flows are preferred for decision making.

There is general acceptance that any serious investment appraisal must consider the time value of money. Sums of money arising at different times are not directly comparable. They must be converted to equivalent values at some common date and DCF methods typically use now i.e. the present time, as the common date.

As an illustration of the time value of money imagine you are owed £100. Would you prefer to be repaid now or in 1 year's time? Naturally you would prefer the money now; you could use it or gain interest on it in a bank if you had it now. The sum of £100 received in a year's time is worth less than the same amount received now. Using DCF terminology the *present value* of £100 expected in 1 year is less than £100; how much less depends on interest rates and other factors.

The two main DCF methods, Net Present Value (NPV) and Internal Rate of Return (IRR) are described below.

NET PRESENT VALUE (NPV)

The NPV method finds the value *in present day terms* of the project cash inflows and outflows expected to occur at different periods in the future. Because all the future cash flows are brought to their equivalent value at a common date, i.e. now, they are directly comparable and can be added together, taking note of pluses and minuses. The resulting answer is known as the Net Present Value (NPV); if positive the project is acceptable, if negative it is unacceptable.

The process by which the present value of a future sum is found is known as *discounting*. Discounting is normally carried out using discount (or present value) tables – Table A. To use the Table it is necessary to know the discount rate and when the future sum is expected to arise.

Table A shows the discount factors (or Present Value factors) for discount rates 1% to 30%, and for periods, normally years, from 1 to 25.

To illustrate the use of Table A.

What is the present value of £10,000 expected in 5 years; at 20%?, at 10%?

Expected in 5 years at 20%
Discount factor from Table   =   0.402
Present value   =   £10,000 × 0.402   =   £4,020

Expected in 5 years at 10%
Discount factor from Table   =   0.621
Present value   =   £10,000 × 0.621   =   £6,210

It will be seen that the higher discounting rate discounts (reduces) the future sum more heavily than the lower rate. This is a general rule.

NPV AND PROJECT APPRAISAL

Projects normally consist of a series of cash inflows or outflows and the objective of project appraisal is to see whether the NPV of the project is positive or negative at the cost of capital of the company. The cost of capital is the cost of financing the project and is the rate at which the project is discounted.

Example 3

A company with a cost of capital of 10% is considering a project with the following estimated cash flows:

Now	After 1 year	2 years	3 years	4 years
– £5,000	+ £900	+ £1,800	+ £2,400	+ £1,600

(minus represents an outflow, positive represents an inflow)

What is the NPV of the project?

Should it be accepted?

Solution

From Table A the discount factors for 10% are

1 year	2 years	3 years	4 years
0.909	0.826	0.751	0.683

NPV   =   –£5,000+(0.909× £900) + (0.826× £1,800)
           + (0.751 × £2,400) + (0.683 × £1,600)

   =   –£5,000 + £818 + £1,487 + £1,802 + £1,093

   =   +£200

As the NPV of the project is positive, at the company's cost of capital it should be accepted. The £200 represents the increase in wealth that could be gained by the project, measured in present day values.

Note: The initial outlay of £5,000 does not need discounting because it is already at the present day value.

REGULAR CASHFLOWS

Regular cash flow patterns are commonly encountered. This means that the same amount of cash is paid out, or received, each year. An example is a lease which requires a payment of £1,200 per year for 10 years. Regular cash flows are known as *annuities* and there is a short cut method of finding their present values, using Table B.

Table B is simply the addition of the individual year's discount factors from Table A.

Take for example, the first 3 years discount factors at 12% from Table A. These are 0.893, 0.797 and 0.712 which added together equal 2.402. From Table B it will be seen that the 3 year factor under 12% is 2.402. The annuity factors from Table B are used as follows:

Example 4

What is the present value at 12% of £2,000 per year received for 3 years?

Solution

Present value $\quad$ = $\quad$ Annual amount × Annuity Factor from Table B

$\qquad\qquad\qquad$ = $\quad$ £2,000 × 2.402

$\qquad\qquad\qquad$ = $\quad$ £4,804

Alternatively and more laboriously, the individual discount factors from Table A could be used, in the normal way by multiplying each year's cash flow by the appropriate discount factor, thus:

Present value $\quad$ = $\quad$ (£2,000 × 0.893) + (£2,000 × 0.797) + (£2,000 × 0.712)

$\qquad\qquad\qquad$ = $\quad$ £4,804

It must be stressed that Annuity factors from Table B can only be used when the cash flows are the same each year. When the cash flows vary from year to year, the discount factors from Table A must be used.

INTERNAL RATE OF RETURN (IRR)

The IRR is an alternative DCF appraisal method. Instead of the answer being in £'s, as NPV, the IRR is a percentage. It can be defined as the discount rate which gives zero NPV. There is no direct method of obtaining the IRR of a project, it requires some trial and error. The normal method is to find a discount rate which gives a positive NPV and one which gives a negative NPV. It follows that some rate between the two will give zero NPV and is thus the IRR.

Example 5

Find the IRR of the project in Example 3, the cash flows of which are reproduced below.

Now	after 1 year	after 2 years	after 3 years	after 4 years
– £5,000	+ £900	+ £1,800	+ £2,400	+ £1,600

Solution

It will be recalled that, at 10%, the NPV was +£200. This will do for the positive NPV so it is now necessary to discount at some higher discount rate which will produce a negative NPV.

Try 15%

At 15%, the discount factors from Table A are 0.870, 0.756, 0.658, 0.572

$$
\begin{aligned}
\text{Net Present Value} \quad &= \quad -£5,000 + (0.870 \times £900) + (0.756 \times £1,800) + \\
&\qquad (0.658 \times £2,400) + (0.572 \times 1,600) \\
&= \quad -£5,000 + 783 + 1,361 + 1,579 + 915 \\
&= \quad -£362
\end{aligned}
$$

It is clear that at some rate between 10%, giving +£200, and 15%, giving -£362, there is a rate which gives zero NPV i.e. the IRR. The value can be found graphically or by *interpolation*, as follows:

$$
\text{IRR} = \underset{(a)}{10\%} + \underset{(b)}{5\%} \times \left[\underset{(d)}{\frac{\overset{(c)}{200}}{562}} \right]
$$

$$
= 11.78\%
$$

Notes:

(a)   The rate which gives a positive NPV. In this case, 10%

(b)   The difference between the two discount rates used. In this case, 15% – 10% = 5%

(c)   The difference between zero and the positive NPV. In this case 200 – 0 = 200

(d)   The total range between the positive and negative NPVs. In this case, between +£200 and –£362 i.e. £562.

If the calculated IRR is greater than the company's cost of capital the project is acceptable. In this case, 11.78% is greater than the cost of capital of 10% so the project is acceptable. If the IRR was below the cost of capital the project would not be acceptable.

NPV AND IRR SUMMARY

NPV and IRR are alternative DCF methods. Both values do not have to be calculated to make an investment decision. Although NPV has certain technical advantages over IRR, IRR is widely used in practice. For most projects, the methods lead to the same accept or reject decision which is summarised below.

	Accept project if	Reject project if
Using NPV (at cost of Capital)	NPV is positive	NPV is negative
Using IRR	IRR is greater than cost of capital	IRR is less than cost of capital

KEY POINT SUMMARY

- Long term decision making is based on similar principles to short term decision making except that the time value of money must be considered
- Accounting Rate of Return (ARR) is a traditional technique and is calculated thus

$$ARR = \frac{\text{average profits p.a.}}{\text{amount invested}}$$

- Payback is the number of periods' cash flows required to recoup the initial investment
- Payback is a measure of liquidity not wealth and is widely used
- All Discounted Cash Flow techniques use cash flows, not profits, and make allowance for the time value of money
- The Net Present Value (NPV) is the net discounted value of all cash inflows and outflows, expressed in present day terms.
- The discount, or present value, tables show discount factors for various interest rates and periods
- If the NPV is positive when discounted at the cost of capital the project is acceptable. If the NPV is negative, it is not acceptable
- Annuities are regular cash flows occurring each year. They can be discounted using Table B
- The Internal Rate of Return (IRR) is that discount rate which gives zero NPV
- The IRR can be found graphically or by interpolation
- NPV and IRR give the same accept or reject decision for the majority of normal projects.

REVIEW EXERCISES

1. What is the time value of money and why is it important in long-term decision making?

2. The cash flows of two projects are given below

	Project A	Project B
Now	− 6,000	− 9,000
Year 1	+ 3,500	+ 1,500
" 2	+ 1,000	+ 2,000
" 3	+ 1,500	+ 2,500
" 4	+ 1,500	+ 4,000
" 5	+ 2,000	+ 2,000
" 6	+ 1,500	+ 1,000

Calculate the Payback periods for the above projects and their N.P.V. assuming that the cost of capital is 10%.

3. What is the present value of the following:

(a) £2,000 received annually for 10 years at 12%

(b) £750 received annually for 8 years at 20%

(c) £500 received annually for 5 years followed by £1,000 received annually for 3 years at 16%.

17 | PERFORMANCE APPRAISAL

OBJECTIVES
After you have studied this chapter you will
- Understand the need for performance appraisal
- Know the reasons for decentralisation
- Be able to define cost, profit, and investment centres
- Understand how controllable, divisional and net profit are calculated and used
- Be able to calculate residual profit and return on capital employed
- Know the circumstances in which residual profit or return on capital are used.

WHAT IS PERFORMANCE APPRAISAL?

Senior managers need to be able to monitor the performance of the operating managers junior to them. They need to know whether the operating management are performing well, if they are meeting company objectives, if they are using the company's assets effectively, if they are earning target profits, if they are controlling costs and so on. Naturally much of this appraisal is done by observation and personal contact but, in addition, relevant information must be available and much of this is supplied by the cost and management accounting system of the firm. This is particularly important when there is decentralised decision making and when the organisation has a divisional structure.

DECENTRALISED DECISION MAKING & DIVISIONAL STRUCTURES

As organisations grow in size and complexity senior management do not have time to make all decisions. In such circumstances, authority for certain types of decision making is delegated to subordinate management. This relieves top management of routine work and gives them more time for strategic matters. In addition, local decision making may well improve because operational management are in closer touch with day to day problems. Having increased responsibility has been found to motivate people and this factor and the need to increase efficiency has led to the growth of divisionalised organisations. Although details vary, there is typically a holding company containing some centralised services and group management and a number of operating divisions. To an extent these operate like independent companies, trading both within and outside the group. At all times group management need to ensure that the individual divisions are taking decisions that do not conflict with the objectives of the group as a whole and need to be able to monitor the performance of divisional management.

It is in these circumstances that well planned performance appraisal systems are vital.

RESPONSIBILITY CENTRES

One type of responsibility centre has already been described. This was the *cost centre*, which forms the basis of budgetary control systems. These are one form of performance appraisal, usually with the emphasis on cost items. In a full performance appraisal system the principles of responsibility accounting are developed beyond cost centres to what are known as *profit centres* and *investment centres*. Figure 17.1 summarises the types of responsibility centres.

Cost Centre	Profit Centre	Investment Centre
Responsible for:	Responsible for:	Responsible for:
COSTS	COSTS	COSTS
—	REVENUES	REVENUES
—	PROFITS	PROFITS
—	—	PROFITS IN RELATION TO INVESTMENT

Figure 17.1

TYPES OF RESPONSIBILITY CENTRE

PROFITABILITY MEASURES OF PERFORMANCE

Profit is a widely used measure of performance which is familiar to management and acceptable to them. When profit is used as a measure of performance it provides a means by which division can be compared with division and one division's performance can be compared period by period. When profit is used it can be defined in various ways. Some of the more important variants are described below: including, controllable profit, divisional profit and net profit.

CONTROLLABLE PROFIT

This is defined as revenues less costs controllable at the divisional level. As this measure includes only those costs for which the local management have primary responsibility, the basis of the measure is sound and it would be a reasonable way of appraising divisional management. What costs and revenues to include depends on the amount of responsibility delegated.

The treatment of particular items is dealt with below.

Variable costs and revenues

These are items controllable by divisional management so would be included.

Divisional overheads

Again these would be included as they are controllable.

Depreciation and fixed asset costs

Normally these would be *excluded* as decisions on the sale and purchase of fixed assets are a strategic responsibility and outside the control of local management.

Apportioned costs

Frequently a portion of central administration costs are charged to the divisions. Clearly these are not controllable by the division, and are thus excluded.

DIVISIONAL PROFIT

Also known as traceable or direct profit. This is the profit which arises from divisional operations without any apportioned central costs. It is controllable profit less depreciation and fixed asset costs. It follows that a number of costs which are identifiable with a division are not controllable by the division.

NET PROFIT

This is the final net profit of the division and is revenues less controllable divisional costs less depreciation and apportioned costs.

Although this method does show the net effect of the division on the group's results it is less useful as a means of appraising the performance of divisional management. This is because so many items are outside the control of local management.

The various types of profit are illustrated in the following example.

Example 1

The following data relate to the B division of the Alphabet Group.

		£
Sales		380,000
Variable costs		75,000
Fixed costs	– Controllable by division	38,000
	– Controllable centrally	29,000
Fixed assets (at cost)		450,000
Apportioned central costs		53,000

It is group policy to charge depreciation at 15% on the straight line basis.

Calculate; controllable, divisional and net profit for B division.

Solution

		£
Sales		380,000
less Variable costs		75,000
= Divisional contribution		305,000
less Divisional fixed costs		38,000
= Controllable Profit		267,000
less Depreciation	67,500	
Non-controllable fixed	29,000	96,500
= Divisional Profit		170,500
less Apportioned central costs		53,000
= Net Profit		£117,500

Note: The depreciation is 15% of £450,000 = £67,500

The calculated actual profits are used as appraisal measures in various ways. For example, actual profit is compared with planned or budgeted profit, the trend in profits is considered, the profit of one division is compared with the profit from other divisions and so on.

PERFORMANCE APPRAISAL AND INVESTMENT

The various types of profit shown above do not take account of the amount of investment in the division i.e. its fixed assets. When local management are responsible both for profits and the amount of investment in the division then this should be taken into account in performance appraisal.

There are two ways this can be done. Either by calculating *residual profit* or the *return on capital employed*. Residual profit (or residual income) is profit less an interest charge calculated on the assets used by the division. Residual profit is an absolute figure i.e. the answer is a number of £'s. Return on capital employed (ROCE) has been mentioned previously and is the ratio of profits to the capital employed by the division i.e. the fixed assets. ROCE is a relative figure and the answer is a percentage.

These measures are illustrated below.

Example 2

The results for three divisions are shown below.

Division	X	Y	Z
	£	£	£
Trading Profits for year	62,000	248,000	57,000
Fixed assets in division	225,000	2,150,000	175,000

The group has a cost of capital of 15%.

Calculate the Residual Profit and Return on Capital employed for each division.

Solution

Residual Profits

Division	X	Y	Z
	£	£	£
Trading Profits	62,000	248,000	57,000
less Interest on capital	33,750	322,500	26,250
Residual Profit (Loss)	28,250	(74,500)	30,750

Note: The interest on the capital used in the division is calculated as follows

$$X = 15\% \text{ of } £225,000 = £33,750$$
$$Y = 15\% \text{ of } £2,150,000 = £322,500$$
$$Z = 15\% \text{ of } £175,000 = £26,250$$

Return on Capital Employed (ROCE)

$$\text{ROCE} = \frac{\text{Profit}}{\text{Capital Employed}}\%$$

$$\text{Division X} = \frac{£62,000}{£225,000} = 27\frac{1}{2}\%$$

$$\text{Division Y} = \frac{£248,000}{£2,150,000} = 11\frac{1}{2}\%$$

$$\text{Division Z} = \frac{£57,000}{£175,000} = 32\frac{1}{2}\%$$

Residual Profit and ROCE give an indication how effectively the assets of the division are being used to earn profits. It will be seen that Division Y although making substantial trading profits, uses its assets much less effectively than the other divisions.

Remember that Residual Profit and ROCE are alternatives; both do not have to be calculated in practice.

RESIDUAL PROFITS AND ROCE COMPARED

Both Residual Profit and ROCE are useful appraisal measures which allow for the impact of the amount invested. Naturally, both have certain limitations and particular advantages and disadvantages. Residual Profit is more flexible and is more likely to encourage managers to take a longer term view of asset investment and asset sales. On the other hand, Residual Profit is less useful for comparisons between investment centres nor does it relate the amount of a centre's income to the size of the investment. In this respect ROCE is a better measure of performance being a relative value.

KEY POINT SUMMARY

- Performance appraisal systems are required so that senior managers can monitor the performance of more junior managers
- Many organisations are separated into operating divisions with many decisions taken at local level
- There are three categories of responsibility centres; cost centres, profit centres and investment centres
- Controllable profit is revenues less costs controllable at the divisional level
- Divisional profit is the profit which arises from division operations, without apportioned costs
- Net profit is the net effect of the division on group results
- Where performance related to investment needs to be appraised, Residual Profit or Return on Capital Employed (ROCE) may be used
- Residual Profit is Trading Profit less an interest charge based on the assets used
- ROCE is $\dfrac{\text{Profit}}{\text{Capital employed}}$ %

REVIEW EXERCISES

1. Describe decentralisation and give its advantages and disadvantages.
2. Distinguish between cost, profit and investment centres.
3. The results of three divisions are given below.

Division	A	B	C
	£	£	£
Trading profit for year	35,000	90,000	65,000
Assets employed	375,000	1,200,000	575,000

Calculate the Return on Capital employed and the Residual Profit for each division assuming that the company has a cost of capital of 8%.

SECTION 3 ASSESSMENT

DECISION MAKING AND PERFORMANCE APPRAISAL

MULTIPLE CHOICE QUESTIONS

1. Relevant information for decision making:
   (a) Can include sunk costs
   (b) Usually includes historical costs
   (c) Is incremental to the decision in hand
   (d) Includes all of the above.

2. Three outcomes of an event are possible:

Value	Probability
£8,000	0.3
£11,500	0.5
£17,000	0.2

   What is the expected value?
   (a) £36,500
   (b) £11,550
   (c) £11,500
   (d) £17,000.

3. The formula for the sales at breakeven point for a single product firm is:

   (a) $\dfrac{\text{Fixed costs}}{\text{Contribution/unit}} \times \text{sales price per unit}$

   (b) $\dfrac{\text{Fixed costs} \times \text{Sales value}}{\text{Contribution}}$

   (c) $\text{Fixed costs} \times \dfrac{1}{\text{CS ratio}}$

   (d) None of these.

4. The margin of safety is:
   (a) The difference between budgeted sales and the breakeven sales
   (b) The difference between actual sales and budgeted sales
   (c) Sales minus variable costs
   (d) The difference between zero sales and breakeven sales.

The following data are used for the next two questions.
A firm makes a single product with a marginal cost of £3 and a selling price of £5 and fixed costs of £25,000.

5. What level of sales will produce a profit of £15,000?
   (a) £120,000
   (b) £20,000
   (c) £100,000
   (d) £40,000.

6. How many units will need to be sold to breakeven?
   (a) 5,000
   (b) 25,000
   (c) 40,000
   (d) 12,500.

7. Which of the following would increase the per unit contribution the most?
   (a) A 5% decrease in total fixed costs
   (b) A 5% decrease in unit variable costs
   (c) A 5% increase in selling price
   (d) A 5% increase in unit volume.

The graph below relates to questions 8 to 11.

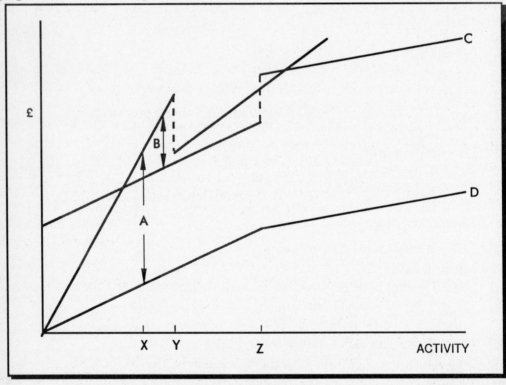

Figure MC/Sect. 3

8. The distance A represents:
   (a) Contribution at activity level X
   (b) Profit at activity level X
   (c) The amount of variable costs at activity level X
   (d) The margin of safety.

9. The distance B represents:
    (a) The contribution at activity level Y
    (b) The amount of variable costs at activity level Y
    (c) The level of sales at activity Y
    (d) The profit at activity level Y.

10. Which of the following are possible causes of the changes in the graph at activity level Z?
    (a) An increase in sales value causing an increase in contribution
    (b) A decrease in fixed costs causing an increase in variable costs
    (c) An increase in total fixed costs and a decrease in variable costs per unit
    (d) An increase in total variable costs and a decrease in fixed costs per unit.

11. What do the lines C and D represent?
    (a) Fixed costs and variable costs respectively
    (b) Total costs and variable costs respectively
    (c) Variable costs and fixed costs respectively
    (d) Sales revenue and total costs respectively.

12. Marginal costing gives a different profit to absorption costing when
    (a) All production costs are fixed
    (b) Opening and closing stocks are different
    (c) All production costs are variable
    (d) There are no opening or closing stocks.

13. A firm manufactures a component with a marginal cost of £6 and a total cost of £11 based on the normal production of 50,000 components. If the firm buys in the component at £8 the change in their results will be:
    (a) Costs will reduce by £150,000
    (b) Costs will increase by £400,000
    (c) Profits will increase by £150,000
    (d) Profits will reduce by £100,000.

14. Which of the following are not relevant for decision making:
    (a) The cost of items bought on credit
    (b) Costs which will change in the future
    (c) Costs already spent
    (d) Costs which do not vary significantly from budget.

Use the following data for the next two questions.

A firm made 6,000 units with a total cost of £10 each. Half the costs were variable and half fixed. 5,000 units were sold at £15 each. There were no opening stocks.

15. Using marginal costing principles what was the profit for the period?
    (a) £20,000
    (b) £25,000
    (c) £50,000
    (d) £5,000.

16. Using absorption costing principles what was the profit for the period?
    (a) £20,000
    (b) £25,000
    (c) £50,000
    (d) £5,000.

17. A project has an IRR of 14% and the firm's cost of capital is 12%. At the cost of capital the NPV will be:
    (a) Positive
    (b) Zero
    (c) Negative
    (d) Equal to the IRR.

The following data are used for questions 18 and 19.

A firm with a cost of capital of 12% is considering a project with the following cash flows:

0	1	2	3	4
–5,000	+2,500	+2,000	+2,000	+1,500

18. What is the NPV of the project?
    (a) 6,204
    (b) 1,204
    (c) 3,896
    (d) 5,000.

19. What is the project's IRR? (nearest %)
    (a) 15%
    (b) 28%
    (c) 12%
    (d) 23%.

20. The NPV of the following investment is Zero:

Cost now	£10,000
Income	£1,490 per year for 10 years

    What is the cost of capital?
    (a) It cannot be calculated without more information
    (b) 10%
    (c) 18%
    (d) 12%.

21. A firm is financed half by shares and half by loans. The cost of the shares is 18% and the cost of the loans is 10%. What would be a reasonable rate at which to discount projects?
    (a) 18%
    (b) 14%
    (c) 10%
    (d) 28%.

The following data are used for the next two questions.

A division of a group has the following results:

	£
Sales	750,000
Variable costs	275,000
Fixed costs:	
– controllable by division	135,000
– controllable centrally	98,000
Depreciation	89,000
Apportioned central costs	43,000

22. What is the controllable profit of the division?
    (a) £340,000
    (b) £475,000
    (c) £110,000
    (d) £153,000.

23. What is the Divisional Profit?
    (a) £340,000
    (b) £475,000
    (c) £110,000
    (d) £153,000.

The following data are used for the next two questions

Division	L	M
Trading Profit £'000s	156	2100
Assets in division £'ms	1.1	12.3

The firm's cost of capital is 12%

24. The ROCE's for the two divisions are (nearest %)
    (a) 17% and 14%
    (b) 10% and 10%
    (c) 14% and 17%
    (d) 4% and 7%.

25. The residual Profits for the two divisions are (£'000s)

   (a) 2 and 9

   (b) 24 and 624

   (c) 156 and 2,100

   (d) 624 and 24.

QUESTIONS WITH ANSWERS

A1. A company is to invest £10,000 in a new project which will have a life of 3 years. The forecasted cash inflows are:

	£
	£
Year 1	3,000
Year 2	10,000
Year 3	4,000

The required rate of return is 10%.

The present values of £1 are:

At:	10%	25%	35%
Year 1	.9091	.8000	.7407
Year 2	.8264	.6400	.5487
Year 3	.7513	.5120	.4064

Required:

(i)   Calculate the net present value of the project at:

   (a) 10%

   (b) 25%

   (c) 35%

(ii) Prepare a graph from which the internal rate of return can be read. State clearly the rate your graph reveals.

(iii) By interpolation, calculate the internal rate of return

(iv) Calculate the profitability index figure of the project at 10%.

(v)   State the payback of the project in years and months.

(vi) Assume the probabilities of the net present values of the project were:

Net present values	Probabilities
£	
4,000	0.5
3,000	0.3
8,000	0.2

Calculate the expected present value.

(vii)   State briefly what you understand by sensitivity analysis.

LCCI Management Accounting

188

A2. XY Ltd makes only one product, which sells at a unit price of £35. For the year just ended, during which 64,000 units were produced and sold, the following information is available:

Total fixed costs	= £560,000
Contribution to Sales %	= 40%
Analysis of total variable costs:	Direct materials 80%
	Direct labour 10%
	Variable overheads 10%

Changes in costs are expected from the start of the current year as follows:

Direct materials	=	increase of 5% per unit
Direct labour	=	increase of 10% per unit
Variable overhead	=	reduced by £0.05 per unit
Fixed costs	=	increase of £12,000

Required:

(i)   Calculate the net profit for the year just ended and the break-even point in units.

(ii) On the assumption that leaving the unit selling price unchanged will result in sales increasing to 66,000 units in the current year, calculate the expected profit and the break-even point in units.

(iii) On the assumption that XY Ltd increased the unit selling price to £38 for the current year, calculate how many units it needs to sell to make the same profit as last year.

LCCI Cost Accounting

A3. F Limited manufactures product G and in the year ended 31st March 1987, 1680 units were made and sold. A statement of the sales, costs and profit for product G for the year was as follows:

	£	£
Sales		134,400
Production cost of goods sold:		
Direct material	38,140	
Direct labour	23,620	
Overhead: variable	4,620	
fixed	29,700	96,080
Other costs:		
Selling & distribution:		
variable	10,900	
fixed	7,200	
Administration, fixed	5,600	23,700
Total costs		119,780
Profit		£14,620

189

You are required:

(a) By calculation or by a breakeven chart to ascertain the number of units to be sold to break even;

(b) To state the profit or loss if 1,100 units were sold;

(c) To calculate the number of units to be sold to make a profit of £27,200 per annum.

RSA Cost Accounting Stage II

A4. A firm produces three products and for the coming year its budget shows:

	Total	Product A	Product B	Product C
	£	£	£	£
Sales	100,000	60,000	25,000	15,000
Direct Material	42,000	23,000	10,000	9,000
Direct Labour	20,000	10,000	8,000	2,000
Variable overhead	10,500	4,000	5,000	1,500
Fixed overhead	15,000	7,500	6,000	1,500
Total costs	87,500	44,500	29,000	14,000
Profit (Loss)	12,500	15,500	(4,000)	1,000

Fixed overheads are absorbed on the basis of a percentage on direct labour. It is suggested that Product B should be eliminated and you are required:

(a) To re-present the above statement if product B is eliminated,

(b) Produce a break-even chart for the company for the coming year, showing the break-even point based upon:
  (i) the original budget
  (ii) if 'B' were eliminated.

(c) Show by calculation the break-even point at the original budget level and the break-even point if Product B is eliminated,

(d) Discuss the limitations that management should be aware of when using break-even charts,

(e) Explain the term 'margin of safety'.

AAT Cost Accounting & Budgeting

A5. The budgets of the Hover and Electric Divisions for the next quarter of Lawncut Mowers plc are shown below. The Electric Division was acquired recently.

	Hover		Electric
	£'000		£'000
Sales 4,000 units at £100	400	16,000 units at £25	400
Variable cost	200		240
Contribution	200		160
Fixed cost	110		70
Profit	90		90
Capital employed	800		720

Each Division is evaluated on a profit performance measure. The manager of the Hover Division believes he could increase sales by 1,000 units if he could reduce his selling price by £5 per unit. At present he buys motors from an outside supplier for £50 each. It has now been proposed that the new Electric Division supply the motor at a price of £45, which is its variable cost. Unfortunately, every motor supplied to the Hover Division would result in five units of sale being lost to the Electric Division.

Required:

(i) Discuss whether you would favour the proposal that the Electric Division should supply the motor at £45 from the position of:
    (a) Lawncut Mowers plc
    (b) The Hover Division
    (c) The Electric Division

Note: Support your answers with suitable figures.

(ii) Calculate the return on investment to the Electric Division
    (a) With the proposal
    (b) Without the proposal

(iii) Assuming an interest rate of 10%, calculate the residual income to the Hover Division after the proposal.

LCCI Management Accounting

A6. For each of the four pairs of costing terms listed below, write a short paragraph which contains a concise definition of each separate term and concludes by clearly identifying the important difference between the two:

(i) Joint product and by-product

(ii) Absorption costing and marginal costing

(iii) Functional budget and master budget

(iv) Flexible budget and rolling budget.

LCCI Cost Accounting

A7. The following information relates to three possible capital expenditure projects. Because of capital rationing only one project can be accepted.

		Project	
	A	**B**	**C**
Initial cost	£200,000	£230,000	£180,000
Expected Life	5 years	5 years	4 years
Scrap value expected	£10,000	£15,000	£8,000
Expected cash inflows	£	£	£
End Year 1	80,000	100,000	55,000
2	70,000	70,000	65,000
3	65,000	50,000	95,000
4	60,000	50,000	100,000
5	55,000	50,000	

The company estimates its cost of capital is 18% and discount factors are:

Year 1	0.8475
Year 2	0.7182
Year 3	0.6086
Year 4	0.5158
Year 5	0.4371

Calculate:

(a) The pay back period for each project
(b) The Accounting Rate of Return for each project
(c) The Net present value of each project
(d) Which project should be accepted – give reasons
(e) Explain the factors management would need to consider – in addition to the financial factors before making a final decision on a project.

AAT Cost Accounting & Budgeting

A8. LC Electronics Ltd has a large retail store providing the use of a maximum total floor space of 20,000 square metres, which is the basis for apportioning the related total fixed expenses of £200,000 per annum.

The store is at present divided into three departments and data concerning each of these for the trading year just ended is as follows:

	Radios	Televisions	Video	Total Recorders
Sales (£'000)	200	320	240	760
Gross profit margin	50%	60%	75%	–
Variable selling expenses	10% on sales	10% on sales	10% on sales	–
Floor space (sq.metres)	4,000	10,000	6,000	20,000

The Directors are keen to start selling microwave ovens which will require the use of 4,000 square metres of floor space, generating sales of £120,000 with a gross profit margin of 70% and incurring variable selling expenses at the rate of 10% on sales. The Directors propose to replace the radio department by this new one to improve profitability.

Required:

(i) For the year just ended, prepare a columnar statement which shows the gross and net profit for each department and also the total for the whole company.
(ii) Produce detailed workings to evaluate the Directors' proposal and then, basing your answers solely on considerations of revised profitability:
  (a) State whether or not you support the proposal and calculate the revised total profit if it were implemented.
  (b) Suggest an alternative re-allocation of the floor space which could be considered, supported by calculations of the revised total profit after implementation.

LCCI Cost Accounting

A9. Your Division has prepared the following budget based upon the production and sale of 200,000 units for the next trading year:

	$000	$000	$000
Sales		400	
Manufacturing costs			
Direct materials	80		
Direct wages	120		
Variable overhead	20		
Fixed overhead	28		248
Budgeted factory profit			152
Selling & Distribution costs			
Variable	40		
Fixed	23	63	
Administration costs – Fixed		39	102
Budgeted Divisional profit			50

Manufacturing, selling and distribution variable costs vary with units sold.

In an effort to improve performance, Group Management have now devised a bonus scheme which would result in a $0.20 per unit increase to direct wages. It is anticipated that, as a result, sales would increase by 20% without additional labour usage.

Required:

(i) Prepare a budget showing the position after the proposed bonus scheme.

(ii) Calculate the break-even point and margin of safety in units after the bonus scheme.

LCCI Management Accounting (part question)

A10. A manufacturing company produces the following information:

	Budget
Direct materials	£150,000
Direct labour	£200,000
Fixed Production overhead	£100,000
Direct labour hours	40,000 hours
Machine hours	25,000 hours

The following estimate, No.1234, has been partially prepared in response to an enquiry:

	Estimate 1234
Direct materials	£3,000
Direct labour	£3,000
Machine hours	800 hours

Actual results for the year included the following:

Total revenue	£600,000
Total cost of materials used	£250,000
Total labour cost	£250,000 (50,000 hours)
Fixed production overhead incurred	£130,000

There were no opening or closing stocks of raw material, and no opening stocks of work in progress. At the end of the period there were a number of jobs still in progress, and these had the following costs charged to them:

Materials	£15,000
Labour	£20,000 (4,000 labour hours)

Required:

(i)   Calculate the budgeted production overhead absorption rate based on:

% direct material cost

machine hour rate

(ii) Calculate the production overhead to be included in estimate No. 1234, using both of the overhead absorption rates which you have calculated in (i) above.

(iii) Assume that overheads are absorbed at the rate of £2.5 per labour hour.

Prepare statements, showing the principles of absorption costing and marginal costing, showing the profit or loss for the year.

AAT Cost Accounting & Budgeting (part question)

QUESTIONS WITHOUT ANSWERS

B1. AFC Ltd makes only two products, called 'Ayef' and 'Efsee', in a very short manufacturing cycle, as a result of which stocks of work in progress and finished goods do not exist. Direct workers are paid at the rate of £3 per hour.

Product details are as follows:

	Ayef	Efsee
Direct material costs per unit	£6	£21
Direct labour hours per unit	12	6
Variable overhead per unit	£6	£6
Unit selling price	£84	£66

Total fixed costs are £125,000 per month and these are absorbed into product costs on a direct labour hour basis calculated on a budgeted monthly activity of 50,000 hours.

Monthly sales demand for the two products has suddenly increased to 3,000 units of Ayef and 5,000 units of Efsee. Steps are being taken to increase the 48,000 direct labour hours currently available, at present rates of pay, to cope with this demand. There are no other constraints and the present level of fixed costs will remain unchanged.

Required:

(i) Calculate the total unit costs of each product and the net profit per unit.

(ii) On the basis of present direct labour hours, decide on the product mix which will maximise profit for next month and calculate the amount of this profit.

(iii) Calculate the amount of additional profit to be made per month if the direct labour force is increased by 20%.

LCCI Cost Accounting

B2 There are two widely accepted measures of performance used by decentralised companies, return on investment (ROI) and residual income (RI). Your company has two divisions:

	Division A	Division B
	$	$
Capital employed	200,000	500,000
Net profit	40,000	90,000

Required:

(i) Calculate the ROI for each of Divisions A and B

(ii) (a) Calculate the RI for each of Divisions A and B, assuming an interest rate of 15%.

(b) Calculate the RI for each of Divisions A and B, assuming an interest rate of 20%.

(iii) Contrast the ROI and RI calculations you have made and discuss the features of each performance measure.

(iv) State and briefly discuss:

(a) Two advantages of decentralisation

(b) Two disadvantages of decentralisation.

LCCI Management Accounting

B3 HL Company has estimated the following for its operations during the year.

Sales of Product X	200,000 units
Selling and Distribution overhead	£500,000
Fixed production overhead	£400,000

Standard data per unit of product X is as follows:

Materials:	kilos of component BW to make 1 unit of X	5
	purchase cost per kilo of Component BW	£3
Direct labour:	hours per unit of product X	4
	rate per hour	£10
Variable production overhead per unit of product X		£16
Selling price per unit of X		£80

Required:
(i) Prepare statements which show the profit or loss for the period based on:
   (a) The initial estimates of cost and standard data;
   (b) A revised plan which reduces selling price by 10% and increases sales volume by 20%;
   (c) An alternative plan which, through increasing advertising by £500,000, increases sales units by 10% over that originally planned.
(ii) Calculate the percentage change from the standard selling price which will cause the firm to break even.

Note: Treat each of the above requirements independently.

AAT Cost Accounting & Budgeting

B4 The Lo Hak company has $1,820,000 to invest on new capital projects next year. The final list of investments to be considered has been reduced to:

INVESTMENT	COST	LIFE (YEARS)	
1	Purchase the licence to manufacture a new high-technology product	$405,000	7	Annual inflows $108,000 per annum
2	Improve the existing production line conveyor system	$510,000	4	Annual cash inflows generated $210,000 per annum
3	Expand and construct new buildings & equipment	$630,000	8	Additional cash inflows $171,000 per annum
4	Replace the microcomputer facilities	$270,000	3	Cost savings $135,000 per annum

All cash inflows will commence in Year 1 except Investment 4, when the first inflows will not be received until the third year. The company's cost of capital is 15%.

The present values of $1 at 15% and 30% are:

	1	2	3	4	5	6	7	8
15%	.8696	.7561	.6575	.5718	.4972	.4323	.3759	.3269
30%	.7692	.5917	.4552	.3501	.2693	.2072	.1594	.1226

Required:
Ignoring residual values:
(i) Calculate the net present values at 15% for each Investments 1-4
(ii) Prepare a profitability index and rank the investments
(iii) Which investment(s) would you reject and why?
(iv) For Investment 3, calculate the internal rate of return
(v) State the payback period for Investment 1
(vi) State 3 other factors that should be considered in making the choice of investments.

LCCI Management Accounting

B5 FGH Ltd makes only one product which sells at £40 per unit and has a budgeted total factory cost of £25 per unit, including factory overheads calculated on the basis of a normal budgeted level of activity of 50,000 units per half year.

Other details from the budget for the current year are as follows:

(1) Opening stock of finished goods – 8,000 units
(2) Work in progress will be constant throughout.
(3)

	First half year	Second half year
Production budget (units)	64,000	42,000
Sales budget (units)	48,000	56,000

(4) Fixed overheads per half year:

	£
Factory	125,000
Administration	160,000
Selling	90,000

Required:

(i) Prepare a ... for each half year and in total for the ye...
    (a) Using ...
    (b) Using ...
(ii) Briefly ex... ...t profit for the year given in your answ...

LCCI Cost Accounting

B6 The following a... ...mpany:

	£'000
Direct mate...	400
Direct wages	600
Variable fact...	250
Fixed factory	400
Fixed admin...	200
Variable selli...	400
Sales	2,750

Required:

(i) On a single graph, plot and label each item of cost separately and the total sales, to indicate the break-even point and area of profit.

(ii) On the assumption that all the above variable costs/expenses vary with the quantity of goods sold, calculate the revised break-even point (to the nearest £'000), if selling prices increased by 10%.

LCCI Cost Accounting

B7 Narburgh Ltd manufactures three products whose average costs of production are as follows:

	X £	Y £	Z £
Direct materials	57	36	54
Direct labour:			
Production at £6 per hour	24	36	12
Assembly at £3 per hour	9	12	6

Maximum potential sales for next year are:

> X 12,000 units at £134 each
> Y 20,000 units at £120 each
> Z 16,000 units at £104 each

Unfortunately, production hours are restricted to 164,000, so the sales demand cannot be met. Assembly hours are not limited.

Required:

(i) In order to maximise profits:

(a) Calculate and state the order in which product demand should be satisfied.

(b) State which product(s) would not be fully supplied and calculate the loss of contribution to the business.

(c) Calculate the anticipated profit for next year, assuming fixed costs are £644,000.

(ii) If production could be sub-contracted, give your views as to what would be the maximum acceptable price(s) for the product(s) that cannot be supplied from Narburgh's own manufacture.

LCCI Management Accounting

B8 Amendit Manufacturing Ltd opened a new factory on 1 May 1988 to produce only one standard product.

The cost accountant prepared the following budgeted Profit and Loss Account for the first three months of trading:

	May	June	July
Sales (000) units	15	20	30
Production (000 units)	20	25	30
	£'000	£'000	£'000
Sales	105	140	210
Cost of sales			
Opening stock of finished products	–	23	46
Direct production costs	60	75	90
Production overhead absorbed	32	40	48
	92	138	184

	May	**June**	**July**
Less: Closing stock of finished products	23	46	46
	69	92	138
Production overhead under/(over) absorbed	8	–	(8)
	77	92	130
Gross Profit	28	48	80
Administration overhead	12	12	12
Marketing overhead	26	31	41
Profit/(Loss)	(10)	5	27

Additional information:

(1) In the factory, total direct costs are assumed to vary with output but the overhead is assumed to be fixed.

(2) All administration overhead is assumed to be fixed but total marketing overhead contains a fixed element, the balance varying with sales.

Required:

(i) Give brief but concise definitions of each of the two alternative principles, ie absorption costing and marginal costing.

(ii) Prepare a budgeted Profit and Loss Account for the first three months in tabular form using the alternative principle to the one used above.

(iii) List three advantages of your revised presentation in (ii) over the original one.

(iv) In what situation will profits or losses be exactly the same regardless of which principle is used?

LCCI Cost Accounting

B9 Alphabet plc makes four components, A, B, C and D. The production budget for the year commencing 1 January 1990 contains the following data:

	A	**B**	**C**	**D**
Production (units)	1,000	2,000	4,000	3,000
Unit cost:	£	£	£	£
Direct material	18	21.50	9	16.50
Direct labour (£4 per hour)	8	10	4	6

Overheads: Variable – at the rate of £1 per direct labour hour.

Fixed – £93,000 in total, to be absorbed on the basis of direct labour hours.

An outside supplier has offered to supply the required units of A, B, C & D at prices of £24, £42, £20 and £28 respectively. If Alphabet plc decides to buy in all of the required units of any component, then fixed overheads could be reduced as follows:

Buy in	**A**	**B**	**C**	**D**
Reduction	£2,000	£10,000	£12,000	£16,000

Required:

(i) Prepare detailed factory costs of each product, finally arriving at the budgeted total factory cost of each.

(ii) For each component, decide whether Alphabet plc should place orders with the outside supplier or continue to manufacture. Support your decision with relevant calculations.

(iii) Calculate the overall saving, as a percentage of the present total production costs budgeted by the company, arising from implementing your recommendation in (ii) above.

LCCI Cost Accounting

B10 A market gardener commenced trading on 1 April 1988 as Acar Products, supplying a mixture of three salad crops. He has only 3,600 square metres of land available and circumstances are such that this area cannot be increased.

He entered into a three year contract with a wholesaler to supply between a minimum of 18,000 and a maximum of 45,000 boxes per annum of each crop and decided in the first year to allocate 50% of space to tomatoes, dividing the remainder equally between lettuces and cucumbers.

At the end of his first trading year, his accountants have produced the following statement:

	Tomatoes	Lettuces	Cucumbers	Total
Square metres	1,800	900	900	3,600
Yield-in boxes per metre	20	30	36	-
Number of boxes sold	36,000	27,000	32,400	95,400
	$	$	$	$
Sales	345,600	129,600	194,400	669,600
Directly Allocated Variable Costs:				
Seeds and Composts	108,000	25,200	62,640	195,840
Direct wages – Growing	64,800	36,000	36,000	136,800
Direct wages – Pick/Box	43,200	14,400	18,000	75,600
Boxes	14,400	10,800	12,960	38,160
Apportioned Fixed Costs	73,660	55,244	66,296	195,200
Total Costs	304,060	141,644	195,896	641,600
Profit (Loss)	41,540	(12,044)	(1,496)	28,000
% on Sales	12.02%	(9.29%)	(0.77%)	4.18%

In their report, they recommend that more tomatoes should be grown in the current year, during which it can be assumed that there will be no change in selling prices, total fixed costs, crop yield and associated variable costs per square metre.

Required:
(i) State whether you agree with the accountants' recommendation, giving brief supporting reasons.
(ii) Decide, providing relevant workings, on the mixture of products which will maximise the current year's profit under the conditions of the present contract.
(iii) Calculate the annual profit arising from your decision in (ii).

LCCI Cost Accounting

ASSIGNMENT 5

FLO-METERS LTD.

An assignment using costs for decision making where limiting factors are present.

Flo-Meters Ltd manufacture a variety of meters and testing devices. They are used in production and packing applications and measure such things as weights, volumes, pressures, moisture and so on. The meters are complex electronic devices which require skilled technicians in manufacturing, especially for calibration. They are considering a new range of grain moisture meters with three capacities; small, medium, large.

The budgeted data are

Meter capacity:	Small	Medium	Large
	£	£	£
Selling price	170	210	295
Direct materials	60	75	95
Labour cost	40	50	75
Maximum demand (units)	2,000	2,000	1,000

The labour is paid £5 per hour and variable overheads are 60% of direct labour costs. Fixed costs are expected to be £55,000 per period.

Each meter requires calibrating using skilled technicians and the number of labour hours required for calibrating each meter are:

Small	2 hours
Medium	3 hours
Large	4 hours

The skilled labour for calibration is in short supply and so, occasionally, are the direct materials.

Flo-meters wish to know if the new range of meters is worthwhile and, if so, what product mix would give the best profit.

STUDENT ACTIVITIES

(a) Prepare a report for the Managing Director advising him whether production is worthwhile and what product mix should be adopted if
(i) The demand constraint applies and either
(ii) The calibration labour is limited to 9,500 hours per period or
(iii) The direct material is in short supply and is limited to £250,000 worth per period.

(b) Calculate the break-even point expressed in sales value, for each mix of sales you have advised and the margins of safety. Explain why the break- even points and margins of safety differ.

(c) Plot the recommended production mixes on separate contribution break- even charts.

OBJECTIVES

The student should show an understanding of

    Limiting factors

    Marginal costing

    Break-even analysis by formula

    Drawing break-even charts.

ASSIGNMENT 6

CORDON BLEU – CATERING PACKS LTD.

This an assignment covering different forms of operating statements, the treatment of fixed and variable costs and the effects of product substitutability.

Cordon Bleu are rapidly expanding specialist food suppliers to restaurants, wine bars, pubs and similar outlets. They buy, prepare and cook the ingredients which are then packaged, deep frozen and supplied to their customers who microwave or boil the meals before serving to their clients who are usually unaware that they are eating pre-packaged meals. Cordon Bleu have five main lines; Chicken Supreme, Boeuf Bourguignon, Duck a l'orange, Chili Con Carne and Chicken Kiev.

Mike Commer has recently been appointed as Managing Director of Cordon Bleu after many years experience as a Director of a major national food manufacturer. He is in the process of reviewing all aspects of operations, especially the financial and sales side which he suspects have been neglected in the formative years of Cordon Bleu, when production and packaging difficulties absorbed most of the attention of John Watson, the founder, who is now Chairman of the company.

Mike asks Bill Hope, who is the Accountant and Office Manager, to prepare a Budgeted Operating Statement for the next period showing the profitability of the main product lines. Up to now there has been no attempt to show separately the profitability of the product lines and the exercise causes Bill a great deal of work. Finally he produces the following statement which, he admits, shows a surprising result and as a consequence he recommends to Mike that he should give serious consideration to cutting out the Boeuf Bourguignon and Duck à l'orange packs to avoid the losses.

The statement produced by Bill Hope was as follows:

Cordon Bleu
Budgeted Operating Statement
£'000s

Product	Chicken Supreme	Boeuf Bourguignon	Duck à l'orange	Chili con Carne	Chicken Kiev	Total
Sales	1,600	1,400	2,100	950	1,900	7,950
Production costs:						
Materials	290	280	370	145	265	1,350
Labour	350	260	390	90	310	1,400
Overheads	368	366	567	122	377	1,800
	1,008	906	1,327	357	952	4,500
Packaging & Transport	183	168	227	83	164	825
Advertising & Office costs	322	406	550	207	415	1,900
	505	574	777	290	579	2,725
Total cost	1,513	1,480	2,104	647	1,531	7,275
Profit (Loss)	87	(80)	(4)	303	369	675

Mike Commer studied the operating statement and suspected that there was more to the problem than the statement showed. Before coming to any decision he felt he needed more detail and sent for Bill Hope. After a lengthy meeting it was agreed that Bill Hope would supply the following additional information:

(a) An analysis of the fixed and variable elements of the various costs
(b) Clear guidance on the methods of allocation and apportionment used in the statement.

Fortunately Bill Hope had kept his working papers and was able to produce the required detail quite quickly. This was as follows:

Supplement to the Budgeted Operating Statement

1. Both labour and material costs are a combination of variable costs and a surcharge of 15% and 10% respectively to absorb general fixed costs. In the case of labour this is for general production supervision and general storage and ordering costs for materials.

2. Production overheads are a combination of variable overheads recovered on the total labour cost, general fixed overheads of £830,000 recovered on labour costs and directly attributable fixed costs as follows:

Chicken Supreme	Boeuf Bourguignon	Duck à l'orange	Chili con Carne	Chicken Kiev	Total
£70,000	145,000	235,000	55,000	115,000	620,000

The directly identifiable fixed overheads would cease if the product was discontinued.

3. Packaging and transport costs consist of £150,000 general fixed overheads absorbed on labour costs, the balance being variable costs absorbed on total material costs.
4. Advertising and Office costs have three elements: Advertising costs absorbed on sales value, general fixed overheads of £100,000 also absorbed on sales value and directly attributable fixed costs as follows:

Chicken Supreme	Boeuf Bourguignon	Duck à l'orange	Chili con Carne	Chicken Kiev	Total
£40,000	160,000	180,000	40,000	80,000	500,000

Once again the identifiable fixed costs would cease if the product was discontinued.

STUDENT ACTIVITIES
1. Comment on the position shown in the budgeted operating statement produced by Bill Hope.
2. Should the decision be taken at this stage to discontinue the two products shown making a loss? If not, why not?
3. What other information, additional to that in the Supplement, might be useful to Mike Commer in assessing the budgeted position?
4. Redraft the budgeted operating statement in a more informative manner assuming that all five products will continue.
5. Comment on your redrafted operating statement explaining why it is more informative.
6. Prepare a new budgeted operating statement assuming that Boeuf Bourguignon and Duck à l'orange are discontinued and sales of the other products continue as budgeted.
7. Comment on the new statement.
8. What decisions should be taken about the product range?

OBJECTIVES
The student should show an understanding of
> Cost behaviour
> Budget preparation
> Decision making
> Marginal costing.

Table A
PRESENT VALUE FACTORS: PRESENT VALUE
OF £1 $(1 + r)^{-n}$

DISCOUNT RATES (r)%

Periods (n)	1%	2%	4%	6%	8%	10%	12%	14%	15%	16%	18%	20%	22%	24%	25%	26%	28%	30%
1	0.990	0.980	0.962	0.943	0.926	0.909	0.893	0.877	0.870	0.862	0.847	0.833	0.820	0.806	0.800	0.794	0.781	0.769
2	0.980	0.961	0.925	0.890	0.857	0.826	0.797	0.769	0.756	0.743	0.718	0.694	0.672	0.650	0.640	0.630	0.610	0.592
3	0.971	0.942	0.889	0.840	0.794	0.751	0.712	0.675	0.658	0.641	0.609	0.579	0.551	0.524	0.512	0.500	0.477	0.455
4	0.961	0.924	0.855	0.792	0.735	0.683	0.636	0.592	0.572	0.552	0.516	0.482	0.451	0.423	0.410	0.397	0.373	0.350
5	0.951	0.906	0.822	0.747	0.681	0.621	0.567	0.519	0.497	0.476	0.437	0.402	0.370	0.341	0.328	0.315	0.291	0.269
6	0.942	0.888	0.790	0.705	0.630	0.564	0.507	0.456	0.432	0.410	0.370	0.335	0.303	0.275	0.262	0.250	0.227	0.207
7	0.933	0.871	0.760	0.665	0.583	0.513	0.452	0.400	0.376	0.354	0.314	0.279	0.249	0.222	0.210	0.198	0.178	0.159
8	0.923	0.853	0.731	0.627	0.540	0.467	0.404	0.351	0.327	0.305	0.266	0.233	0.204	0.179	0.168	0.157	0.139	0.123
9	0.914	0.837	0.703	0.592	0.500	0.424	0.361	0.308	0.284	0.263	0.225	0.194	0.167	0.144	0.134	0.125	0.108	0.094
10	0.905	0.820	0.676	0.558	0.463	0.386	0.322	0.270	0.247	0.227	0.191	0.162	0.137	0.116	0.107	0.099	0.085	0.073
11	0.896	0.804	0.650	0.527	0.429	0.350	0.287	0.237	0.215	0.195	0.162	0.135	0.112	0.094	0.086	0.079	0.066	0.056
12	0.887	0.788	0.625	0.497	0.397	0.319	0.257	0.208	0.187	0.168	0.137	0.112	0.092	0.076	0.069	0.062	0.052	0.043
13	0.879	0.773	0.601	0.469	0.368	0.290	0.229	0.182	0.163	0.145	0.116	0.093	0.075	0.061	0.055	0.050	0.040	0.033
14	0.870	0.758	0.577	0.442	0.340	0.263	0.205	0.160	0.141	0.125	0.099	0.078	0.062	0.049	0.044	0.039	0.032	0.025
15	0.861	0.743	0.555	0.417	0.315	0.239	0.183	0.140	0.123	0.108	0.084	0.065	0.051	0.040	0.035	0.031	0.025	0.020
16	0.853	0.728	0.534	0.394	0.292	0.218	0.163	0.123	0.107	0.093	0.071	0.054	0.042	0.032	0.028	0.025	0.019	0.015
17	0.844	0.714	0.513	0.371	0.270	0.198	0.146	0.108	0.093	0.080	0.060	0.045	0.034	0.026	0.023	0.020	0.015	0.012
18	0.836	0.700	0.494	0.350	0.250	0.180	0.130	0.095	0.081	0.069	0.051	0.038	0.028	0.021	0.018	0.016	0.012	0.009
19	0.828	0.686	0.475	0.331	0.232	0.164	0.116	0.083	0.070	0.060	0.043	0.031	0.023	0.017	0.014	0.012	0.009	0.007
20	0.820	0.673	0.456	0.312	0.215	0.149	0.104	0.073	0.061	0.051	0.037	0.026	0.019	0.014	0.012	0.010	0.007	0.005
21	0.811	0.660	0.439	0.294	0.199	0.135	0.093	0.064	0.053	0.044	0.031	0.022	0.015	0.011	0.009	0.008	0.006	0.004
22	0.803	0.647	0.422	0.278	0.184	0.123	0.083	0.056	0.046	0.038	0.026	0.018	0.013	0.009	0.007	0.006	0.004	0.003
23	0.795	0.634	0.406	0.262	0.170	0.112	0.074	0.049	0.040	0.033	0.022	0.015	0.010	0.007	0.006	0.005	0.003	0.002
24	0.788	0.622	0.390	0.247	0.158	0.102	0.066	0.043	0.035	0.028	0.019	0.013	0.008	0.006	0.005	0.004	0.003	0.002
25	0.780	0.610	0.375	0.233	0.146	0.092	0.059	0.038	0.030	0.024	0.016	0.010	0.007	0.005	0.004	0.003	0.002	0.001

Table B
PRESENT VALUE ANNUITY FACTORS: PRESENT VALUE OF £1
RECEIVED ANNUALLY FOR n YEARS $\left(\dfrac{1-(1+r)^{-n}}{r} \right)$

DISCOUNT RATES (r)%

Years (n)	1%	2%	4%	6%	8%	10%	12%	14%	15%	16%	18%	20%	22%	24%	25%	26%	28%	30%
1	0.990	0.980	0.962	0.943	0.926	0.909	0.893	0.877	0.870	0.862	0.847	0.833	0.820	0.806	0.800	0.794	0.781	0.769
2	1.970	1.942	1.886	1.833	1.783	1.736	1.690	1.647	1.626	1.605	1.566	1.528	1.492	1.457	1.440	1.424	1.392	1.361
3	2.941	2.884	2.775	2.673	2.577	2.487	2.402	2.322	2.283	2.246	2.174	2.106	2.042	1.981	1.952	1.923	1.868	1.816
4	3.902	3.808	3.630	3.465	3.312	3.170	3.037	2.914	2.855	2.798	2.690	2.589	2.494	2.404	2.362	2.320	2.241	2.166
5	4.853	4.713	4.452	4.212	3.993	3.791	3.605	3.433	3.352	3.274	3.127	2.991	2.864	2.745	2.689	2.635	2.532	2.436
6	5.795	5.601	5.242	4.917	4.623	4.355	4.111	3.889	3.784	3.685	3.498	3.326	3.167	3.020	2.951	2.885	2.759	2.643
7	6.728	6.472	6.002	5.582	5.206	4.868	4.564	4.288	4.160	4.039	3.812	3.605	3.416	3.242	3.161	3.083	2.937	2.802
8	7.652	7.325	6.733	6.210	5.747	5.335	4.968	4.639	4.487	4.344	4.078	3.837	3.619	3.421	3.329	3.241	3.076	2.925
9	8.566	8.162	7.435	6.802	6.247	5.759	5.328	4.946	4.772	4.607	4.303	4.031	3.786	3.566	3.463	3.366	3.184	3.019
10	9.471	8.983	8.111	7.360	6.710	6.145	5.650	5.216	5.019	4.833	4.494	4.192	3.923	3.682	3.571	3.465	3.269	3.092
11	10.368	9.787	8.760	7.887	7.139	6.495	5.938	5.453	5.234	5.029	4.656	4.327	4.035	3.776	3.656	3.543	3.335	3.147
12	11.255	10.575	9.385	8.384	7.536	6.814	6.194	5.660	5.421	5.197	4.793	4.439	4.127	3.851	3.725	3.606	3.387	3.190
13	12.134	11.348	9.986	8.853	7.904	7.103	6.424	5.842	5.583	5.342	4.910	4.533	4.203	3.912	3.780	3.656	3.427	3.223
14	13.004	12.106	10.563	9.295	8.244	7.367	6.628	6.002	5.724	5.468	5.008	4.611	4.265	3.962	3.824	3.695	3.459	3.249
15	13.865	12.849	11.118	9.712	8.559	7.606	6.811	6.142	5.847	5.575	5.092	4.675	4.315	4.001	3.859	3.726	3.483	3.268
16	14.718	13.578	11.652	10.106	8.851	7.824	6.974	6.265	5.954	5.668	5.162	4.730	4.357	4.033	3.887	3.751	3.503	3.283
17	15.562	14.292	12.166	10.477	9.122	8.022	7.120	6.373	6.047	5.749	5.222	4.775	4.391	4.059	3.910	3.771	3.518	3.295
18	16.398	14.992	12.659	10.828	9.372	8.201	7.250	6.467	6.128	5.818	5.273	4.812	4.419	4.080	3.928	3.786	3.529	3.304
19	17.226	15.678	13.134	11.158	9.604	8.365	7.366	6.550	6.198	5.877	5.316	4.843	4.442	4.097	3.942	3.799	3.539	3.311
20	18.046	16.351	13.590	11.470	9.818	8.514	7.469	6.623	6.259	5.929	5.353	4.870	4.460	4.110	3.954	3.808	3.546	3.316
21	18.857	17.011	14.029	11.764	10.017	8.649	7.562	6.687	6.312	5.973	5.384	4.891	4.476	4.121	3.963	3.816	3.551	3.320
22	19.660	17.658	14.451	12.042	10.201	8.772	7.645	6.743	6.359	6.011	5.410	4.909	4.488	4.130	3.970	3.822	3.556	3.323
23	20.456	18.292	14.857	12.303	10.371	8.883	7.718	6.792	6.399	6.044	5.432	4.925	4.499	4.137	3.976	3.827	3.559	3.325
24	21.243	18.914	15.247	12.550	10.529	8.985	7.784	6.835	6.434	6.073	5.451	4.937	4.507	4.143	3.981	3.831	3.562	3.327
25	22.023	19.523	15.622	12.783	10.675	9.077	7.843	6.873	6.464	6.097	5.467	4.948	4.514	4.147	3.985	3.834	3.564	3.329

EXAMINATION TECHNIQUE

INTRODUCTION

If you are a genius and/or can calculate and reproduce facts and figures with the speed of a computer and/or know the examiner then there is no need for you to read this section. On the other hand if you do not fall into any of the above categories then you will stand more chance of passing your examinations first time if you study this section carefully and follow the simple rules.

WELL BEFORE THE EXAMINATION

No amount of examination room technique will enable you to pass unless you have prepared yourself thoroughly beforehand. The prior of preparation may be years or months long. It is no use expecting to pass with a feverish last minute bout of revision. By this stage you should have worked through all of tho manual and you should be thoroughly familiar with your syllabus and the type of examination questions that you have been set in the past.

By the end of your study and revision you should be able to answer every question in this manual.

IMMEDIATELY BEFORE THE EXAMINATION

a.   Make sure you know exact time, date and location of examination.

b.   Carefully check you travel arrangements. Leave yourself adequate time.

c.   Check over your examination equipment: Calculator? Spare Battery? Pens? Pencils? Slide Rule? Tables? Watch? Sweets? Cigarettes? etc, etc.

d.   Check your examination number.

IN THE EXAMINATION ROOM

If you have followed the rules so far you are well prepared; you have all the equipment you need; you did not have to rush – YOU ARE CALM AND CONFIDENT.

Before you start writing:

a.   Carefully read the whole examination paper including the rubric.

b.   Decide what questions you are going to answer.

c.   Decide the sequence you will tackle the questions. Generally, answer the easiest question first.

d.   Decide the time allocation for each question. In general the time allocation should be in direct proportion to the marks for each question.

e.   Read the questions you have decided to answer again. Do you know exactly what the examiner is asking? Underline the key words in the question and keep these in you mind when answering.

Dealing with the questions:

a.   Make sure you plan each question first. Make a note of the main points or principles involved. If you are unable to finish the question you will gain some marks from these points.

b.	Attempt all questions required and each part of each question.

c.	Do not let your answer ramble on. Be as brief as possible consistent with covering all the points you know.

d.	Follow a logical sequence in your answers.

e.	Write neatly, underline headings and if the question asks for a particular sequence of answer then follow that sequence.

f.	If diagrams graphs or tables are required give them plenty of space, label them neatly and comprehensively, and give a key to symbols, lines etc used. A simple clear diagram showing the main points can often gain a good proportion of the marks for a question.

When you have finished writing:

a.	Check that you have followed the examination regulations regarding examination title, examination number, candidates number and sequence of answer sheets.

b.	Make sure you include all the sheets you require to be marked.

c.	If you have time carefully read each and every part of each answer and check each calculation.

General-points.

a.	Concentrate on answering the questions set not some related topic which you happen to know something about.

b.	Do not leave the examination room early. Use every minute for checking and rechecking or adding points to questions answered.

c.	Always attempt every question set and every part of each question.

EXAMINERS' REPORTS

After every examination an Examiner's Report is prepared and you are urged to obtain a copy and thoroughly digest the contents. Much useful advice is given not only about the detail of individual questions, but about the general approach to be adopted.

Ever since examinations were invented examiners have complained, with justice, about similar problems and deficiencies. The more common ones include:

- failure to read the question
- failure to answer the question as set
- careless work, especially with calculations
- bad English
- poor writing
- poor charts/diagrams with no titles or keys
- rote learning rather than real understanding
- inadequate time planning resulting in the failure to answer all questions
- inclusion of irrelevant material
- failure to relate theory and practice

You are *strongly-advised to* note carefully the above list of common failings and to make sure that you are not guilty of any of them.

ANSWERS

REVIEW EXERCISES

CHAPTER 1

1.

Information	Use
Cost per unit of production or service	In pricing, cost control, planning.
Cost of department or section	Cost control, management.
Cost of materials and scrap.	Materials, cost control, production planning.
Cost of wages and idle time.	Wages cost control, production planning.
Cost behaviour with changes in activity.	Profit planning, decision making.

2. Two way analysis of expenditure:
   - *Type* of expenditure
   - *Location* or *use* of expenditure.

3. Planning precedes control and control is necessary to ensure that operations proceed according to plan.

4. Key features of decision making
   - relates to future
   - choice between alternatives
   - needs to deal with uncertainty
   - needs relevant information.

CHAPTER 2

1. Prime cost = Direct materials + direct labour + direct expense.

2. A location or function in relation to which costs may be gathered. Its main function is part of the build-up of overheads and for cost control.

3. Cost apportionment is the division or splitting up of a common cost so that the cost centres receiving benefit from the common cost bear some of the cost.

Basis of apportionment	Typical costs apportioned on basis
Floor area	Rates, rent, cleaning costs etc.
Number of employees	Canteen costs, Personnel department costs, Safety.

CHAPTER 3

1 Stores account using LIFO

	Qty	Price	£		Qty	Price	£
1st May stock	5,000	20p	1,000	2nd May Issue	3,000	20p	600
6th May receipt	1,600	22p	352			Note	
18th May receipt	1,800	23p	414	16th May Issue	2,100	1	452
				Closing stock	3,300	2	714
	8,400		1,766		8,400		1,766

				£
Note 1	Issues	1,600 @ 22p	=	352
		500 @ 20p	=	100
		Total		452
Note 2	Stock	1,800 @ 23p	=	414
		1,500 @ 20p	=	300
		Total		714

Stores account using Average Price

	Qty	Price	£		Qty	Price	£
1st May stock	5,000	20p	1,000	2nd May Issue	3,000	20p	600
6th May receipt	1,600	22p	352			Note	
18th May receipt	1,800	23p	414	16th May Issue	2,100	1	439
				Closing stock	3,300	2	727
	8,400		1,766		8,400		1,766

Note 1.　Balance of stock after 3,000 issue is 2,000 @ 20p = £400

+ (receipt 1,600 @ 22p = £352) = £752

∴ average price $\dfrac{£752}{3,600} = 0.2088$

∴ Issue = £439

Note 2.　Balance of stock after 2,100 issue is 1,500 @ 0.2088 = £313

+ (receipt 1,800 @ 23p = 414) = £727

This has an average price of $\dfrac{£727}{3,300} = 0.22$

2.　Time based wages are paid by hour, day, shift or week regardless of output. Wages based on production are related to the number of units produced, or tonnage or some other measure of production. Production related wages may be based on individual production or production of a team or gang.

3.　Only good production is paid so output level is 596 − 22 = 574

Wages		£
First 300 @ 40p	=	120
Next 200 @ 45p	=	90
74 @ 48p	=	35.52
Total		£245.52

CHAPTER 4

1. Overhead apportionment is the spreading of a common cost, for example, rates, among the cost centres which benefit from the cost.

   Overhead absorption is the process by which each cost unit passing through a cost centre is charged with a proportion of the overheads of the cost centre.

2. Machine hour overhead absorption rate $= \dfrac{£85,000}{7,700} = \underline{£11.04}$

3.
Overheads absorbed = 7,328 × £11.04	=	£80,901
Actual overheads	=	£82,681
Under absorbed overheads	=	£1,960

4. Depreciation is the decrease in value of an asset due to wear and the passage of time.

   Depreciation is not a cash cost as other overheads such as Rates, Electricity, Salaries and so on.

   Straight line depreciation per year $= \dfrac{\text{cost of asset}}{\text{estimated life.}}$

CHAPTER 5

1. In job costing direct costs are charged straight to the cost unit (i.e. the job). Indirect costs or overheads are first accumulated by cost centre and then charged to the various jobs passing through the cost centres, using overhead absorption.

   In continuous costing *all* costs, direct and indirect, are accumulated by cost centres and then averaged over the cost units passing through the cost centres. This procedure is possible because the cost units are identical.

2. The general effect would be that the jobs containing mostly labour would be over-costed (and so over-priced) and the ones containing little labour would be under-costed (and priced too low). As prices are cost related the firm would tend to receive more of the mainly machinery jobs and would tend to make lower profits or even losses because an incorrect costing basis has been used. The remedy is to use more individual costing procedures and absorb overheads using either the labour hour or machine hour basis depending on the nature of the job.

3. If a profit is anticipated for the contract when completed, having regard to costs already incurred and costs expected, then it is reasonable to take a conservative proportion into account for the current period. If the assessment of the project outcome shows that a loss is expected then the whole of the loss must be included in the current period's accounts.

CHAPTER 6

1.

	Kilos	£
Input material	540	2,160
Labour & overheads		2,900
	540	5,060
less Normal loss (15%)	81	81 (scrap sale)
= Net good production	459	4,979

$$\therefore \text{Cost per kilo of good production} = \frac{£4,979}{459} = \underline{£10.85}$$

2.

$$
\begin{aligned}
\text{Abnormal loss} \quad &= \quad \text{Actual loss} - \text{Normal loss} \\
&= \quad (540\text{-}450) - 15\% \text{ of } 540 \\
&= \quad 90 - 81 \quad = \quad 9 \text{ Kilos}
\end{aligned}
$$

	Kilos	£	
Input material	540	2,160	
Labour & overheads		2,900	
	540	5,060	
less Normal loss	81	81	
less Abnormal loss	9	97	Note 1
	450	4,882	Note 2

Note 1. The abnormal loss is costed at the cost of good production, £10.85 per kilo. The 9 kilos of extra scrap can be sold for £1 per kilo so the net cost of the abnormal loss (£97 – 9) £88 is charged to the firm's P & L account.

Note 2. The output of 450 kilos at £10.85 per kilo is charged as material input to the next process.

3.

Product	Output	Physical unit basis Cost calculation		Product cost £
X	500	$\frac{500}{1,800} \times £62,500$	=	17,361
Y	1,000	$\frac{1,000}{1,800} \times £62,500$	=	34,722
Z	300	$\frac{300}{1,800} \times £62,500$	=	10,417
	1,800			£62,500

Product	Sales value £	Sales Value basis Cost calculation		Product cost £
X	45,000	$\dfrac{45,000}{87,500} \times £62,500$	=	32,143
Y	35,000	$\dfrac{35,000}{87,500} \times £62,500$	=	25,000
Z	7,500	$\dfrac{7,500}{87,500} \times £62,500$	=	5,357
	87,500			£62,500

CHAPTER 7

1. Planning can be summarised as: *aims* and *means*.

    Control can be summarised as: *measure, compare and adjust*.

    Control is the way that operations and activities are monitored to see if plans are being followed and achieved. The control process relies on information feedback.

2. (a) Fixed cost: one that remains unchanged even though activity alters. Variable cost: one that changes in sympathy with activity variations. Semi-variable cost: one that contains a fixed element and a variable element.

    (b)

Cost	Cost difference between 10,000 & 15,000 units £	Cost type
L	13,750	Variable £2.75 per unit
M	5,000	Semi variable £3,750 fixed & £1 per unit variable
N	22,500	Semi variable £5,000 fixed & £4.5 per unit variable
O	NIL	Fixed

3.

	£		£
Highest sales value	216,500	Distribution costs	18,650
Lowest sales value	149,500	Distribution costs	15,590
Difference	67,000		2,700

$\therefore$ Variable element per £1,000 sales $= \dfrac{£2,700}{67} = £40.3$

Fixed element

$$= £18,650 - (£40.3 \times 216.5)$$
$$= £18,650 - 8,725 = £9,925$$

Accordingly distribution costs are a semi-variable cost with a fixed element of £9,925 and a variable element of £40.3 per £1,000 sales value.

Distribution costs at £230,000 sales:

$$= £9,925 + (£40.3 \times 230) = \quad \underline{£19,194}$$

CHAPTER 8

1. A budget is a quantitative or financial expression of a plan. A financial budget shows the expected cost of every type of expenditure necessary to meet the plan.

    The benefits of budgeting include: Co-ordination, communication, cost control, exception, management, increased motivation.

2. A limiting factor (or key factor or principal budget factor) is the factor which constrains or limits the activities of the organisation. It may be lack of finance, space, skilled staff and so on or it may be sales demand.

3. A master budget is the budgeted Operating Statement and Balance Sheet of the organisation. The Operating Statement shows the profit/loss expected from the activities of the period and the Balance Sheet shows the assets and liabilities at the end of the period. These two statements provide a summary of all the period's activities.

CHAPTER 9

1. A fixed budget is one designed for a single activity level. A flexible budget enables the various costs to be adjusted or flexed to suit the actual level of activity. The adjustment is made possible by separating all costs into their fixed and variable components.

2.

Flexible Budgets

Activity level (units)	13,000		17,000
	£		£
Prime cost (13000 × £4)	52,000	(17,000 × £4)	68,000
Production overheads			
(£20,000+13000 × £1.50)	39,500	(£20,000 × 17,000 × £1.50)	45,500
General overheads (fixed)	35,000		35,000
	£126,500		148,500

3.

	Flexed budget for 16,100 units £	Actual costs for 16,100 units £	Budget variances £
Prime cost	64,400	62,790	+ 1,610
Prod.Overheads	44,150	47,370	– 3,220
General overheads	35,000	36,300	– 1,300
	£143,550	146,460	– 2,910

CHAPTER 10

1. Typical contents of a cash budget

All cash receipts; for example

cash sales

receipts from debtors

loans received

sale of assets

dividends/interest received etc.

All cash payments; for example

cash purchases

payments to creditors

purchase of fixed assets

tax payments

payments of dividends/interest, etc.

Cash budgets are prepared so that the organisation has advance notice of possible cash shortages or surpluses.

2.

Cash Budget

	March	April	May
Opening Balance	27,000	29,000	38,340
+ Receipts from debtors*	77,700	81,840	90,100
+ Cash sales	20,000	22,000	25,000
= Total cash available	124,700	132,840	153,440
– Salaries	9,500	9,500	10,000
– Fixed overheads	25,000	25,000	27,000
– Purchases	61,200	60,000	69,000
Total disbursements	95,700	94,500	106,000
Balance c/f	29,000	38,340	47,440

The receipts from debtors are calculated as follows:

March	£	April	£	May	£
40% March	32,000	40% April	36,000	40% May	40,000
45% Feb	36,900	45% March	36,000	45% April	40,500
12% Jan	8,800	12% Feb	9,840	12% March	9,600
	£77,700		£81,840		£90,100

CHAPTER 11

1. A standard cost is derived from a detailed technical/engineering/financial analysis of each aspect of manufacture, each material used, every type of labour required. The analysis includes the methods, volumes, times and prices expected.
    A standard cost is a target cost, it is not an average of past costs.

2. Variance analysis is the sub-division of the total difference between actual and standard cost into variances (differences) caused by material, labour, overheads and so on. Variance analysis is carried out to assist management in improving efficiency and controlling costs.

3. The key principle of variance analysis is the following comparison.
    Actual cost of Actual Quantity is compared with the **standard cost** of *Actual Quantity*.

4. Labour Variances

    Labour Rate Variance
    (Actual hours @ Standard Rate) – Actual wages
    $$= \quad (35{,}792 \times £6.50) - £229{,}069$$
    $$= \quad £232{,}648 - 229{,}069 = £3{,}579 \text{ FAV}$$

    Labour Efficiency Variance
    (SHP – Actual hours) × Standard Rate
    $$\text{SHP} = 2{,}186 \times 16 = 34{,}976$$
    $$(3{,}4976 - 3{,}5792) \times £6.50 = £5{,}304 \text{ ADV}$$
    Total Labour Variance = + £3,579 – 5,304 =   £1,725 ADV

    Proof of Total Variance
    (SHP × Standard Rate) – Actual wages
    $$= (3{,}4976 \times £6.50) - £229{,}069$$
    $$= £227{,}344 - £229{,}069 = £1{,}725 \text{ ADV}$$

The variances show that the labour was paid below the standard rate (or a lower grade of labour was used) resulting in a gain due to rates of £3,579.
On the other hand efficiency was below standard resulting in a loss of £5,304.
If a lower and cheaper grade of labour was used the overall effect was adverse so that it probably would be beneficial to use the correct grade of labour.

CHAPTER 12

1. The decision process can be divided into the following stages
    - definition of objectives
    - consideration of alternatives

     –   evaluation of alternatives
     –   choice of best option(s).

2.   Relevant costs and revenues for decision making are:
     –   Expected future costs and revenues
     –   Differential costs and revenues i.e. those that will *change* as a result of the decision being considered.

3.

Expected Values

Option X			Option Y			Option Z		
	£			£			£	
0.4 × £10,000	=	4,000	0.2 × £3,000	=	600	0.3 × –£1,000	=	–300
0.6 × £15,000	=	9,000	0.7 × £13,000	=	9,100	0.4 × £13,000	=	5,200
			0.1 × £22,000	=	2,200	0.3 × £5,000	=	7,500
Expected Values		13,000			11,900			12,400

On the basis of expected values Option X would be preferred.

CHAPTER 13

1.   (a) Separation of fixed and variable costs. Calculation of contribution for each of the options. (Contribution = Sales – variable cost)
    (b) Maximise contribution per unit of the key factor.

2.   Decision to close department should be based on the contributions of departments, not their profit.

Revised statement showing contribution

	Dept. M.	Dept. N.	Dept. O.	Total
	£	£	£	£
Sales	280,000	415,000	146,000	841,000
less Variable costs	193,200	202,800	67,200	463,200
= contribution	86,800	212,200	78,800	377,800
less Fixed costs				308,800
= Profit				£69,000

It will be seen that Department M produces a contribution of £86,800 and, if closed, the firm's total contribution would fall by this amount changing the profit of £69,000 to a loss of £17,800.

The assumption in the above is that the fixed costs were all general fixed costs which would not reduce if M was closed. If some of the fixed costs were applicable solely to Dept. M, these would have to be taken into account.

3.

Operating statements for period -Based on Total Costing

	£	£
Sales		900,000
less Production costs	570,000	
less Closing stock	57,000	513,000
= Gross Profit		387,000
less General overheads		180,000
= Profit		£207,000

Note 1. The closing stock of 2000 kilos is valued at full production cost i.e. $\dfrac{£570,000}{20,000}$

$\times 2,000 = £57,000$

Based on Marginal Costing

		£	£
Sales		900,000	
less	Variable production cost	350,000	
less	Closing stock	35,000	315,000
	= Contribution		585,000
less	Fixed costs		
	Production	220,000	
	General	180,000	400,000
	= Profit		£185,000

Note 2. The closing stock is valued at variable production cost i.e. $\dfrac{£350,000}{20,000} \times 2,000$

$= £35,000$

The difference between the two profits is (£207,000 – 185,000) £22,000. This is entirely due to the difference in stock valuation i.e. £57,000 – 35,000 = £22,000. Using Total Costing, fixed production costs are included in the stock valuation whereas using marginal costing only variable costs are included.

CHAPTER 14

1. Contribution = £12 – £5 = £7.

   (a) Units to breakeven

   $$= \frac{\text{Fixed costs}}{\text{contribution per unit}} = \frac{£80,000}{7} = \underline{11,429 \text{ units}}$$

   (b) Sales to produce £100,000 profit

   $$= \frac{\text{Fixed costs + Target profit}}{\text{unit contribution}} \times \text{selling price}$$

   $$= \frac{£80,000 + 100,000}{7} \times £12 = \underline{£308,571}$$

2.

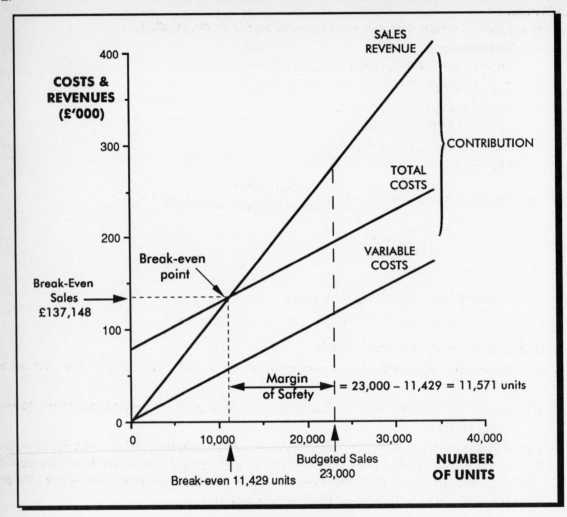

Figure 14/1/Answer
CONTRIBUTION BREAK-EVEN CHART

3. The main limitations of B-E analysis are:
    (a) The cost patterns, i.e. linear variable costs and unchanging fixed costs are over simplified and unrepresentative.
    (b) A single product firm or a firm with an unchanging sales mix is assumed. This is unrealistic.
    (c) B-E analysis only provides a rough guide to performance around normal activity. Outside this range it is unreliable.

CHAPTER 15

1. Some factors which may need to be considered in pricing decisions
   – The market
   – The position of firm in the industry
   – The product
   – The demand for the product
   – The state of the economy
   – Government/legal regulations
   – The costs.

2. (a) Percentage mark-up on cost $= \dfrac{\text{capital employed}}{\text{Total Annual costs}} \times \text{Target ROCE}$

   $\qquad = \dfrac{\text{£6m}}{\text{£3.75m}} \times 16\%$

   $\qquad = \underline{25.6\%}$

   (b) Selling price $=$ £150,000 + 25.6%
   $\qquad\qquad\qquad\; = $ £188,400

3. Transfer prices should be set which

   (a) Encourage divisional management to act in the best interests of the firm as a whole

   (b) Enable the performance of both the transferring and receiving divisions to be fairly assessed

   (c) Enable the divisions to act as independently as possible. The best transfer price to use is a true Market Price if this is available. In many cases there is not a market price because the transferred item is not sold on the open market or is not sold in the exact form or state in which it is transferred.

CHAPTER 16

1. Money received earlier is worth more than the same amount received later. This is because the money received earlier can be put to use. The time value of money must be considered in long term decision making because sums of money (costs or income) occurring at different periods in the future cannot be compared directly; they must be reduced to some equivalent value at a common date. Now, the present time, is normally used.

2. Payback calculations.

		Project A		Project B	
		Cash flow	Cumulative cash flow	Cash flow	Cumulative cash flow
		£	£	£	£
Now		− 6,000	− 6,000	− 9,000	− 9,000
Year	1	+ 3,500	− 2,500	+ 1,500	− 7,500
"	2	+ 1,000	− 1,500	+ 2,000	− 5,500
"	3	+ 1,500	−	+ 2,500	− 3,000
"	4	+ 1,500	+ 1,500	+ 4,000	+ 1,000
"	5	+ 2,000	+ 2,000	+ 2,000	+ 3,000
"	6	+ 1,500	+ 3,500	+ 1,000	+ 4,000

Payback periods

Project A   3 years

Project B between 3 and 4 years. Assuming that the Year 4 cash flows are evenly spread throughout the year the exact payback period is 3¾. years.

NPV calculations at 10%

	Project A			Project B		
	Cash flow	Discount Factors (Table A)	Present value	Cash flow	Discount Factors	Present Value
	£		£	£		£
Now	− 6,000	1	− 6,000	− 9,000	1	− 9,000
Year 1	+ 3,500	0.909	+ 3,181	+ 1,500	0.909	+ 1,363
" 2	+ 1,000	0.826	+ 826	+ 2,000	0.826	+ 1,652
" 3	+ 1,500	0.751	+ 1,126	+ 2,500	0.751	+ 1,878
" 4	+ 1,500	0.683	+ 1,025	+ 4,000	0.683	+ 2,732
" 5	+ 2,000	0.621	+ 1,242	+ 2,000	0.621	+ 1,242
" 6	+ 1,000	0.564	+ 564	+ 1,000	0.564	+ 564
Net Present values			+ 1,964			+ 431

3. Present Values of annuities.

Present value = Amount of annuity × Discount Factor (Table B)

(a) Present value of £2,000 p.a. for 10 years at 12%

=   £2,000 × 5.650 =   £11,300

(b) Present value of £750 p.a. for 8 years at 20%

=   £750 × 3.837 =   £2,878

(c)   Present value of £500 p.a. for 5 years followed by £1,000 p.a. for 3 years at 16%

= £500 × 3.274 = £1,637 to which must be added the P.V. of the next three years income

= £1,000 × 2.246 = £2,246 which must be discounted because this is its value at Year 5.

∴ Present value = £2,246 × 0.476 (Table A)

= £1,069

Thus the present value of the two annuities is £1,637 + £1,069 = £2,706

For clarity the above is shown diagrammatically, thus:

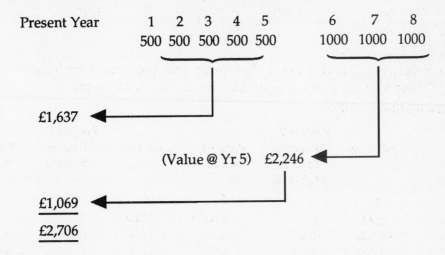

Present Year | 1 2 3 4 5 | 6 7 8
500 500 500 500 500 | 1000 1000 1000

£1,637

(Value @ Yr 5)   £2,246

£1,069

£2,706

CHAPTER 17

1.   Decentralisation occurs when some decision making occurs at local level rather than all decisions being taken at the centre by top management.

Advantages:
–   Frees top management from low-level work
–   Improves local decisions which are taken close to the action
–   Provides motivation and training for junior management

Disadvantages:
–   Local decisions may be taken which conflict with the objectives of the organisation as a whole
–   Needs information system to monitor results of local decisions.

2.   Cost centres are responsible for costs.

Profit centres are responsible for costs, revenues and profits Investment centres are responsible for costs, revenues, profits and profits in relation to investment.

3. Return on Capital Employed (ROCE)

$$ROCE = \frac{Profits}{Capital\ Employed}\ \%$$

Division	A	B	C
	£35,000	£90,000	£65,000
	£375,000	£1,200,000	£575,000
ROCE	= 9.3%	= 7.5%	= 11.3%

Residual Profit

Trading Profit – Interest on Capital = Residual Profit

Division	A	B	C
	£	£	£
Trading profit	35,000	90,000	65,000
8% on capital	30,000	96,000	46,000
= Residual Profit(Loss)	£5,000	£(6,000)	£19,000

ANSWERS

SECTION 1 ASSESSMENT

ANSWERS TO MULTIPLE CHOICE QUESTIONS

1 b	6 a	11 d	16 c	21 a
2 c	7 b	12 b	17 a	22 c
3 c	8 c	13 c	18 d	23 d
4 a	9 b	14 c	19 b	24 a
5 d	10 a	15 b	20 c	25 b

SOLUTIONS TO EXAMINATION QUESTIONS

A1. (a) Details can be taken from the Chapter (LIFO, FIFO and Average Price)

(b) Effect in times of inflation:

Method	On stock valuation	On cost of product	On profit
LIFO	understates	more realistic	more realistic
FIFO	more realistic	understates	overstates

Weighted Average produces a position between LIFO and FIFO

(c) When producing work to special requirements special materials are usually required and specific material prices used.

A2. (i) Closing stock values (given Opening stock is 20 at £80 each)

			FIFO			LIFO		W.AV
Jan	50×70	=	£3,500	20×80	=	£1,600	$\dfrac{£9,880}{130}$ =	£76
	30×82	=	£2,460	20×81	=	£1,620		
				40×70	=	£2,800		
	80		£5,960	80		£6,020	80×76	£6,080

			FIFO		LIFO			W.AV
Feb	30×85	=	£2,550					
	30×85	=	£2,550		as above	$\dfrac{6,080+8,680}{180}$ =		£82
	20×94	=	£1,880					
	80		£6,980	80		6,020	80×82 =	£6,560

(ii) Workings for March closing stock using Weighted Average

$$\frac{£6,560 + 9,280}{180} = \underline{£88}$$

∴ Deficit $= 2 \times £88 = \underline{£176}$ and Closing Stock $= 28 \times 88 = \underline{£2,464}$

Profit & Loss Account for March

	£	£
Sales (150 × £150)		22,500
Opening stock	£6,560	
+ Purchases	9,280	
– Deficit & Closing Stock	(2,640)	13,200
= Gross Profit		9,300
less Variable costs (10% of 22,500)		(2,250)
Fixed costs		(4,000)
Stock deficit		(176)
= Net Profit		£2,874

A3. (i) Four possible overhead absorption rates.

$$\text{(Overhead absorption rate} = \frac{\text{Total Overheads}}{\text{Total of absorption base}}$$

OAR per labour hour	$= \dfrac{£500,000}{50,000}$	$=$	£10
OAR per machine hour	$= \dfrac{£500,000}{100,000}$	$=$	£5
OAR Direct Wages Percentage	$= \dfrac{£500,000}{£200,000}\%$	$=$	250%
OAR Prime Cost Percentage	$= \dfrac{£500,000}{£1,200,000}$	$=$	42%

Price quotations for Job 456

Using Labour hour basis:

	£
Direct material	1,000
" labour (60 × £4.50)	270
= PRIME COST	1,270
Factory overheads	
60 × £10	600
= Factory cost	1,870
+ 100% Mark-up	1,870
= Selling price	£3,740

Using Machine hour basis:

		£
Prime cost		1,270
Factory overheads		
72 × £5		360
= Factory cost		1,630
+ 100% Mark-up		1,630
= Selling price		£3,260

Using Direct Wages Percentage

		£
Direct material		1,000
Direct labour		270
= PRIME COST		1,270
Factory overheads		
£270 × 250%		675
		1,945
+ 100% Mark-up		1,945
		£3,890

Using Prime Cost Percentage

		£
Prime cost		1,270
Factory overheads		
£1,270 × 42%		533
		1,803
+ 100% Mark-up		1,803
		£3,606

(ii) The Machine Hour basis is likely to be the most appropriate as there is expensive machinery which will account for much of the overheads.

A4   **Operation**

	1	2	3	4	*Total*
Time/component(Hrs)	1	1	1	1	
	3	2	6	4	
No of components	2,400	2,400	2,400	2,400	
=Total time (Hrs)	800	1,200	300	600	

228

NO OF OPERATIVES

| (Hrs + 40) | Grade A | 20 | 30 | | | 50 | |
| | Grade B | | | 10 | 15 | 25 | |

COSTS

Grade A (Hrs × £4)	£3,200	4,800			£8,000	GRADE A
Grade B(Hrs × £3.20)			1,280	1,920	£3,200	GRADE B
					11,200	Total

COST/COMPONENT

| (cost + 2400) | £1.33 | £2 | 0.53 | 0.8 | £4.66 |

A5. (a)

Departments

	Total £	A £	B £	C £	X £	Y £	Apportionment basis
Rent and rates	12,800	6,000	3,600	1,200	1,200	800	Floor area
Machine insurance	6,000	3,000	1,250	1,000	500	250	Machine value
Telephone charges	3,200	1,500	900	300	300	200	Floor area
Depreciation	18,000	9,000	3,750	3,000	1,500	750	Machine value
Supervisors salaries	24,000	12,800	7,200	4,000			Labour hours
Heat and light	6,400	3,000	1,800	600	600	400	Floor area
Allocated		2,800	1,700	1,200	800	600	
	77,500	38,100	20,200	11,300	4,900	3,000	
		2,450	1,225	1,225	(4,900)		
		600	900	1,500		(3,000)	
	£77,500	41,150	22,325	14,025			
Budgeted D.L.hours		3,200	1,800	1,000			
Absorption rates		£12.86	£12.40	£14.02			

(b) & (c)

	Job 123 £		Job 124 £
D.Material	154.00		108.00
D.Labour			
Department A	76.00		60.80
Department B	42.00		35.00
Department C	34.00		47.60
Total Direct Cost	306.00		251.40
Overhead			
Department A (20 × 12.86)	257.20	(16x12.86)	205.76
Department B (12 × 12.4)	148.80	(10x12.4)	124.00
Department C (10 × 14.02)	140.20	(14x14.02)	196.28
Total cost	852.20		777.44
Profit	284.07		259.15
Quoted selling price	1,136.27		1,036.59

229

(d) Detailed controls are necessary at each stage of the whole material cycle from Purchasing to material usage. For example;

Purchasing: Materials of the appropriate quality and specification should be purchased only when required and authorised. There should be an appropriate balance between price, quality and delivery.

Materials should be properly received and inspected. Storage should be secure and efficiently organised. There should be well designed documentation used at every stage. The stock control system should monitor stock levels, re-order quantities, usage rates, delivery times and so on to ensure that just enough stocks are held to service operations.

A6. (a) Method of pricing used.

Weighted Average Price

e.g. The issue of 20 units is made at £28.5 per unit made up from the stock of 16 @ £28 and 16 @ £29.5

(b)

	Stores Ledger Account using Weighted Average Pricing								
Date	Receipts			Issues			Stock		
	Units	Price £	Total £	Units	Price £	Total £	Units	Price £	Total £
Mar									
2	34	28	952				34	28	952
4				18	28	504	16	28	448
9	16	29	464				32	28.5	912
14				20	28.5	570	12	28.5	342
17	24	27	648				36	27.5	990
19				22	27.5	605	14	27.5	385
21	28	29	812				42	28.5	1,197
23				32	28.5	912	10	28.5	285
25	30	30.5	915				40	30	1,200
28				26	30	780	14	30	420
30	42	32	1,344				56	31.5	1,764
	174		5,135	118		3,371	56		1,764

(c) Value of closing stock using FIFO is (42 × £32) + (14 × £30.5) = £1,771. This is because the 56 units left must be from the latest batches received i.e. on 30th and 25th.

A7 **(a)** **(i)**

	Total cost £	Develop-ment £	Data Preparation £	Computer Operations £
Salaries	200,000	60,000	50,000	90,000
Compilation	60,000	60,000	–	–
Maintenance	20,000	–	2,000	18,000
Materials	10,000	1,000	2,000	7,000
Power	10,000	–	2,500	7,500
Office	10,000	2,000	2,000	6,000
	310,000	123,000	58,500	128,500
Chargeable rates				
staff hours		12,000		
1,000 key depressions			24,300	
usable hours				4,200
charge rate		£10.25	£2.407	£30.595

(ii)

	Job 1234 £	Job 5678 £
Development	4,100	205
Data Preparation	–	192.56
Computer	–	152.98
	4,100	550.54

(b) **(i)** Cost unit
- a unit of product or service in relation to which costs can be calculated.

Cost centre
- a means by which costs are collected together for control and charging to cost units. Cost centres are an essential part of the overhead gathering, recording and charging system.

(ii) Examples:

	Cost unit	Cost centre
From the question	Key depressions	The Divisions
	Development hour	
Others	Kilogram of output	Machining department
	Meal	Wages department
	Patient night	

(c)

			£	
Actual hours worked	(34+5)	@ £5 per hour	195	Direct
Overtime premium	5	@ £2.5 per hour	12.50	Indirect
Idle time	6	@ £5 per hour	30	Indirect
Group bonus			4	Direct
			£241.50	

231

A8 (i) Cost centre and cost unit can be taken directly from the chapter.

(ii)

Organisation	*Typical cost units*
Brickmaking	Per 100 or 1,000 bricks or per Pallet
Oil Refining	Per barrel, per litre or 1000 litres
Boiler house	Per lb of steam raised
Works canteen	Per meal or per customer
Coalmining	Per tonne of coal
Heavy goods transport	Per tonne/kilometre or mile
School/College	Per full time equivalent student
Professional accountant	Per chargeable hour or per job.

A9 (a) This can be answered directly from the book.

(b) Room occupancy $= \dfrac{\text{Rooms occupied}}{\text{Rooms available}} = \dfrac{200 + 30}{240 + 40} = 82.1\%$

Bed occupancy $= \dfrac{\text{Beds occupied}}{\text{Beds available}} = \dfrac{6,450}{15,600} \times 2 = 82.7\%$

(Beds available $= (240 \times 2 \times 30) + (40 \times 30) = 15600$)

Average guest rate $= \dfrac{\text{Revenue}}{\text{Guests}} = \dfrac{£774,000}{6,450} = £120$

Revenue utilisation $= \dfrac{\text{Revenue}}{\text{Maximum revenue}} = \dfrac{£774,000}{876,000} = 88.4\%$

(Maximum revenue $= 30(240 \times £110) + (40 \times £70)$)

Cost of cleaning supplies $= \dfrac{£166.6}{230} = £0.7$

Average cost per occupied bed $= \dfrac{£127,500}{12,900} = \underline{£9.9}$

(c) A cost unit is a unit of product or service in relation to which costs are ascertained. A cost centre is part of the cost collection system especially important in collecting overhead costs.

(d) Typical cost centres and cost units:

Cost centre	Cost unit(s)
Restaurant	per meal, per customer
Laundry	per item processed.

ANSWERS

SECTION 2 ASSESSMENT

ANSWERS TO MULTIPLE CHOICE QUESTIONS

1 c	6 d	11 a	16 d	21 b
2 d	7 a	12 d	17 b	22 a
3 a	8 b	13 c	18 a	23 d
4 c	9 a	14 b	19 d	24 b
5 b	10 c	15 b	20 c	25 a.

ANSWERS TO EXAMINATION QUESTIONS

A1 Workings to find the Fixed and Variable elements of Labour Costs using the High/Low technique.

	Direct labour hrs	Total cost	Variable	Fixed
High	110,000	£330,000	£275,000	£55,000
Low	80,000	255,000	200,000	55,000
Difference	30,000	£75,000		

Variable element: £2.50 per direct labour hour.

Flexible Budgets

Activity level:	90%	100%	110%	120%
	£	£	£	£
Depreciation	22,000	22,000	22,000	22,000
Staff salaries	43,000	43,000	43,000	43,000
Insurances	9,000	9,000	9,000	9,000
Rent and rates	12,000	12,000	12,000	12,000
Power	32,400	36,000	39,600	43,200
Consumables	5,400	6,000	6,600	7,200
Direct labour	378,000	420,000	462,000	504,000
Semi-variable				
Fixed element	55,000	55,000	55,000	55,000
Variable element	270,000	300,000	330,000	360,000
Total	826,800	903,000	979,200	1,055,400

A2 (i) (a), (b), (c), (d) and (e) £50,000, (f) £67,500, (g) £72,750 (h) £76,250, (i) £78,000, (j) £79,750, (k) £42,500, (l) £55,250, (m) £59,500, (n) £63,750, (o) £72,250, (p) £76,500, (q) £24,000, (r) £36,000.

    (ii) Group 1 – Fixed costs £50,000 per month

             2 – Semi–variable (MC hrs × 35p) + £50,000

             3 – Variable (MC hrs × 85p)

             4 – Stepped Fixed cost. Rising in £4,000 steps for each 10,000 hours.

(iii) First necessary to calculate the budget for a normal month of 85000 hours i.e.

(e + j + o + £36,000) = £238,000

$$\therefore OAR = \frac{238,000}{85,000} = £2.8 \text{ per hour}$$

Variance calculations.

Actual overheads	£216,450	
		Expenditure variance £6,130 (ADV)
Budgeted overheads (Note 1)	210,320	
		Volume variance £18,240 (ADV)
Actual hours x OAR (69,600 x £2.8)	192,080	
		Efficiency variance £10,080 (FAV)
SHP x OAR (72,000 x £2.8)	202,160	

Total variance £14,290 (ADV)

Note 1:   The Flexed budget allowance for 68,600 hours is:

	£	
Group 1	50,000	(Fixed)
2	74,010	(£50,000+68,600x0.35)
3	58,310	(68,600x0.85)
4	28,000	(7 x £4,000)
	£210,320	

A3 (a) (i) Standard direct labour cost per product

Dept.	Product Grade		H £		J £
F	1	(2 × 2.50)	5	(12 × 2.50)	30
	2	(4 × 3)	12	(6 × 3)	18
G	1	(8 × 2.50)	20		
	3	(10 × 2.30)	23		
		Total	60		48

(ii) Total standard labour cost of actual production

Product	H	200 × £60	=	£12,000
	J	300 × £48	=	£14,400
				£26,400

235

(b)   Labour total variances for each department

Dept. F

Actual wages	£17,950
less Standard wages for actual output	17,800 *
= Total variance	£150 ADV

* In Dept. F, standard labour cost of 1 unit of H is £17 and £48 for 1 unit of J.
∴ Standard labour for actual output is (200x£17) + (300x£48) = £17,800

Dept. G

Actual wages	£8,500
less Standard wages for actual OP*	8,600
= Total variance	100

* (200 × £43) = £8,600

(c)   Rate and Efficiency variances

Dept. F

Actual wages	£17,950
less actual hrs at standard rates (4,028 x £2.5) + (2,570x£3)	17,780
less SHP x standard rate (400x£2.5)+(3,600x£2.5)+ (800x£3)+(1,800x£3)	17,800

Rate variance £170 (ADV)

Efficiency variance £20 (FAV)

Total £150 (ADV)

Dept. G

Actual wages	8,500
less actual hrs at standard rates (1,610 x £2.5) + (1,980x£2.3)	8,579
less SHP x standard rate (1,600x£2.5)+(2,000x£2.30)	8,600

Rate variance £79 (FAV)

Efficiency variance £21 (FAV)

Total £100 (FAV)

A4 Note that the Production and Materials Purchase Budget are *quantity* budgets.

(i)
Production budget (sacks)

	Compo 1	Compo 2	Compo 3
Sales quantity	50,000	40,000	60,000
+ stock increase (i.e. 60% of opening stock)	3,000	3,300	4,500
= Production quantity	53,000	43,300	64,500

(ii)
Materials Purchases Budget

	G kg		R kg		0 kg
Quantity required for production					
*Compo 1 53,000 sacks: × 25 =	1,325,000	× 20 =	1,060,000	× 5 =	265,000
*Compo 2 43,300 sacks: × 15 =	649,500	× 25 =	1,082,500	× 10 =	433,000
*Compo 3 64,500 sacks: × 5 =	322,500	× 30 =	1,935,000	× 15 =	967,500
= Production requirement	2,297,000		4,077,500		1,665,500
less stock decrease	31,000		36,500		28,500
(20% of opening stock = Purchase quantity	2,266,000		4,041,000		1,637,000

* Each sack weighs 50kgs and contains the materials in the standard mix percentages given. These have been converted to kilos per sack. For example;

Compo 1	50% G	=	50% × 50kg	=	25kg
	40% R	=	40% × 50kg	=	20kg
	10% O	=	10% × 50kg	=	5kg.

(iii)
Production cost budget

		Compo 1	Compo 2	Compo 3	Total
Production (sacks)		53,000	43,300	64,500	
$ per sack		$	$	$	$
1. Materials					
	18	954,000			954,000
	19		822,700		822,700
	20			1,290,000	1,290,000
2. Labour	0.4	21,200	17,320	25,800	64,320
3. Prod.OH	1.6	84,800	69,280	103,200	257,280
Total		1,060,000	909,300	1,419,000	3,388,300

Note 1. The material costs per sack are calculated from the quantities in the Materials Purchase budget and the given standard prices. For example;

Compo 1

25kg	of	G	@ 0.40 per kg	=	$10
20kg	of	R	@ 0.20 per kg	=	4
5kg	of	0	@ 0.80 per kg	=	4
			Total		18

Note 2. Labour cost $= \dfrac{\$12}{30} =$ <u>$0.40 per sack</u>

Note 3. Production overhead = 400% of labour

= 400% of 0.4 = <u>$1.60</u>

A5 (i) It is necessary first to calculate the Standard Hours (SH) contained in the actual output

X	–	672 × 35 standard minutes	=	392 SHP
Y	–	615 × 40 standard minutes	=	410 SHP
		Total		802

Variances £

Actual wages 2,926

Actual hours × SR (760 × £3.50) 2,660

SHP × SR (802 × £3.50) 2,807

Rate variance £266 (ADV)

Efficiency £147 (FAV)

Total variance £119 (ADV)

(ii) Typical reasons

Rate Variance

1. Using higher grade labour than planned
2. Interim wage award
3. Incorrect standard

Efficiency Variance

1. Better grade of worker being more skilled
2. Better material
3. More efficient production due to fewer breakdowns
4. Incorrect standard.

A6 (i) Cash budget

	Jan	Feb	Mar	April	May	June
Cash balance	2,000	(4,500)	(3,200)	(3,800)	2,300	9,800
+ Cash from sales	18,000	19,000	22,000	24,000	25,000	29,000
= Cash available	20,000	14,500	18,800	20,200	27,300	38,800
– Cash payments						
Materials	9,000	10,000	7,000	9,000	11,000	4,000
Labour	3,900	4,000	4,200	4,700	3,700	4,100
Overhead	3,600	3,700	3,900	4,200	2,800	3,500
Capital			7,500			27,200
Tax	8,000					
Total payments	24,500	17,700	22,600	17,900	17,500	38,800
Closing balance	(4,500)	(3,200)	(3,800)	2,300	9,800	–

(ii) Need to arrange possible overdraft for the first three months given the cash shortage. Also the firm is paying promptly for purchases but allowing two months credit to its customers.

The June balance also suggests possible future liquidity problems.

Generally the distinction between reasonable budgeted profit figures and not so good cash balances needs constant monitoring.

A7

Labour variances	£
Actual wages	102,350
less Act.hrs × Std Rate (24,600 × £4)	98,400
less SHP × Std Rate (25,200 × £4)	100,800

Rate variance £3,950 (ADV)

Efficiency variance £2,400 (FAV)

Total variance £1,550 (ADV)

Overhead variances

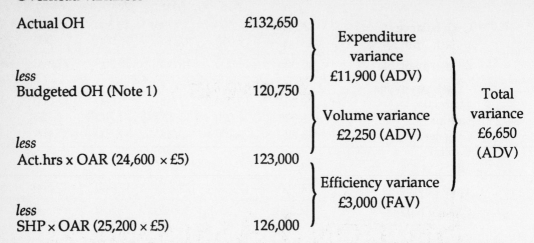

Actual OH   £132,650

Expenditure variance £11,900 (ADV)

less
Budgeted OH (Note 1)   120,750

Volume variance £2,250 (ADV)

Total variance £6,650 (ADV)

less
Act.hrs x OAR (24,600 × £5)   123,000

Efficiency variance £3,000 (FAV)

less
SHP × OAR (25,200 × £5)   126,000

Note 1. The budgeted overheads are found by flexing the budget in the normal way i.e. Fixed costs + actual hours × variable OAR =£90,000+24,600 × £1.25 = £120,750.

The £90,000 fixed costs are found by multiplying the budgeted fixed OAR by the budgeted hours i.e. £3.75 ×24,000 = £90,000.

ANSWERS

SECTION 3 ASSESSMENT

ANSWERS TO MULTIPLE CHOICE QUESTIONS

1	c	6	d	11	b	16	b	21	b
2	b	7	c	12	b	17	a	22	a
3	a	8	a	13	d	18	b	23	d
4	a	9	d	14	c	19	a	24	c
5	c	10	c	15	a	20	d	25	b

A1 (i)   NPV @ 10%

$= -£10,000+(.9091 \times 3,000)+(.8264 \times 10,000)+(.7513 \times 4,000)$

$= £3,996$

NPV @ 25%

$= -£10,000+(.8 \times 3000)+(.64 \times 10,000)+(.512 \times 4,000)$

$= £848$

NPV @ 35%

$= -£10,000+(.7407 \times 3,000)+(.5487 \times 10,000)+(.4064 \times 4,000)$

$= -£665$

(ii)

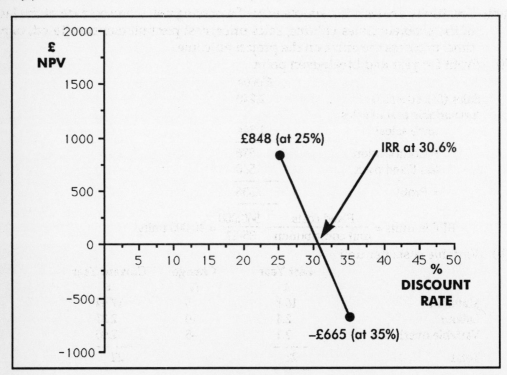

FIGURE A1/3/Ans

(iii) IRR by interpolation

$$= \quad 25\% + 10\% \frac{848}{1,513} = 30.6\%$$

(iv) Profitability Index at 10%

$$= \quad \frac{\text{NPV (or PV of cash inflows)}}{\text{investment}}$$

$$= \quad \frac{3,996}{10,000} = 0.3996 \text{ or } \frac{13,996}{10,000} = 1.3996$$

(v) Payback is 1 year 8.4 months

(vi) Expected Present Value

	£
£4,000 × 0.5	2,000
£3,000 × 0.3	900
£8,000 × 0.2	1,600
Expected NPV	£4,500

(vii) Sensitivity analysis is a simple way of assessing risk whereby each of the factors of the problem (sales volume, sales price, cost per unit etc) are altered, one at a time, to assess the effect on the project outcome.

A2 (i) Profit for year and break-even point

	£'000s
Sales (64,000 × £35)	2,240
less variable cost of sales	
(60% sales)	1,344
= Contribution	896
less Fixed costs	560
= Profit	£336

$$\text{BEP in units} = \frac{\text{Fixed costs}}{\text{unit contribution}} = \frac{560,000}{35-21} = 40,000 \text{ units}$$

(ii) Variable costs per unit

	Last Year £	Change %	Current Year £
Materials	16.8	5	17.64
Labour	2.1	10	2.31
Variable overheads	2.1	–5	2.05
Total	21		22

Revised contribution = £35–22 = £13

243

	£'000
Total contribution 66,000 × £13	858
less Fixed (560 + 12)	572
= Expected profit	286

$$\text{BEP in units} = \frac{£572,000}{13} = 44,000$$

(iii) Required contribution

= Fixed costs + Profit = £572,000+£336,000 = £908,000

Unit contribution = 38 – 22 = £16

$$\therefore \quad \text{Required quantity} = \frac{£908,000}{16} = \underline{56,750 \text{ units}}$$

A3 (a) To find contribution and profit

	£	£
Sales	134,400	
less Variable costs		
Materials	38,140	
Labour	23,620	
Var.Ohds.prod.	4,620	
Var selling ohds	10,900	77,280
= Contribution		57,120
less Fixed costs		
Production	29,700	
S & D	7,200	
Admin.	5,600	42,500
= Profit		14,620

$$\text{Unit contribution} = \frac{£57,120}{1,680} = £34$$

$$\therefore \text{Break-even point} = \frac{\text{Fixed costs}}{\text{unit contribution}}$$

$$= \frac{£42,500}{34} = \underline{1,250 \text{ units}}$$

(b) Expected profit if 1100 units sold

	£
Total contribution = 1,100 × £34 =	37,400
less Fixed costs	42,500
= Loss	5,100

(c) Units required for profit of £27,200

$$= \frac{\text{Fixed costs} + \text{Target profit}}{\text{unit contribution}}$$

$$= \frac{£42,500 + 27,200}{34} = \underline{2,050 \text{ units}}$$

A4 (a) Statement with B eliminated

	Total £	A £	C £
Sales	75,000	60,000	15,000
less variable costs			
Direct materials	32,000	23,000	9,000
" labour	12,000	10,000	2,000
Var.ohds	5,500	4,000	1,500
= Total variable costs	49,500	37,000	12,500
= Contribution	25,500	23,000	2,500
less Fixed costs	15,000		
= Profit	10,500		

(b) See Figure A4/3/Ans on following page.

(c) Break-even point

	3 products	2 products
Sales	£100,000	£75,000
less var.costs	72,500	49,500
= contribution	27,500	25,500

C/S ratio $\quad \dfrac{27,500}{100,000} = 27\tfrac{1}{2}\% \quad \dfrac{25,500}{75,000} = 34\%$

Break-even point $\quad \dfrac{£15,000}{.275} = £54,545 \quad \dfrac{£15,000}{.34} = £44,118$

(d) Main limitations
  - Assumes single product or unvarying sales mix
  - Assumes linear cost patterns
  - Assumes that cost/revenue relationships, technology remain unchanged
  - Short–term only
  - Ignores uncertainty

(e) Margin of safety is the difference between normal sales and break-even point.

245

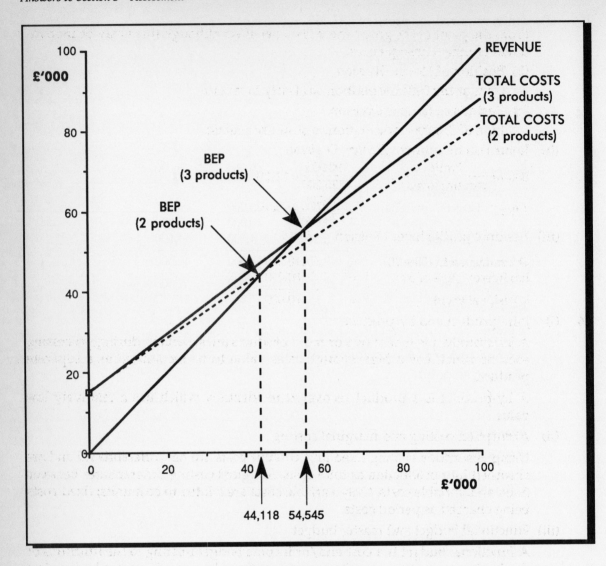

Figure A4/3/Ans

BREAK-EVEN CHART

A5   Supply of motor at £45
(i)   (a)   Position of Lawncut mowers plc

		£	
Gain in contribution from Hover sales 1,000 × £50	=	50,000	+
Loss in contribution by Electric = 5 × £10 × 1,000	=	50,000	–
		NIL	

From the point of the group there is no net effect although there may be motivational or other consequences.

    (b) Position of Hover Division

        Gain of £50,000 contribution so clearly in favour.

    (c) Position of Electric Division

        Loss of £50,000 contribution so strongly against.

  (ii) Return on investment Electric Division

$$\text{Before: } \frac{\text{Profit}}{\text{cap.employed}} = \frac{90,000}{720,000} = 12\tfrac{1}{2}\%$$

$$\text{After} = \frac{40,000}{720,000} = 5.6\%$$

 (iii) Residual profit Hover Division

Operating profit (50 + 90)	=	140,000
less Interest (10% of 800)	=	80,000
= Residual Profit	=	60,000

A6 (i)   Joint product and by-product

A joint product is where two or more products are separated during processing each of which has a high enough sales value to be recognised as a separate product.

A by-product is a product recovered incidentally which has a relatively low value.

  (ii) Absorption costing and marginal costing

Using absorption costing fixed and variable costs are not differentiated and are absorbed into production as total costs. Marginal costing differentiates between fixed and variable costs. Only variable costs are alloted to cost units; fixed costs being charged as period costs.

 (iii) Functional budget and master budget

A functional budget is a cost and/or income budget relating to the functions of the business eg. sales, purchasing, research and so on. A master budget is a summary of the functional and departmental budgets and comprises the budgeted Operating Statement and the budgeted Balance Sheet.

 (iv) Flexible budget and rolling budget

A flexible budget is a budget where the cost characteristics have been analysed so that the budget can be adjusted to various activity levels. A rolling budget is one where, on a continual basis, a budget is added for a further period whilst the oldest period is deleted. It is done so that budgets are up-to-date.

A7 (a) Pay back periods (assuming cash flows received evenly throughout the year)

Project	A	B	C
Payback	2yrs 9mths	3yrs 2mths	2yrs 8 mths

(b) Accounting Rate of Return (ARR)

$$= \frac{\text{Average Profits p.a.}}{\text{Net Capital Investment}} \%$$

where

$$\text{Average profits p.a.} = \frac{\text{Total Income} - \text{Net Capital Cost}}{5}$$

PROJECT A

$$\text{Average profits} = \frac{£330,000 - 190,000}{5} = £28,000$$

$$\therefore \text{ARR} = \frac{£28,000}{190,000} = \underline{14.7\%}$$

PROJECT B

$$\text{Average profits} = \frac{£320,000 - 215,000}{5} = £21,000$$

$$\therefore \text{ARR} = \frac{£21,000}{215,000} = \underline{9.7\%}$$

PROJECT C

$$\text{Average profits} = \frac{£315,000 - 172,000}{5} = £35,750$$

$$\therefore \text{ARR} = \frac{£35,750}{172,000} = \underline{20.8\%}$$

(c) NPV of Projects

Project A	Cash flows	Discount Factor	Present Value
Year 0	– 200,000	1.00	– 200,000
1	+ 80,000	0.8475	+ 67,800
2	+70,000	0.7182	+ 50,274
3	+ 65,000	0.6086	+ 39,559
4	+ 60,000	0.5158	+ 30,948
5	+ 65,000	0.4371	+ 28,411
		NPV =	+ 16,992

Project B	Cash flows	Discount Factor	Present Value
Year 0	– 230,000	1.00	– 230,000
1	+ 100,000	0.8475	+ 84,750
2	+ 70,000	0.7182	+ 50,274
3	+ 50,000	0.6086	+ 30,430
4	+ 50,000	0.5158	+ 25,790
5	+ 65,000	0.4371	+ 28,411
		NPV =	– 10,345

Project C

Year			
0	– 180,000	1.00	– 180,000
1	+ 55,000	0.8475	+ 46,613
2	+ 65,000	0.7182	+ 46,683
3	+ 95,000	0.6086	+ 57,817
4	+ 108,000	0.5158	+ 55,106
		NPV =	+ 26,819

(d) Assuming that 18% is the correct cost of capital Project C should be chosen as it has the largest NPV. ARR and Payback are not as reliable as NPV for investment appraisal.

(e) Numerous other factors may be considered:
  – Riskiness of projects
  – Effects on current operations
  – Effects on staff, environment, suppliers etc.
  – Reliability of estimates
    and so on.

A8 (a) (i) Profit statement

		Radios £'000		TVs £'000		VRs £'000	Total £'000
Sales		200		320		240	760
Cost of sales	50%	100	40%	128	25%	60	288
= Gross Profit		100		192		180	472
less Expenses							
Variable (10%)		20		32		24	76
Fixed (on space)		40		100		60	200
= Net Profit		40		60		96	196

(ii) Necessary to find contribution per sq metre

	Radios	TVs	VRS	Microwaves
Sales (£'000s)	200	320	240	120
less variable costs				
Cost of sales	100	128	60	36
Variable ohds	20	32	24	12
= Contribution	80	160	154	72
Area (sq.metre)	4,000	10,000	6,000	4,000
Contribution per sq.m.	£20	£16	£25.67	£18

It will be seen that the proposal to replace Radios by Microwaves is not worthwhile as the contribution per sq.m. is lower and total contribution is £8,000 lower. If adopted total profit would fall by £8,000.

(b) Microwaves earn £2 per sq.m. more than TVs so 4,000 sq.m could be taken from TVs and used for selling Microwaves. This would result in 4,000 × £2 = £8,000 extra profit.

A9 The new budget will show the position after the bonus scheme. Variable costs will increase by 20% except for wages, and the fixed costs will remain the same.

Budget after Bonus Scheme

	£'000s	
Sales (240,000 units)	480	
Manufacturing costs		
Materials (+20%)	96	
Wages see note	192	
Var.ohds (+20%)	24	
Fixed ohds (unchanged)	28	340
Factory profit		140
Selling and Distribution		
Variable (+20%)	48	
Fixed (unchanged)	23	
Admin.costs (unchanged)	39	110
Budgeted divisional profit		30

Note:

$$\text{Wages before bonus} = \frac{120,000}{200,000} = \text{60p per unit}$$

$$+ \text{ bonus} \qquad \text{20p}$$

$$= \text{80p}$$

$$\therefore \text{Total wages} = 240,000 \times 80p = £192,000$$

(ii) $\text{Break-even point} = \dfrac{\text{Fixed costs}}{\text{Contribution per unit}}$

Fixed costs = £28,000+23,000+39,000 = £90,000

Contribution per unit   = Sales – Variable costs p.a.
                                 = £2 – £1.5 = 50p

(Variable cost p.a. = (£96,000+192,000+24,000+48,000) ÷ 240,000 = £1.5)

$$\therefore \text{B.E.P} = \frac{£90,000}{5} = 180,000 \text{ units}$$

∴ Margin of safety = 240,000–180,000 = 60,000 units.

INDEX

Accounting and Finance for Business Students
M BENDREY, R HUSSEY & C WEST

400pp £6.95 1989

This book provides a comprehensive introduction to accounting and finance. It includes numerous examples, with solutions in the text, to assist the student in understanding each topic. Also, for directed private study, there are student activities (assignments, objective tests, etc.).

Courses on which this book is known to be used

BTEC National and HNC/D Business and Finance; BA Business Studies; CMS/DMS; IPM; BSc Engineering; BSc Computing; BEd in Business Studies; BA in Modern Languages and other management development courses.

CONTENTS

SOURCES AND USES OF FINANCE
Personal Finance
Business Finance
Project Appraisal
FINANCIAL ACCOUNTING
Sole Traders
Concepts and Control

Limited Liability Companies
Other Organisations
MANAGEMENT ACCOUNTING
Using Costs for Planning and Control
Using Costs for Total Costing
Using Costs for Decision Making

LECTURERS' COMMENTS

'..concise and easy to follow by students..' '..good, comprehensive coverage..' ' superior in number of examples and explanations compared with alternative texts..' '..book is very good for nonspecialists..' '..assignments are excellent for classroom activities..' '..very clearly written..' '..I have recommended your book for all students on HND...' '..gives a good introduction at an excellent price.'

Free Lecturers' Supplement

A First Course In Marketing

Frank Jefkins

192pp £4.95 1989

This book has been specially prepared for those with no prior knowledge of marketing and who need to get to grips with the subject in a simple and straight forward manner. It has quickly gained wide use as support material on BTEC First and National courses.

Courses on which this book is known to be used

BTEC First and National; RSA; LCCI; CAM Certificate in Communication Studies.

CONTENTS

LECTURERS' COMMENTS

'Another superb DPP book - ideal for the BTEC National Diploma Introduction to Marketing module!' '...useful on any basic marketing course...' 'Well planned - is British with British examples...' '..accessible to students ...'

Free Lecturers' Supplement

A First Course In Statistics
D BOOTH

304pp £4.95 1988

This book provides a core text for introductory level courses in statistics. It assumes the student has no prior knowledge of statistics whatsoever and no more than an ability to handle simple arithmetic.

Courses on which this book is known to be used
BTEC Business and Secretarial Studies; RSA; LCCI; AAT Certificate.

CONTENTS

REVIEW EXTRACTS

'The book is a breath of fresh air to those who think statistics is an essentially practical subject, as it has not only a section on the derivation of individual statistics but also three sections dealing with the practical details and problems associated with 'Asking the question', 'Collecting the data' and 'Communicating the results' which are so often given such little emphasis in introductory statistical texts ... Each chapter of each section ends with a short series of exercises, answers being provided only to alternate questions, a nice touch to cut out the 'right answer/wrong calculation' effect, yet still giving students some answers.'
The Mathematical Gazette

Free Lecturers' Supplement

Costing
3rd edition
T LUCEY

620pp £8.95 1989
(Also available as ELBS edition in member countries at
local currency equivalent price of £3.00)

This book provides a thorough coverage of cost accountancy. It is
widely used as a course text on both accountancy and other courses.
The text includes many self-testing exercises, examination questions
and case studies.

Courses on which this book is known to be used

ACCA; CIMA; AAT, BSc Combined Studies; BA (Hons) Accounting; BA
(Hons) Business Studies; BA (Hons) Business Administration; BTEC HND
Business and Finance; RSA Costing; SCOTVEC HND Accounting;
Institute of Purchasing and Supply..
On reading lists of ACCA, AAT and SCCA

CONTENTS

LECTURERS' COMMENTS

*'Lucey has bravely attempted to bring the subject into the 1990s ... There is
a useful new chapter on Costing and Computers ... The price is right, and
the technical quality is there. What more could a student ask?'*
ACCA Students Newsletter December 1989
'Brilliant!'
Lecturer

Free Lecturers' Supplement

Management Accounting
2nd Edition
T LUCEY

560pp £7.95 1988

This book provides comprehensive coverage of the Management Accounting syllabuses of the major professional bodies. It includes many graded exercises, examination questions (with and without answers) and case studies.

Courses on which this book is known to be used
ACCA; CIMA; CIPFA; ICSA; BTEC HNC/D; BA Accounting; BA Business Studies..
On reading lists of CIMA and ICSA

CONTENTS

WHAT IS MANAGEMENT ACCOUNTING?
COST ACCOUNTING AND COST ASCERTAINMENT - A REVISION
COST BEHAVIOUR
INFORMATION AND MANAGEMENT ACCOUNTING
PLANNING - SYSTEM CONCEPTS
LONG TERM PLANNING
BUDGETING
NETWORK ANALYSIS
CONTROL - CONCEPTS AND SYSTEM PRINCIPLES
BUDGETARY CONTROL
STANDARD COSTING
STOCK CONTROL
DECISION MAKING - AN INTRODUCTION
MARGINAL COSTING AND CVP ANALYSIS
PRICING DECISIONS
LINEAR PROGRAMMING
INVESTMENT APPRAISAL
DIVISIONAL PERFORMANCE APPRAISAL
TRANSFER PRICING
RATIO ANALYSIS
MANAGEMENT ACCOUNTING AND COMPUTERS
MANAGEMENT ACCOUNTING CASE STUDIES
EXAMINATION TECHNIQUE
SOLUTIONS TO QUESTIONS SET AT END OF CHAPTERS

REVIEW EXTRACTS
'This text is astonishingly comprehensive, well written and nicely laid out. As a manual for professional examinations it has no obvious competitor.'
British Accounting Review Service

Free Lecturers' Supplement